Partnership Parenting

PARTNERSHIP PARENTING

How Men and Women Parent Differently— Why It Helps Your Kids and Can Strengthen Your Marriage

Kyle Pruett, MD
Marsha Kline Pruett, PhD, MSL

Da Capo
LIFE
LONG

A Member of the Perseus Books Group

Produced in conjunction with Downtown Bookworks, Inc.
Design and production by Eclipse Publishing Services
Set in 9 point Imperial

Page 72: Gatekeeper Quiz for Moms © National Fatherhood Initiative, reprinted by
          permission
Page 74: Doonesbury (c) 1986 G. B. Trudeau. Reprinted with permission of Universal
          Press Syndicate. All rights reserved.
Pages 80–83, 205: Copyright 2000 ZERO TO THREE. Questions reproduced with
          permission of the copyright holder. What Grown-ups Understand About
          Child Development. Further reproduction requires express permission from
          ZERO TO THREE (www.zerotothree.org/permissions).
Page 151: David Alpert, 2006 D&A Records. Other Alpert Music Publishing/ASCAP.
Page 199: Ideas About Parenting reprinted with permission of Gertrude Heming,
          Philip A. Cowan, and Carolyn Pape Cowan

**Cataloging-in-Publication data for this book is available from the
Library of Congress.**

First Da Capo Press edition 2009
ISBN: 978-0-7382-1326-2

Published by Da Capo Press
A Member of the Perseus Books Group
www.dacapopress.com

Da Capo Press books are available at special discounts for bulk purchases in the U.S.
by corporations, institutions, and other organizations. For more information, please
contact the Special Markets Department at the Perseus Books Group, 2300 Chestnut
Street, Suite 200, Philadelphia, PA, 19103, or call (800) 810-4145, ext. 5000, or e-mail
special.markets@perseusbooks.com.

10 9 8 7 6 5 4 3 2 1

For Lisa and Emily,
with whom we started our co-parenting lessons;
and for Liv and J.D.,
who closed the circle and continue to fill in the gaps.

Contents

Foreword   ix

Acknowledgments   xi

Introduction   xiii

PART ONE

 1   **Becoming Parents Together**   3
     Life B.C. (before children) and A.C. (after children)

 2   **Cuddling vs. the Football Hold**   15
     Why Parenting Differences Are Not Deficiencies

 3   **Building a Partnership That Works**   35
     The Relationship Is the Solution, Not the Problem

 4   **Managing Conflict and Fighting Fair**   49
     The Dynamics of Healthy Disagreement

 5   **Valuing Your Spouse's Contribution**   65
     So Glad I Chose You

 6   **Assumptions and Actions**   79
     What Grown-ups Do and Don't Know About Raising Kids

PART TWO

 7   **Discipline**   99
     "Wait 'til Your Father Gets Home!"

 8   **Care and Feeding**   115
     Keeping Your Child Healthy in Body and Mind

 9   **Co-parenting and Sleeping Children**   133
     Learning to Be on One's Own

10   **Safety**   151
     From Within and Without

11 Education 169
The Co-parenting Foundation to Lifelong Learning

12 Epilogue: For Divorce Prevention 191
Keeping the Parenting Partnership First So It Lasts

Appendix A: Ideas About Parenting 199
Appendix B: Parental Profile Answers 205
Notes 207
Index 213

Foreword

I've BEEN PRIVILEGED as a pediatrician to witness tremendous changes in the well-being of children over the course of my lifetime. As I've held newborns in my hands and watched their parents hold them in theirs, one change stands apart from the rest: These days, fathers are more actively engaged right from the start. This, as Kyle and Marsha Pruett so beautifully set forth in *Partnership Parenting*, is great news for all concerned. Watching a mother, father, and baby fall in love with one another right after birth is to see a miracle unfold. When I hold a newborn up in front of me and talk to him or her, he or she always turns to my voice. If I have the father compete with me, 80 percent of the babies will turn to their father's voice. If they don't, I tip their heads. Then, more often than not, the father takes his baby from me and exclaims, "You know me already!"

In my lifetime, I have seen changes in the way fathers have been expected to behave with their children. Before the 1960s, fathers were expected to work all day and be home at night. Most children were lucky if a father even read them a story at bedtime. My own father used to take me to swim with him, but otherwise I rarely saw him.

All of us who care about the young owe a debt of gratitude to the Pruetts' pioneering work. Their contributions over the past decades have enhanced our understanding of babies, their mothers, and fathers. In this book, Marsha and Kyle have combined clinical research (their own and others') with their uncanny knack for synthesizing and interpreting the science for today's young families. Fathers and mothers have made big strides in sharing the care and feeding of their families. But along with the women's movement and the narrowing of the equality gap, there have been unforeseen challenges that the Pruetts address head on—and in wonderfully pragmatic ways.

Not unlike an experience Kyle describes in this book, I remember when my first baby was born. I allowed our obstetrician to send me home, while my wife labored at the hospital. Even though I had examined newborns in this same nursery, I was not allowed to hold my own baby. It was a dawning moment for me: Our biases were operating to keep fathers away from their newborns, and that was not a good thing for anyone—especially the baby.

We needed to change that attitude and practice, and we have (with thanks, in no small part, to the women's movement). Now, with 71 percent of mothers working outside the home, fathers are much more likely to feed, change, and push their babies around in their strollers. But we still have a lot of work to do. Based on their own experiences and memories, and still evolving social expectations about what it means to be a "good" mother and "good" father, mothers are often ambivalent about "sharing the care."

Kyle and Marsha are each gifted clinicians and researchers as well as the parents of four terrific kids themselves. Whether you are a mother, father, parent-to-be, or a person who simply cares about the way children are raised, there is much to be gained from the insights, advice, and strategies throughout this book. And, I'm happy to point out, your children and my grandchildren will be the ultimate beneficiaries.

T. Berry Brazelton, MD
Professor of Pediatrics, Emeritus, Harvard Medical School
Founder, Brazelton Touchpoints Center

—————— ▼ ——————

Acknowledgments

WHILE THE REAL WORLD of co-parenting is hardly acknowledged in books for parents, a body of literature and research does exist that has nourished our clinical and empirical understanding, laying the foundation for much of our own thinking. Many wonderful thinkers have influenced us, but we wish to acknowledge here those on whose work we drew most heavily for this book and whose influence flows through many chapters.

We particularly wish to acknowledge the work of our dear friends and colleagues, Phil and Carolyn Cowan, who had the vision years ago to see "it's the couple" that drives child and family development, and have since worked tirelessly to link research and intervention in this area. Their friendship and wisdom sustain and feed us. We also draw on the work of pioneering couples interventionists Julie and John Gottman, the inspired research of James McHale, and the eloquently considered history of marriage authored by Stephanie Coontz. The contributions made by these creative thinkers will be evident in many places throughout this book. Rather than earmark each one, we choose to give them each heartfelt credit for their leadership in this continually evolving field.

We thank Mindy Werner for her tasteful editing, and our agent Pam Abrams and Perseus editor Katie McHugh for bringing our vision to reality. Like some of the parents mentioned in our book, we learned as we went that as long as we keep believing in the same things, we could learn to see eye to eye on the "small stuff." On a more personal note, special thanks to Mareike Muszynski for her intelligent research, Karen Yatsko for her diligent help on the bibliography, and Rachel Simpson for her experienced and talented reading and advice and her abiding friendship. Lastly, we want to acknowledge both sets of our parents with deep appreciation—they created exceptional co-parenting role models in their equally loving ways—and the families whose voices are heard throughout this book sharing their struggles and triumphs and pains and pleasures in co-parenting young children.

Introduction

Our FAMILY CONSISTS OF four children spanning a generation (from ages seven to thirty-something), two sons-in-law, four grandchildren, and us, Kyle and Marsha—two older-parent mental health professionals. Over the years, we've shared in the pleasures and challenges of writing, doing research, working with children and couples, and educating myriad organizations about the well-being of families. Much of our work has focused on couples and families who are entering the unknown territory of new parenthood together or, in the case of separation and divorce, ending their familiar life as a family and establishing a new one.

One thing became quite apparent to us some time ago: Most of the parenting books written to date have offered advice and wisdom to parents—typically to mothers—while largely ignoring the implications of the steady advance of fathers' active role in raising their children. Many changes in family life have occurred over the past decades—especially the spectacular increase in the number of women in the workforce, including as many as 75 percent of mothers with young children. Despite the changes, parenting advisers have generally overlooked what it's actually like for couples to try to parent *together* as a team, given different genders, personalities, temperaments, and childhood experiences. Couples talk to us most often about these very issues, seeking help for their loneliness, frustration, and confusion: How do you raise your children well, while keeping your marriage strong and happy at the same time?

The idea for *Partnership Parenting* crystallized when we realized that co-parenting advice is more common in the literature on *divorce*. Divorcing parents need help negotiating after they have split up, but so many parents, including happily married ones, need (and could more constructively use) help much earlier. After all, the vast majority of co-parenting occurs within the context of marriage and cohabitation.

The real and hard questions about parenting begin when procreation creeps inevitably into a couple's life, often after they visit family or friends who have a child or two. Then the questions begin to percolate:

▼ Can we be good parents, have jobs or careers, and still stay happily married?
▼ Will we both feel the thrill that makes having children worth all the trouble?
▼ Do we agree on when it would be good for us to become parents?
▼ Do we feel equally prepared for becoming parents?
▼ Will we delight in having kids to the same degree, and will it matter if we don't?
▼ Will we both do whatever it takes to help our marriage thrive?
▼ Will the marriage and child-rearing decisions be made in ways that feel equally fair and desirable to both of us?

So, how do you create a marriage that feels like home and family to both partners?

Our Journey

When Kyle became a father for the first time, it was clear to him from day one that life was different for men who wanted to be involved in their baby's lives. On the "preconfinement" visit to the hospital where his first daughter, Elizabeth, was to be born, he was told that he'd need signed permission from the chief of obstetrics and gynecology if he wanted to be present in the delivery room during the birth. (A year earlier, as an intern in that same hospital, he'd delivered six babies there, in those same delivery rooms with the same nurses.) Several years later, when Kyle's second daughter, Emily, was born, there was still no paternity leave for residents at the Yale Child Study Center, but there was a softer hand on the delivery-room door, and he was welcomed in without signed permission.

The world of marriage and parenthood has changed greatly in a generation or so. When we got married twelve years ago, we did so in our home, which was stuffed to the brim with friends and family. The older children (Marsha's stepdaughters) gave her away to their dad. When we became parents together ten years ago, some things had changed radically. Not only was Kyle expected in the delivery room the entire time, but because the labor was long and arduous, Marsha's parents and, at Marsha's behest, our daughter, Emily, also took part. Marsha's father was overwhelmed by the changes that allowed him to be a more integral part of his grandchild's birth than the birth of his own child. By the time our son was born, Kyle handled much of the birth himself.

Three decades ago, when Kyle began to review the scientific literature about involved fathers and the effects of fathers' engagement on babies and families, he realized that the topic was not just understudied, but seemingly avoided. He commented to his renowned child analyst supervisor, "Why do we know more about the fruit fly genome than we do about the effects of fathers' involvement on their children?" He got the following reply, "Kyle, I think it must be obvious to you [it wasn't] that very young children can't have two separate intimate relationships at the same time. So, when the father is emotionally engaged, it is likely to lead to maternal deprivation. You'd be smarter to be looking for pathology in these families rather than insights." Kyle then knew he had discovered just what he wanted to study: What exactly *did* emotionally engaged fathering contribute to child development (because he was already pretty sure that it wasn't deprivation)? Since then, research has shown just how important involved men are to the raising of healthy children, increasing the chance that they will be healthier emotionally and socially, stronger cognitively and academically, and stable throughout their lifetimes.

Parenthood wasn't the only institution undergoing rapid change during this period; marriage itself seemed to be less resilient in the face of demands of "modern" parenting. Early in the 20th century, sociologist E.E. LeMasters had found that over 80 percent of couples he surveyed had experienced a "moderate to severe crisis" in making the transition from partnership to parenthood. Books on the transition to parenthood may question whether it is a crisis, but even today experts agree that the transition throws the couple into a whirlwind of change in values, roles, and expectations, not to mention emotions, from which some couples land on their feet and nearly as many do not.

LeMasters highlighted for the first time the naked, unsympathetic, nonromanticized truth of babyhood: It is very hard on a couple to be at home alone with an infant who is crying and needy most of the time, especially at night. It's particularly hard because neither parent really knows exactly what to do. Sometimes the baby "responds" and simply stops crying. Other times, it's hard to tell if anything anyone does makes any difference. Sleep deprivation is inevitable from the outset. Stress begins to accumulate because there is never sufficient respite or recovery. Of course, there are many incredible moments of intense joy and intimate connection too. The task for couples is to maneuver through the difficult, exhausting parts of parenting, while holding fast to the joys and their dreams.

A Common Vision

The underlying message of *Partnership Parenting* is that when two adults (*any* two adults) share the parenting of a child, the nature and quality of the relationship *between* those adults will have a strong impact on the child's development, for good or ill. While this might seem like common sense, it wasn't so long ago that mental health professionals would focus on the well-being of a child and rarely considered the relationship between his parents.

This concept seemed so obvious to both of us early on in our careers—as a child psychiatrist (Kyle) and a psychologist (Marsha)—that we sought supplemental marital and family therapy training beyond what was offered in our formal clinical training programs. The additional training taught us that families are whole entities larger than the sum of the pairs (mother-child, father-child, or couple). The system of relationships *between and among* all these smaller parts of the nuclear family make up the dynamics and determine so much about how each member adjusts to family life, day by day.

Kyle's Research

Kyle had to dig to get such instruction. From the beginning of his clinical training, he had repeatedly encountered the toxic effects of significant marital dysfunction on the development of the infants, toddlers, and children with whom he worked in therapy and in consultation. Children who were sad, anxious, or angry often had parents who felt the same way—about each other. In the majority of children's mental health and guidance clinics of the 1970s and 80s, social workers were typically assigned to work with the mother on such issues as her parenting style, her self-esteem, and the upsets to mothering that she brought from her own childhood. The children, meanwhile, entered into a separate, one-on-one therapeutic relationship with another clinician. Fathers were not encouraged or expected to participate, the prevailing assumption being that the mother was the only parent who needed to be involved. Why? Presumably because only she understood the child's problems and would therefore be able, with help, to devise and provide the solutions. Her emotional limitations were likely part of the child's trouble, making her improvement a necessary part of the solution to the child's problem(s). The father typically sat in the waiting room, took care of the bills and transportation, and was generally assumed to be supportive, if clueless.

Kyle saw a stark contrast in the perspective of the children with whom he worked in the *other* therapy office. Typically, these children felt raised by, in love with, and accountable to *both* parents. They had elaborate and distinct emotional relationships with their fathers and mothers that mattered to them. Often the relationship with one was seen as a counterweight or complementary to the other, even if one of the parents (typically the father) seemed not to be "very involved," at least according to the child guidance clinician. This was code for "we aren't going to bother to include him in the therapeutic work" or "we're not sure what to do with him anyway." Yet, how the parents "got along" was of primary interest to the vast majority of children, since that was the foundation of—and safety net for—how well their family functioned day-to-day. This discrepancy drew Kyle into his decades-long curiosity about the effect of paternal engagement (and its absence) on child development and the family as a whole.

Marsha's Research
Marsha, by contrast, entered the field through education and psychology disciplines, and was taught early on that both parents were critical to the lives of their children. In her family therapy training at the Philadelphia Child Guidance Clinic, then a mecca for famous family clinicians and researchers, she studied families that had very close relationships between mothers and children, along with disengaged or excluded fathers or preadolescents who had more authority than their fathers or both parents. These families had symptoms ranging from aggression and asthma to eating disorders in children or adolescents to substance-abusing parents, and so on. She learned to examine how the parental relationship formed the basis for all the relationships in the family. When it became weak or imbalanced in ways that detracted from the parental alliance, relationships ran amok in various ways that led to children in pain and trouble.

Marsha then became interested in divorcing families and custody matters, and discovered that family lawyers and judges were clinging to the notion that only mothers were significant as the primary caretakers of very young children. Fathers were relegated to secondary status, and little was understood or put into place to maximize parents' shared parenting in the face of serious disagreements about childrearing. When this happened early in the children's lives, their relationships with their fathers were frequent casualties of the divorce. Topics ranging from overnights, to how to keep fathers involved after a mother had relocated, to children's rejection of their fathers permeate family conflict enacted in the legal system. The theme is typically the same: How a father can find a lasting place in his children's lives while negotiating his place with the mother. And so Marsha's and Kyle's worlds met. It was this keenly shared interest in the power of the parenting partnership to place children on a secure or slippery path of development that drew us together intellectually. The rest is history, much of which resulted in this book. The ultimate focus on what we call the "parenting partnership" is the natural evolution of our preoccupations with the intimate intermingling of marital, maternal, paternal, and child well-being.

From Parents to Partners . . . Fighting the Tide

What exactly is the parenting partnership? To us, it encompasses the parental alliance formed on behalf of the couple and the children, an alliance requiring negotiation, respect, and support that benefits immensely from affection and commitment—all toward the desired end of raising happy and healthy kids. Our professional journey was informed by our personal one as we struggled with and learned from stepparent and then co-parenting issues ourselves. Eventually we joined to do research and interventions on vulnerable families with young children. *Partnership Parenting* is based on the lessons learned from doing that clinical work and research and from talking with a broad and diverse range of families.

This book is about husbands and wives as mothers and fathers. Though the focus is on marriage and gendered parenting, much of what we discuss will certainly pertain to *any* two people raising younger children together: a grandparent and his or her adult children, same sex couples, noncohabiting couples, and other combinations of connected, committed adults. These relationships often struggle with the same issues and patterns we will illuminate on these pages, and if you are not in a male-female partnership, we still hope and believe that you'll find much useful wisdom in the chapters that follow. We invite all parents to join us as we explore the foundations of co-parenthood and partnerships that are loving, lasting, and joyful.

Partnership
Parenting

PART

I

1

Becoming Parents Together
Life B.C. (before children) and A.C. (after children)

My wife and I have always been happy and close. She's one of the
most loving people in the universe. That's why I'm a bit rattled
about how unloved she can make me feel. She doesn't mean to, but
she makes me feel incompetent, like a mediocre parent. . . . She just
has a way of correcting what I say and do; it's subtle sometimes,
and she always pretends she's supporting me while fixing
things. . . . I can feel myself withdrawing, and it scares me.

—Father of a seven-month-old daughter

I think my husband is the world's best, and he's really a great
father, too. I am surprised, though, how often I feel annoyed at him
when he's parenting our little girl. It's like he doesn't get who she
really is, so I try to be helpful and steer him in a direction that will
help her feel closer to and have more confidence in him. Then he
gets this glazed look and I think he's gone off inside his head.
I know he gets mad at those moments, but he doesn't realize
how often I make things work between them.

—Mother of the same seven-month-old daughter

IN HOLLYWOOD, "happily ever after" typically means that the celluloid
couple embraces in a passionate kiss after uttering their marriage vows.
We don't often see what happens once those couples have children. In
fact, movies about family life are often light comedies about inexperi-
enced parents, focusing on the good-hearted but bumbling father and
the competent but overwhelmed, long-suffering mother. And yet, in real
life, if the goal is happily-ever-after, there is solid evidence for freezing
the blissful picture before the children are born. Long-term studies in the
United States and other Western countries show that a couple's happiness
begins to slip away with the birth of their first child and continues down-
ward through the child's fourteenth year. Even though this steady decline
doesn't stop parents from reporting that having children is the best thing

they have ever done and is one of life's most rewarding experiences, for many couples, juggling the demands of marriage and family can also make them angry, resentful, annoyed, and unhappy with their mates. Is it any wonder that the average marriage ends after eight years, which coincides with the early years of parenting?

James McHale of the University of South Florida has done some illuminating research on marriages once kids enter the picture. In his "Families Through Time" project, begun in 1997, McHale and his colleagues talked with expectant couples and then followed up when the infants were three months, one year, and then two and a half years old.[1] They began with the assumption that the folks lucky enough to be in what they called "super marriages" would make the happiest parents. But as it turned out, they were wrong.

Some of the best-prepared couples found themselves "quite surprised by how challenging the early months of new parenthood actually were."[2] Despite gentle warnings from family, friends, and the occasional health professional, many found the exhaustion more depleting than they "could have ever imagined." This was exponentially true if the baby suffered colic or sleep troubles. Postpartum blues were evident in the mothers *and* the fathers, and their disappointments with their lack of independence and intimacy were legion. Both mothers and fathers viewed very ambivalently the beloved jobs that had been put on hold for parental leave. Mothers missed the social life and the esteem that emanate from an active career, as well as the salary, but still weren't sure they were ready to leave their babies for hours each day. Similarly, fathers wanted mothers to return to work for their own happiness and the family income, but also liked the idea of mothers being at home with their children, as they had agreed before having them.

McHale's research underscored that marriages that were strong before the baby arrived weren't guaranteed to remain so. With findings similar to McHale's, *And Baby Makes Three*, a book by researchers John Gottman and Julie Schwartz Gottman reports on a dozen studies following parents before and after the baby's arrival. Despite the incredibly beautiful moments of their new lives, there emerged hard truths and unspoken expectations. The Gottmans heard from men who hoped that "now that Mom had 'her' baby and 'her' family was underway, she'd be happy from this point forward," especially with him for making this baby with her. Maybe she'd even want to express her feelings *to* him more often. Meanwhile, they heard from women who hoped that, now that her man had been through this incredibly intense emotional and physical event with her, "he'd be more loving and sensitive, even more open and available emotionally to her and their new baby."[3]

Such conflicts are exacerbated by a new mother's sudden dip in sexual desire after labor and delivery. That dip is not short-lived, especially if she is nursing every few hours. Not surprisingly, sexual behavior changes radically, and most women don't recover much libido until the end of the first year. Although most men have heard the jokes, it's not very funny when it takes over your bed. Likewise, there's a lack of the *other* activity that also used to take place there—sleep. The intimacy gap widens with these changes in sexual and sleep patterns and conflicts about being at work—or not.

Regardless of when a couple marries, parenthood is the dawn of an entirely new epoch in their lives. *How* new is often what most stuns new parents. Today's expectant couples typically anticipate that it won't be that difficult to communicate regularly about the needs of their baby and other child-related decisions, all in support of each other's daily parenting behaviors. It sounds simple enough. But in reality, it is hard to imagine a more difficult family task: to establish patterns of behavior that will meet the needs of each family member, regardless of the child's age, each parent's individual history, or the state of the marriage.

XX vs. XY

When partners become parents, their gender differences come into play in a strong and familiar way, harking back to grade school and the first realization of differences in how the other gender thinks and behaves. Partly because of the differences, mothers and fathers tend naturally to parent in diverse ways. Not surprisingly, then, relationship conflicts increase in number and intensity during the first year after the baby arrives. These differences, though often at the heart of frustrations, disappointments, and conflicts, not only are daily fare for comedians, but offer parents an opportunity to work together to achieve a balance in styles and behaviors.

A child will eagerly embrace these parental differences, play to them, and—if given the chance—delight in them: "Mom is great at comforting me when I'm hurt, and Dad helps me get right back in the game." A child who has the support of each parent to take the best from the other has a large and flexible repertoire of cognitive, social, and emotional behaviors from which to draw. The result is a healthier and often happier child.

Learning to identify gendered parenting differences and sort out which are problematic and which are emblematic of two parents acting in concert is what this book is about. We hope to help you recognize that the problem is really the solution; that the difference is the pathway to happily-ever-after and to co-parenting as true partners.

Both mothers and fathers typically begin parenting with ideas about how the job ought to be done and why it ought to be done in a particular way for this particular child in this particular family. Should the baby sleep in our bed? Should she be allowed to cry at night and for how long? Should we have babysitters who are not family members? Ideas about how to parent are often based on one's own childhood, seasoned with lessons from relationship experiences along the way. Since no two people have ever grown up in exactly the same way, there are bound to be variations on how to raise the baby.

Mothers' and fathers' inherent parenting differences, as well as their own intense desires to do what is right to maximize their children's potential, inevitably lead them into some degree of conflict over parenting decisions both big and small. A mother wants her daughter to be more assertive and socially adept because her own shyness felt like such a handicap growing up. A father wants his son to be a more flexible, roll-with-the-punches kind of guy because his own rigidity cost him some important career opportunities. And the influences are not just from their respective pasts; marital experience counts too. A father wants his daughter to learn how to speak for herself and say what she wants because he is weary of trying to read his wife's mind. A mother wants her son to be more emotionally available and vibrant because her husband can be so withdrawn sometimes.

Parents' emotionally loaded aspirations for their child may not routinely generate consensus. Because of your own dreams for changing yourself and your partner for the better *through your child*, some of these ideas may not be sufficiently clear to you, let alone to your partner. Not appreciating these differences and expecting that your spouse will do things your way can lead to frequent miscommunications and misunderstandings, unmet expectations, and increased tension, resentment, and frustration.

Jennifer and Frank, a couple in their mid-thirties, describe themselves as passionately in love with life and each other. When they first met, they were both heavily engaged in their work, he as a management consultant and she as a high school math teacher with a knack for teaching gifted students. Coming from a big family with children always around, Jennifer had long dreamed of having her own children—lots of them. Her plan had been to stop working outside the home once her first child was born. She figured she'd stay at home for a few years and then return to her beloved job, maybe part time or maybe full time; the details weren't clear in her head.

Frank grew up in a small but close-knit family; his only sibling, a brother, is a few years younger than him. As kids, the two of them were involved in sports and music together. Frank admitted he didn't think much about being a father before he met Jennifer; he just took it for granted that he would be one someday. He attributes the lack of discussion about parenting to having grown up around three men and only one (outnumbered) woman, his mother.

When Jennifer became pregnant, it was a joyous time for them both. Looking back, though, Jennifer recalls that she was a bit shocked at Frank's independence, his willingness to take risks during the pregnancy—going skydiving, for instance—despite her anxiety for him and the future of their family. Both admit, however, that she always loved that "devil may care" quality about him before they had their son, Benjamin.

When we first spoke to them, Ben was two and a half. Jennifer was upset about how much Frank allowed Ben to do—pushing him too hard on the swings and allowing him to go on his own to the top of their jungle gym without Frank standing right beneath it. On the other hand, Frank was upset that their child still slept in their bed, and Jennifer said she agreed with him, but life circumstances (a recent move to a new condo, Ben's lingering cough and flu) caused a delay in their plan for Ben's sleeping arrangements. Frank feels she is more emotional than he noticed before the birth; Jennifer feels he is colder and more into discipline than she expected.

It's the Little Things . . .

These kinds of disagreements about the right way to raise a child typically smolder in the new family, somewhat under the radar. The more obvious struggles occur in sorting out the heavy lifting of who does what for the child. Chief among the surprises for many mothers in the McHale study was how much credit the fathers gave themselves for family duties.[4] Equally surprising to the fathers was how little credit their spouses gave them for their nonwork contributions to family life and its endless chores. This was especially troubling to the fathers, because they seemed to be getting so little appreciation from their partners for giving up the things they'd rather be doing, like getting exercise, hanging out with friends, or reading a book.

But of particular interest to us is less the nature of the complaints themselves than the fact that most of the distressed mothers had "rarely shared their frustrations with their husbands" and "even fewer husbands had shared their concerns with their wives."[5] Couples said they just didn't have the time, energy, or opportunity to talk about those things. Jobs, family errands, the lack of sleep, and the intensely preoccupying focus on the baby all add up to a formula for communication time slipping away unnoticed and minor conflicts starting to chip away at the foundation of the relationship. Often couples choose to ignore the small hurts or misunderstandings to keep the peace and not get petty. Such virtuous motivations can backfire, though, as the backlog of small insults piles up, and resentment and anger set in.

Partnership Parenting: A New Approach

What can you do to ensure harmony as a couple, while devoting most of your time and energy to raising young children? Like any new and demanding task, it is harder to accomplish alone; the team approach works best. To use a business metaphor, working as a team or a full partnership for the long haul, invested in the company's growth and the quality product that results is the way to achieve harmony. There are many approaches and many pitfalls along the way. This, too, is what this book is about.

Taking the long view—focusing more on the big picture than the minor daily annoyances—lies at the heart of a successful parenting partnership. When two people decide to start a company together, their arrangement is based on the assumption that both have the same goal: to work together to create a successful enterprise. This doesn't mean that both will act as the money guy who provides the capital and crunches the numbers; nor will they both provide the technical know-how to come up with the product they're going to sell. Each partner has unique talents and resources, without which the business could not be sustained. The strength of the operation lies in these complementary and supplementary differences.

So it is with parenting. Both parents need to come to the marriage expecting that their mates will contribute comparably, but uniquely, to building a life together that supports and sustains their most important product—their children. A successful parenting partnership requires:

▼ Making decisions together.
▼ Sharing child-care responsibilities.
▼ Striving to agree on who your children are, what they need and want, and how you'll go about giving it to them.

▼ Valuing the other parent for his or her differences and accepting the differences as part of what makes family life interesting.

▼ Recognizing and appreciating gender differences that lead you both to think, feel, and behave in distinct ways with respect to child rearing and how you express love, anger, fear, and sadness.

▼ Putting your children's well-being first when disagreements arise.

▼ Finding a way to talk about conflicts so that you both feel heard and understood.

▼ Sticking together even when the going gets rough; making your relationship's health a clear priority.

▼ Committing to finding ways to grow individually and in tandem in response to your ever-changing family's developmental stage.

Building the Partnership

Although couples face enormous challenges as parents and partners, our years of clinical and research experience have shown us repeatedly that there are many ways to stack the deck in your favor.

1. Put the Other First

Couples need time *as couples* to recharge their common, collective battery and to talk about their partnership outside the world their child inhabits or pervades. Many mothers and fathers bring an intensity and tunnel vision to parenting that renders them myopic; that is, they focus too much on the children. Parents need time away from their children in order to thrive, grow, and evolve together as a couple. Such times should have certain parameters:

▼ Choose activities or adventures which you each enjoy.

▼ Spend time individually and together with family and friends, without children.

▼ Banish talk about logistics for an evening.

▼ Check in with each other about any feelings that may be simmering but not expressed. Do not attempt this during time reserved for fun. Instead, find a few quiet moments at the end of the day over herbal tea or decaf to talk with each other, while your children are engaged in an activity.

Wives often first bring up the need to talk in order to make changes in the marriage. Husbands' ability to change in response to these requests is, as it turns out, one of the strongest indicators of whether the couple will be happy and stay together. So, for men, it isn't whether they get it right the first time that matters; it's whether they are willing to be responsive.

2. Practice Resilience

Another important factor for maintaining stability at home is resilience. Resilience renders us less vulnerable when we hit life's unexpected speed bumps, such as illness (ours or the family's), unemployment, or the loss of a loved one. Of course, we're going to encounter one or more of these bumps, but our ability to recover without getting bitter or traumatized is a function of our resilience. How does this relate to parenting? Research[6] has shown that men and women differ in their ability to maintain resolve and focus under stress. James McHale found that resilient dads were more likely to stay collaboratively involved during the difficult first three months of a newborn's life. For these fathers, existing marital distress was less likely to spill over and negatively affect the couple's co-parenting relationship at the end of the baby's first year. Hence, fathers' resources appear to be particularly important assets for the developing parenting partnership.

When a mother is resilient, she often tries to make things better for everyone in her family as they all absorb stress, but the collaborative nature of her parenting isn't always strongly affected or enhanced in any particular way. What McHale's research shows, however, is that resilient fathering is especially important for protecting the whole family, precisely because it strengthens the bedrock parents' relationship itself. Although it's not easy, a person can learn to remain cool; it's not simply a trait you inherit.[7]

3. Recognize That a Sturdy Parenting Partnership Leads to a Strong Family

Couples with the strongest parenting partnerships support one another, make and stick to agreements about how to raise their children, and refrain from undermining each other by deviating from these agreements. In addition, those couples who work well together as parents report less distress in their parent-child relationships; both partners—but mothers in particular—report greater personal well-being.[8] Thus the old adage applies: What is good for one is good for all.

Fathers are a critical part of this equation. The benefits of a strong parenting team work in individual parents' and the couple's favor and flow to the child. When parents feel less distress in their relationships with their children because the parental alliance is strong, everyone benefits. Interestingly, this improvement is particularly true for fathers who are uncertain about how to be intimate with their spouses. These realities highlight the basic premise of this book: A solid parenting partnership can strengthen a couple's intimacy and, without such intimacy, it is nearly impossible to co-parent well over time. The two go together, and problems in one area magnify problems in the other.

4. Acknowledge That Good Fathering Is Part of Good Co-Parenting

Being an active father and a more responsive husband leads to a healthier family. When men assume an active role in fathering, it positively affects them personally and tends to strengthen their marriage. For example, men who become fathers are in a new category of health and risk. They live longer, suffer fewer accidents, and their suicide rate drops dramatically (Where's the reduction in health and life insurance premiums when men become fathers?). Coworkers and bosses rate fathers as more reliable and productive workers.[9] Fathers are less aggressive and less prone to act impulsively. As soon as the nurturing needs of children activate the nurturing potential in men, many seemingly unrelated aspects of their personalities begin to soften and open.

Women, of course, are also profoundly changed by mothering. Emotional, social, physical, and economic vulnerabilities come to the fore in ways unseen since adolescence. Because both adults are in such flux, it would be easy to assume that the parenting partnership would simply be composed of the sum of their various strengths and vulnerabilities. But the whole is greater than the sum of its parts. Sometimes one parent's strengths provide what the child needs at just that moment, while other times, the other parent's strengths are required.

5. Forget Bean Counting and Splitting Tasks

You need to consider everything you and your spouse do for the good of the family, and stop keeping track of what your partner is *not* doing. Put a temporary, if not permanent, halt to bean counting or insistence on "sharing." Sharing is often code for an expectation of a (verifiable) fifty-fifty split in tasks. For example, if Mom packed the lunchboxes this week, it's Dad's turn to do it next week. After all, the deal is that they share the parenting tasks, right? While there's some logic here, this kind of thinking ignores the realities of people's lives. What if Dad has a grueling commute and has precious few hours at home while the kids are actually awake? Or what if Mom works hard too, but her commute is less taxing and she is able to pack lunches without stressing about which kid still likes what kind of jelly? The point is not that each parent needs to take a turn making sandwiches, but, overall, are they both committed parents doing the best they can to support one another *as* parents?

But what about fairness, you ask? How can an uneven split be fair?

If you are lucky enough to live many years together, there will be a time when the roles will reverse and your partner will need to pick up the slack. The important issue is not whether the burdens are unevenly distributed now, in these formative years. Rather, it is whether your partner is responsive when you ask for change, and whether he or she is the kind of person who can and will assume a share of the work when necessary, now and in the future.

How Strong Is Your Partnership?

Do you know how strong your parenting partnership is? Ask yourself if you (or your spouse) have fallen into any of the following traps:

▼ Believing that your partner is only second in command and therefore of lesser importance in nurturing the children or the marriage.

▼ Keeping a running tab of how much your mate actually does around the house and for the children and what he or she owes you in return—otherwise known as bean counting.

▼ Treating your mate like an employee, someone who is less invested in the family, rather than a stockholder with a stake in the venture. This means micromanaging your spouse's relationship with your children.

▼ Conveying frustration or disdain when interacting with your partner about an unresolved issue. Do your tone of voice, facial expression, and body language convey a negative, disrespectful attitude, rather than a belief that the two of you can successfully settle the problem? Does the time you choose to bring up the problem (for instance, during the children's soccer game rather than on a quiet evening after they are in bed) convey the message that talking about the problem thoroughly isn't really a priority?

▼ Expressing your unhappiness with your spouse in front of others, whether your kids, extended family, or friends.

▼ Using work or other adult responsibilities as an excuse for not pulling your weight at home, especially for the tasks that aren't especially fun or fulfilling (doing dishes, folding laundry).

▼ Putting up a metaphorical wall or withdrawing from the conversation when the two of you face a difficult decision, whether it's selecting a preschool or figuring out if you should hire a new caregiver.

▼ Withholding information from your spouse to see if he or she will figure it out for him- or herself, such as neglecting to remind your partner that your child needs to take his swimsuit to preschool that day.

▼ Protecting your children at the expense of your spouse's authority or creativity. For example, giving your spouse detailed instructions about which apparatus your toddler has mastered at the playground and which climbing equipment should be avoided because you consider it too risky for the child. Although this will keep your child safe, it may also limit her opportunities to build new competence and confidence, while undermining your spouse's ability to parent effectively.

If you found yourself wincing as you read the list, fear not. This book is full of information that will help you see your partnership in a new light and make it easier to work with your spouse, understand your different perspectives, and communicate more effectively. In the next chapter, we discuss in detail the natural differences between how mothers and fathers parent. Then we'll describe the main components of partnership parenting—how couples can better manage their conflicts and value their spouses' contributions. We end the first part of the book by looking at what we know and don't know about effective child-rearing practices.

The second part takes a closer look at the five key realms where parents' gender differences really come into play: discipline, care and feeding, sleep, safety, and education. In addition, we offer advice on how to work through the most common problems that can arise in each area. In the epilogue, we offer some final thoughts about how to create enduring parenting partnerships.

Happily-ever-after stories lie in understanding and appreciating the differences as well as the similarities between moms and dads, and using them in support of raising a healthy, interesting child. The differences are keys to our happiness as families. Let's take a closer look at what you can do to build a successful partnership.

2
▼

Cuddling vs. the Football Hold
Why Parenting Differences Are Not Deficiencies

FOR FATHERS AND MOTHERS, it is not simply our personalities that make us unique as partners and as parents; it is also our gender, even beyond its quintessential role in procreation. After accounting for personality, temperament, and upbringing, science shows that our gender strongly influences our appetites, aptitudes, and social roles. So it's fair to say that mothering and fathering, both nurturing and instinctually influenced activities, are ultimately different. Mothers do not father, and fathers do not mother.

A newborn, moments old, is placed on his mother's belly. The cord is cut, he latches onto his mother's breast, hears her voice, and seems to recognize her. For nine months, he has heard and felt her talk, laugh, and cry; measured time by her heartbeat; and grown accustomed to her movements. Mother and baby have shared body fluids, ups and downs, illness, food, and tissue—even emotions. For mothers and babies, birth is less a beginning than a continuation of an ongoing relationship.

This physical connection has, for decades, led psychologists and researchers from various disciplines to focus almost exclusively on the mother-child relationship, which was so fascinating and seemingly important that it eclipsed all attention paid to fathers. Not until we began to question why so many fathers were playing a secondary role in their children's lives—or worse, dropping out—did we begin to wonder more about the nature of their connection. How does dad fit in with baby and with mom?

More recently, the presence of men in children's lives has slowly but steadily increased, especially in the lives of younger kids. In the past ten years, school personnel from day care to elementary levels, medical receptionists, librarians, playground supervisors, birthday party vendors, and checkout clerks all have seen more men bringing kids to school, attending parent-teacher conferences, going on school field trips, and just being around kids. Advertisers have begun to pander to men. Fifteen years ago, they did not exist in cereal, diaper, children's medicine, or toy and game commercials; now they are commonplace. When Madison Avenue pays attention, something important has changed. This shift toward focusing on fathers as well as mothers highlights the fact that we are in the midst of a co-parenting revolution, wreaking that quiet havoc that so often accompanies structural and dynamic changes in the family.

Gender Differences

Men typically bring different values, behaviors, and attitudes into parenting, though perhaps they are based as much on roles as on gender. Fathers have a lot of ground to make up after their child's birth, given the head start that mothers and babies have from sharing the same body for months. Women experience significant hormonal changes during pregnancy: Sustained levels of progesterone support the pregnancy, prolactin is essential for nursing, and oxytocin plays a crucial role in preparing for the new emotional relationship that the mother will have with her infant. The brain itself undergoes changes that will make it easier for a mother to understand her infant's cries and preverbal cues,[1] while she is ever more preoccupied with her baby's well-being.

But fathers' bodies work hard to catch up, even before the baby is born. In the hormonal systems of men as they prepare for parenthood, during the last month of the pregnancy, the father's estrogen levels rise;

they stay elevated for three months after the baby's birth. After the baby arrives, a father's testosterone level drops by a third and stays low for a month. His prolactin levels increase by 20 percent at birth and stay high for the first three weeks of the baby's life.

Having only recently discovered these changes in expectant fathers, we are just beginning to understand what they mean. The testosterone drop—and the likely subsequent decrease in competitiveness and aggression—may make it easier for the father to adapt to his new family's nesting period. The estrogen increase probably plays a role in drawing his interests into that nesting place.

The prolactin surge might be one of the more interesting changes occurring in the new father's overall physiology. The *relationship hormone*, as some researchers now call prolactin, is also high at another time in life when attention is riveted on intimate connections: during the first episode of puppy love. The hormone seems to strengthen the emotional power of intimate relationships, intensifying the connections among memory, feeling, and sensory input. This is a sensitive period in the relationship between baby and dad, so any labor and delivery guardians or caregivers (midwives, doulas, nurses) should ensure that their welcome help does not marginalize him during this phase. Furthermore more men should be encouraged to take paternity leave to maximize the efficacy of this hormone, which helps them connect quickly and tightly to their new families during the first three months.

In addition to hormonal fluctuations, a man's average weight gain during his spouse's pregnancy is usually within ounces of their baby's eventual birth weight. All these physical and chemical changes seem to draw men and women together in ways they have not previously experienced in their marriage, in cooperative readiness as they anticipate and then celebrate the arrival of the baby.

Despite the hormonal changes, fathers are not mothers in any real sense. And babies can tell the difference early on. A baby's first impression of her father is more likely determined by his novelty than by his familiarity. Yet he's not a complete stranger; there is something identifiable about his voice. New research corroborates the father's conviction that his unborn baby can and does recognize the difference between his parents' voices and continues to notice that difference after birth.

Kyle had about six songs he'd sing regularly to his kids while they were still in the womb. It made him feel close to them to do so, though he was initially skeptical that it would be much of a conversation. But Marsha, who helped choose the songs (since she had to listen, too), was convinced that the babies would quiet down and were clearly "listening" during these serenades. After they were born, Kyle continued to sing to them and "swears" they recognized the tunes by the way they responded.

Within weeks, a baby will attune himself more closely to his father's voice, smell, and textures. Harvard pediatrician Michael Yogman demonstrated that by six weeks of age, babies respond differently to each parent. In his research, babies would partially close their eyes, slow their heart rates, and relax their shoulders as their mothers approached to pick them up, as if they were sighing, "Ahhh, Mom." When fathers approached, the babies hunched their shoulders, their heart rates rose higher, and they opened their eyes wider, as if to say, "It's Dad . . . party time!" But for most of these early weeks and months, dad is less familiar than mom, more of an undiscovered country ripe for exploration, distinguished not so much for himself but simply for the fact that he is not mom.[2]

This joint sense of novelty and wanting to discover each other serves as the foundation of the father-child connection because it belongs to *both* of them. They are on this journey together, making it completely theirs as they progress. Sometimes we take trusted, depended-on relationships for granted; new ones can be very enticing. The lifelong affair of the heart begins for father and child, preferably in a mother's presence and with her countenance and support.

Learning How to Cope

Over time, a father's difference turns into a huge advantage in certain areas, especially when helping children develop autonomy and master separation. If dad is not mom, who is he? What's unique about the ways moms and dads approach their children? Why do these differences matter so much to children and families? One difference is in the way they help their children feel good about themselves and handle frustration.

Alicia, two-and-a-half, sat at the small clinic table between her mother and Kyle, who was doing developmental testing with her. She was not happy; pouting, her head rested in her right hand. She'd spent the past three minutes trying to assemble a challenging eight-piece jigsaw puzzle. Because the puzzle had no frame, Alicia had to pay close attention to the only clues she had—the fragmented images on the irregularly shaped pieces. The puzzle was part of a developmental assessment Alicia was undergoing because her parents were concerned about her speech delay. Although she was of normal, if not slightly above-average intelligence, Alicia was behind her peers in expressive language, which made her subject to bouts of frustration and more than a few tantrums. She was asked to solve the puzzle to assess her problem-solving abilities and her frustration tolerance.

Right now, Alicia was very frustrated. She couldn't finish the puzzle because the last piece was on the edge of the table, hidden from her view by her right elbow. Several minutes elapsed while Alicia dithered, becoming more agitated by the moment. Then, her mother, who was seated to Alicia's right, put her left hand on her daughter's left shoulder and nudged the missing piece from its hiding place behind Alicia's right elbow into the center of the table. Kyle, seated on Alicia's left, saw this intervention in the one-way mirror facing the table. As soon as Alicia saw the piece, she solved the puzzle. Glowing with pride, she said, "'licia do, 'licia do!" Her mother was proud, too, and happy for her daughter's success.

Teddy, another two-and-a-half-year-old who had issues with frustration tolerance as well, had come to the same kind of assessment with his dad. When he was asked to solve the same puzzle Alicia had struggled with, he nearly had a meltdown. But Teddy's father, who was sitting next to him, leaned back in his chair and said, "I've seen you do harder puzzles than this at home. You'll do fine . . . stick with it . . . you'll get it." Hearing this, Teddy began to whine and complain with even more intensity, but his father stayed calm. "I know you can do it, son," he said, crossing his arms over his chest. On the verge of a full-blown tantrum, Teddy picked up one of the remaining pieces—seemingly at random—and suddenly saw where it fit. Then he picked up another piece and, through his tears, saw where it fit, too. Soon the puzzle was completed. "I did it, I did it, Daddy!" Teddy said. And his father said, with pride, "See, I knew you could do it."

These two approaches are typical. Mothers tend to tip the playing field in the direction of their children's needs and self-confidence, actively helping their children solve problems. Mothers feel it is their job to be proactive. Fathers, however, tend to directly intervene less often but still offer verbal and nonverbal support. About their children, they say things like, "I wasn't totally sure he could do it, but I did think it was important for him to really try his best."

Ask most dads what they think of how Alicia's mother handled the same situation, and they'll describe mothers who are too eager to help their kids. "I just didn't feel like I'd be helping Teddy much by making the task easier for him, when it was his job to do his best," Teddy's dad explained. Dads worry that if they intervene in the way Alicia's mother did, their kids won't develop the skills they need to conquer problems on their own, especially those they encounter out in the world. They want their children to experience and triumph over adversity. Moms, on the other hand, scoff at their husbands' criticism. They argue that they're more attuned to their children's needs than men are. They fault dads for not paying attention, being too reluctant to help, too passive, too withdrawn, or just plain lazy.

On the first day of school in our neighborhood, both mothers and fathers walk or drive their children to school. Excitement fills the air. The children all go into the gym, where they stay until sent off to their classrooms. Kyle and another father are saying, "Okay, a successful launch. Time to go." Marsha and her friend Sally linger, wanting to walk to the classroom to get one last glance, to see who the children are sitting next to, and how they are managing the transition. The fathers shuffle behind, muttering that the kids are doing just fine. The moms look knowingly at each other. Of course the kids are fine, but how glorious to be nearby in *case* they need something.

Dads are seemingly more reluctant to assist their children, and moms are supposedly more reliably attuned to their children's needs. Fathers are more likely to allow a certain amount of frustration to build while a child works to solve a problem. Most mothers, on the other hand, are more likely to intervene as soon as a child's irritation develops in order to protect the child from too much frustration and failure. This leaves fathers to complain that early intervention prevents the child from ever learning to manage or cope with failure. Dad worries that mom is spoiling the child, while mom says that dad is ignoring the child's request for help or support, which will cause the child to become more insecure and create more meltdowns with which mom will then have to cope. It's at this point that the recriminations start.

These parenting styles seem miles apart. Yet, let's consider the similarities. Both parents want their kids to have a sense of accomplishment and positive self-esteem; they simply use different tactics. Perhaps most important, as in the case of Alicia and Teddy, both children end up saying the same thing—"I did it!"

When Ben was approaching his third birthday, his parents, Jennifer and Frank, began talking about moving him to a new preschool. Frank felt the move fit in well with their commuting and work schedules, and, according to him, "Ben is really quite a coper. He makes friends easily, is likable, and will not have a problem." Jennifer acknowledged all of that to be true, but wondered if this was the best time for him to have to make new friends and change teachers, and whether the new schedule would interfere with his nap times. "It's such a huge decision," she lamented. Frank disagreed. "This is nothing for him, you'll see," he said, trying to comfort his wife.

Ben will undoubtedly cope well in his new school, despite his mother's anxiety. She will also be instrumental in his adjustment as she turns her anxiety into caring gestures just as Alicia's mother did. It's interesting that after Alicia's mother helped her with the puzzle, she didn't look directly at Kyle again, as if she was less than proud of her slightly illicit support of her daughter's performance. Or she was not open to discussing it, but felt justified that she was simply being a supportive mother, "doing whatever it takes to help my child succeed." If there's a paternal version of this "whatever it takes" mentality, we've yet to encounter it, at least as it relates to young children. Men often feel that they need to do everything it takes to provide enough financial support for their families to live securely, even if that entails spending hours at work and irritating their wives with their absence. Or they do whatever it takes to complete a household chore, even if it takes up most of Saturday.

So who's right? In our opinion, they both are. It's important that children hear from *both* parents about how the world is going to respond to the things that they find hard to do. We want them to learn that they have to work hard, but that they can both expect and count on help. In other words, they can do it alone, but they are not alone. That is our version of a balanced message that incorporates the typical male and female methods of responding and coping.

In the rest of this chapter, we examine what's unique about how men and women parent, and dispel some of the more pervasive myths that keep men and women from communicating well with each other. And then we talk about these differences in the context of a working marriage.

Pre-Baby Attitudes

Differences in the ways men and women parent don't just suddenly appear when children are three years old. They start before the baby is born. Pregnant women obsess about baby names, wake up at night thinking about the kinds of sheets to buy for the crib, and can't walk by a toy store without staring at the stuffed animals. Most men don't react in this way. In many cases, men focus more on their wives than on their future children. Some women quickly conclude that their husbands aren't ready for fatherhood, or that there will be problems in the marriage when dad has to share mom with the baby. Those conclusions may be a bit hasty and misplaced, but knowing how ready a father is for his paternal role can tell a lot about how life will go after the birth.

Phil and Carolyn Cowan, pioneering researchers from the University of California-Berkeley, studied how a couple's relationship changes when children are born. A strong predictor of a child's successful transition to kindergarten is how much that child's father embraced the pregnancy. A father's prenatal attitudes affect a child's entry into school, and everything up to that point. This finding also suggests a more subtle point: When a father desires and is ready to have a child, the couple is happier. Happier couples provide more sensitive nurturing and higher-quality parenting, and the child goes on to do better in her own transition to school. She enters feeling ready, loved, and focused—echoing the feelings her father had about her arrival and her parents have about their life together.[3]

A father's emotional closeness to the baby and mother has an impact even during delivery: Nursing literature is full of examples of mothers who require less anesthesia and experience fewer birth complications when the father is present at the birth.[4] Again, when a man supports his wife during childbirth, it enhances her sense of well-being, which in turn, supports the infant.

Holding Patterns

Once the baby arrives, differences between a mother's and father's styles of handling the baby become even more pointed. For example, a mother tends to approach and pick up her baby in a predictable fashion. Nine times in ten, she puts both hands under the baby's upper back and shoulders, cradling the child in her hands and arms as she lifts the baby to her upper chest and into the crook of her neck. Sometimes referred to as the "Madonna position" (a la Renaissance art), it's a position most babies and mothers appreciate; it gives them an opportunity to have maximum contact in which their faces are together, their hearts are almost touching, and they can smell each other's scent.

When fathers go to pick up their children, their approach is unpredictable. They may hold the baby at arm's length, look the baby in the eye, or activate the baby physically by rolling the baby over in their arms. And when a man does (finally) bring the baby to his body, it is less often into the crook of his neck than against his upper chest or thorax, supporting the baby's weight on the upturned palm of his hand.[5]

Interestingly, both mothers and fathers hold the baby on their left side so the baby is closer to their hearts. This holds true even with most left-handed parents. However, the mother's holding position, with the baby's face turned inward, gives the baby more ready access to the mother's face and body, but less to the world beyond this compact little unit. The father's position, sometimes called the "football position," with the baby's buttocks in the father's upturned palm, the body tucked between the father's upper arm and the side of his chest, gives the baby a different view of the world—the same view that the father has. They are approaching the world together head on. As one first-time father told us, "I can take care of my son and have a big impact on him, and I don't have to turn into a woman to do it."

Responses to Distress

Mothers and fathers respond differently to a distressed infant or toddler. Mothers are more likely to pick up their children and soothe them. Fathers usually pick up their children and distract them. Again, these are general tendencies that relate to the way men and women solve problems according to their own talents and abilities; they are not absolute differences related to gender or chromosomes.

Play, Playfulness, and Exploration

Although mothers tend to pick up their babies to feed or care for them, fathers pick up their children to *do* something with them. That something often involves more play or discovery than pure maintenance. Fathers tend to make something happen when they have their children's attention, rather than just interacting with them in the rhythm of everyday care. Fathers enjoy surprising their children with unexpected facial expressions, verbal surprises, or physical action—picking the child up without warning or first making eye contact. Babies—if they're up for it—often respond actively, even rambunctiously. This can evoke the mother's amusement or frustration, depending on whether she has a different agenda for the baby at that moment.

Eighteen-month-old Petey would know immediately when his dad Simon returned from work each day. Upon seeing each other, they'd begin to giggle uncontrollably, leaving Petey's mother to complain that the two of them liked to get wired before they even said hello. "Simon likes to get Petey so turned on that by the time they are interacting, they're both at a barely manageable level of excitement," Marilyn explained. But when asked to reflect on whether her husband's behavior was good for her son, despite how much it might irritate her, she did say, "Petey has a gleam in his eye when he is in his father's arms that I don't see when I'm playing with him. They clearly have something special going on between them, and I can't imagine that it isn't good for either of them. I was a little jealous of this at first, but now I realize that it's just their thing, and it really does seem to help Petey keep a high level of interest in the world around him."

The way Simon plays with his son, prompting Petey to become ever more engaged with him, is a hallmark of how many fathers behave. Raising the activity level helps solidify the connection men have with their children: they see and feel how they are positively engaged with each other. Not all fathers and sons interact as vigorously as Simon and Petey; men (to say nothing of children) vary considerably in how they approach each other.

Marilyn's response—admiration mixed with jealousy—is also typical of many mothers. Others are aggravated, especially if they are annoyed at their spouse for other reasons. Jennifer commented, "I love [that] Frank is so crazy with Benjamin, because Ben just loves it. But I often don't love his timing. He riles him up when I've said it is bedtime, or when I was about to read Ben a book. Suddenly, Ben's not interested in that anymore." But Jennifer doesn't always find this lack of synchronicity annoying. At other times, she experiences the same sense of head-shaking wonder and acceptance that Marilyn expressed.

> "The other day I wouldn't give Ben some sweet he wanted when it was close to dinner. He just wouldn't let go of it, getting louder and more boisterous. He even tried to hit me. I was getting ready to discipline him when along came Frank and cranked up the decibel level. He told Ben if he really wanted something, he shouldn't just whine. He should shriek. Soon they were both shrieking at the top of their lungs, then laughing, then Ben forgot all about the candy. I was truly amazed, and once I got over my smidgeon of annoyance, I realized it was funny, too."

When parents are pressed to explain their individual styles of interaction with their children, each give equally strong rationales. Mothers often act on an impulse to prepare their children for the relationships and the emotional connections that will keep them safe, predisposed to learning, and feeling loved and secure. For instance, moms focus on teaching children manners and the importance of showing appreciation. In this way, they convey the notion that politeness facilitates social interaction, and that establishing good habits and routines early in life will be beneficial in the future. Fathers, on the other hand, tend to explain their distracting, risk-taking, and problem-solving behavior as purposeful preparation of their children for the real world into which the children will eventually be propelled. This behavior can take many forms.

According to Marilyn, "Simon is playful even when he is comforting Petey, like the time he [Petey] fell down at the playground." He really hurt himself, it seemed to Marilyn, and an older child whose parents they didn't know had something to do with it, she was sure. But when she wanted to comfort Petey and talk to the other parent, Simon simply brushed Petey's pants off and told him to go back to playing, saying, "Sometimes the big kids knock you down, you just have to get back up." To Marilyn's bemusement, the incident was over almost before it started. She realized Petey would probably have appreciated being comforted by his father, but it also would have turned his spill into a bigger production.

Simon would explain his behavior as helping his child toughen up, since the world won't accommodate his moods and minor aches and pains as readily as his mother does. He wants Petey to know that sometimes you just have to "buck up" and accept that the world isn't always about *you* or even always fair. At that moment, Simon was less interested in whether his child understood the whole message than he was in imparting this valuable lesson.

When it comes to these issues, by the time their children have reached toddlerhood, fathers are often aware they are on a somewhat different trajectory from mothers. Fathers of toddlers have already spent more time playing with their children, particularly compared to the mothers who, despite all the recent changes in roles, are still more highly engaged in maintenance and transportation. And fathers are willing to let their children take more risks in playing.

Behavioral scientists have known for decades that fathers encourage their children, regardless of gender, to explore the world more vigorously than mothers do. Many children identify physical activity and exploration, like bike riding or petting a friendly dog, more with their dads than their moms, thinking that their father will give them more latitude. Still, it can be the opposite. When a mother puts in time at the playground, she sees what other children are doing, which expands her notion of what her own can do. Fathers, who may spend less time observing other children and amassing information about what's appropriate behavior at various ages, may be less certain about the playground culture.

As children age, some differences persist in parents' different styles, although they do come closer together to adjust to the developmental challenges of toddlerhood. Men continue to encourage and support novelty-seeking, even marginally risky behavior in their children, both boys and girls. Rough-and-tumble play is a widely recognized characteristic that distinguishes fathers' actions. Men's typically larger size and muscle mass may predispose them to manage their children's bodies differently. They often carry toddlers on their shoulders. Being hung upside down or high in the air and just tossed about is the common fate of well-fathered children of either gender.

The father as a jungle gym generally delights children. Toddlers and preschoolers seem interested in using their father's body as a play space more readily than their mother's. Mothers are typically less invested in physical play, largely because they feel that after carrying the baby, giving birth, and often nursing, their bodies have already been used by their children. Wrestling doesn't come as naturally to them. Boys like to wrestle—even big boys. For fathers, feeling physically close to their children is a novelty to be explored.

Language and the Art of Communication

Many differences between mothers and fathers appear in the way they each use and teach language. Often younger children put more effort into explaining themselves—what they want to do, things they need, or problems they'd like to solve—to their dads. This pattern begins early, often with a child's repertoire of gestures. Children seem to anticipate that their mothers can figure out sooner what they want, so they work less hard at explaining to her what they need.

Mothers often feel attuned to their children's earliest attempts to speak. They know what their children mean to say, even from minimal cues, and sometimes jump into the conversation before the child finishes speaking. Intuition like this—to feel that you know your child better than she knows herself and better than anyone else does—can be especially important to a working mom.

If Petey's mom, Marilyn, and Benjamin's mom, Jennifer, ever met, they would quickly realize that they have much in common. Both take great pride in knowing what their children need and in providing it almost before they ask. Marilyn knows when Petey is about to have a hunger "meltdown," and she usually has Ritz crackers on hand to prevent it. Similarly, Jennifer knows when Ben is getting so tired that, although he is still raring to go, he will soon embarrass himself (or her) with a temper tantrum that means, "I've had enough. Can't you tell?" They place limits on their children so that they can prevent the meltdowns. The children don't have to use their language to explain these emotions; their mothers supply it for them: "I know you are just hungry (tired), and that's what's really bothering you." It is wonderful to be so understood, and the children are aware of their mothers' love at those moments and grateful for their understanding (even if they don't show or express it).

In some marriages, this type of communication can become a source of some contention. Mothers complain that their children work harder to communicate with their fathers but "expect their moms to read their minds and feed them before they themselves even know they're hungry," as Marilyn described it. There is some evidence that by the middle of toddlerhood, when toddlers are mastering speech more actively, they use more advanced speech patterns with fathers than they do with mothers. Once again, it appears as though dad can't understand without help, while mom is responsible for getting it right the first time.

> It was lunchtime, and a group of us were picnicking with our kids. Three-year-old Jack was having a tantrum in front of his father. His dad picked him up, held his arms pressed against his body so he couldn't wiggle around, put his face close to the toddler's, and said, "Now tell me what you want. Don't whine or hit, just tell me, and then I can help you." Jack was pouty for another moment; then he said, "I'm very hungry, Daddy, and I don't want any of those things for lunch." Having witnessed this episode, Marsha later asked Jack's dad if he knew what the youngster had wanted. "Of course," he said. "But I wanted him to tell me. I say all the time to him, 'Use your words.' So does my wife, but she means, 'Don't whine.' I mean, 'Explain what you want.'"

Differences Are Not Deficiencies

For decades, child development experts, especially experts on bonding and attachment, have focused exclusively on the mother-child pair. As a result, we've been inclined to think of parental behavioral differences as deficiencies. It's a cultural given, it seems, that mothers are the main caregivers and fathers are assistants—able or otherwise. A father is relied on at many times, not least when it is his turn or a mother needs a break. But culturally, babies have generally been seen as prime maternal property.

Some surprising research findings bear this out. One distinguishing characteristic between maternal and paternal behavior becomes evident after parents divorce and relates to the primary physical custody of the children. California psychologist Warren Farrell, in analyzing parenting plans set up by sole physical custody parents, showed that fathers who have primary physical custody—for whatever reason—are nine times more likely than mothers to support the other parent's engagement in the lives of their children.[6] Similarly, Mogens Christofferson, in a 1995 study, showed that when divorced fathers become primary caregivers, the parents are far less likely to have ongoing conflict than when the children remain in the primary care of their mothers.[7]

Plato opined that mothers are closer to their children than fathers because they are more certain they are their own. This opinion is supported in extremely acrimonious custody disputes and results in fathers being marginalized or excluded from their children's lives. But the reality is that mothers and fathers view their parenting roles and their relations with their children differently. Children typically value what each parent gives them.

Fathers Are Not Substitute Mothers

Fathers themselves perpetuate the stereotype that mothers are in charge by relegating themselves to second-class parental status as their preferred default position. Instead of trying to figure out his own way of relating to his baby, a father may assume the role of support staff and try to mimic what the mother does or acquiesce when she tells him to copy what she does. After all, she knows best, right?

But this approach to parenting rarely, if ever, works for children or the family as a whole. Men we've interviewed who choose this path almost always end up saying that it felt "wrong," it "didn't fit," they "couldn't get the rhythm," and "relating to their children, they felt like socks that were too small." Kyle first encountered this phenomenon when he began studying infants and toddlers raised by stay-at-home dads in stable families. Many men reported that after a week or two of trying to be a replacement mom, they decided to do it their *own* way—changing, feeding, comforting, bathing, dressing, talking and singing with, carrying, and playing in ways they thought "fit us guys better." Interestingly, most of them kept this feeling to themselves, fearing that their wives might become upset if they realized that their husbands were not following their instructions to the letter. We now know that these parenting differences do not harm children, mothers, fathers, or their marriages. A Swedish research group systematically reviewed twenty-two studies and found father engagement was linked to fewer behavioral problems in sons, better psychological health and cognitive outcomes for daughters, less delinquency, and a higher standard of living for families with lower incomes.[8]

> Hank, a father, told us: "When I cut the cord in the delivery room, the nurse looked at me and asked me if I was ready to hold Sam. I'm exhausted and confused, enormously relieved my wife

and baby seem okay, and still plenty scared, but somehow I said yes. The nurse wrapped him in a pink blanket—they were out of blue—and she plunked him in my arms, eyes still closed, hair greasy with amniotic fluid. I was trembling, afraid I might drop him. Right away I had this overwhelmingly powerful feeling—having this life which I helped create going from inside of Susan's body straight into my arms. I felt totally inept, clueless if I was even holding him right. How tight should I hold him? I was suddenly aware of the warmth of my own body and wondering how to get it to him through the blankets. I wasn't the only one shivering and shaking at the moment.

"A nurse came to take him out of my arms to give him a bath. My first instinct was to give Sam to her—she obviously knew more of what she was doing than I did. But I hesitated; Sam was mine and would be for the rest of his life. I felt this tidal wave of possessiveness come through me. I balked at handing him over. That feeling would be a constant companion for the next months as I overcame my reticence to always back away and let Susan do the work. She took such pride in caring for him. She had waited so long for this job, and I wanted her to love every blessed moment of it. But not at the expense of my getting to know my son. It was fancy footwork. I wonder if Sam will ever be aware of these early tensions between his mom and me over who was going to learn what about him and what he needed."

Hank sounds like a lot of men; he cannot believe that he is falling in love with his child at first sight. Many men retreat from asserting claims on their babies, often out of love for their wives and their desire not to impinge on her special moment. We helped Hank realize that doing so wouldn't take anything away from Susan—not by a long shot. Plenty of evidence exists that, although the mother-child bond persists across many cultures and circumstances, it is strong enough to allow children to have significant relationships with other people. Whenever fathers and children have the space to figure out who they are to each other, without mothers micromanaging the relationship, children thrive and mothers get the break they need.

Even more important, the tie that develops between a father and his child strengthens—not weakens—the couple's relationship. When dads take the initiative with their children, many women report feeling as if their husbands are caring for them directly. Many women report that they never loved their husbands as much as they do when their husbands care for their children.

Even among divorced couples, their relationship and the father's relationship to his child is aided by being as cordial as possible. Research indicates that when fathers and mothers feel most positively about each other (romantically or otherwise), fathers get—and stay—more involved with their children.[9] Being a nurturing parent helps the couple, and being a happier couple helps the mothering and the fathering. It is a circular interaction that keeps feeding on itself, positively or negatively.

When divorced parents fight, gender-based parenting differences become more rigid and are attributed to a defect in the ex-spouse. For example, divorced mothers often complain that fathers rile up their children instead of calming them at bedtime, which they commonly attribute to a defect in the father's parenting skills. This complaint often becomes mothers' reason that divorced fathers should bring their children back to them earlier in the day. Angry mothers complain that their husbands' hands-on play is immature and their discipline style is aggressive. Often such criticism hurts the child as much as the parent for whom it is intended. After all, she shares half of her gene pool with each parent.

It's Not Just Gender

Even though the parenting differences between fathers and mothers are important, we should acknowledge that they are only part of the story. Who we *are*—our unique history, temperament, and personality—influences the first most important thing we as parents do: choose a partner or mate. This in turn affects our working together (or not) and our choices when life is difficult. Gender is less important than who a particular man or woman is *as an individual*, and how he or she became that person. Our advice is to be yourself first and consider your gender second.

When we ask couples to consider this idea, it is not very popular. It is easier for most of us to blame X or Y chromosomes in their various combinations for our less-than-attractive habits as parents and partners than to own our sometimes nutty, self-serving behavior. Temperament, personality, and character trump gender in many of our most important human endeavors, and nurturing is no exception.

Nurturing is a central human instinct, but it is not exclusively female. The drive to nurture appears early in the development of both boys and girls (sharing binkies with their beloved fuzzies), and keeps on growing until they are men and women, well on into grandparenthood. The bedrock of any nurturing behavior—the capacity to be loving and consistent, selfless and patient, flexible and expectant and, primarily, the ability to sacrifice and share one's own emotional, spiritual, and intellectual assets and dreams for the well-being of one's child—all quickly transcend gender as the dominant factor in nurturing. Our own personal histories as men and women, the cultures that have prepared us to behave in ways consistent with those beliefs and values, and our own families all drive us toward expressing these abilities in relationships.

That's why we say a man's relationship with his mother reveals a great deal about how he acts as a husband. If the relationship is one of mutual respect, regard, and emotional vitality and warmth, he is more likely to bring such qualities to his marriage and seek them in a mate. How a woman feels about her own upbringing will be reflected in her behavior. If, for example, she thinks her own mother placed too much emphasis on how much attention she garnered for her brains, looks, or a certain aptitude, she may strive to ensure her own children don't have to face similar pressures.

Vive la différence!

That men and women parent differently, for whatever complicated reasons, is in most cases a great advantage for children. However, there is one area of parents' competence in which there seems to be little or no difference. Research has underscored that it is the *quality*, not quantity, of the interactions between you and your child that determines the overall value of your involvement in his or her life.[10]

A mother's or father's sensitivity to a child's needs is far more important than counting the minutes each spends or calculating each parent's share of work or play. Children value how their fathers play with—and care for—them and what they learn, not the total amount of time they log together. That kind of calculation tells us practically nothing about the ultimate influence of the parent on the development of the child. What parents actually *do* while they are with their children, *how* they do it, and most importantly how they *are* with their children matters more than how often or how long they are doing it.

Children know this. Most who have had involved fathers in their lives (and mothers who have supported that arrangement) do not think their fathers are second-class parents. Our niece, who has an involved dad, explains, "When my friends who don't have much to do with their dads are over at the house, the first thing they ask me is why I ask *Dad* if stuff is or isn't okay to do. It always surprises me, 'cause I don't think of my dad as standing in for my mom—like holding down the fort till the real parent gets back. He's the real deal all on his own. I think it's cool and so does Mom. Sometimes it even makes my friends jealous."

Even very young children understand that there's a strong parenting partnership. Toddlers show greater self-reliance and ability to manage daily frustrations (which toddlers face a lot) if there is good co-parenting rapport between their parents.[11] Their day-care providers also notice that such children have stronger pre-academic skills and are more attentive and less hyperactive than those whose parents' relationships are more acrimonious. And toddlers may not be the youngest ones affected. Cris Scull, a University of North Carolina psychologist, suggests that infants whose parents don't function well as a team may be more distressed and less well adjusted as toddlers.[12]

The differences between how fathers and mothers typically parent—especially when the co-parenting partnership remains strong—are associated with a number of benefits for children. Research on marriage and divorce has shown for many decades that a mother's relationship with her children is critical for their development in terms of their sense of self, sense of security in the world, and so on; a consistent and loving mother is one of the strongest predictors of a well-adjusted adult in single- and dual-parent homes.

But the research on fathers and subsequent co-parenting considerations were negligible until a few decades ago. Current research on the paternal role shows that paternal involvement tends to make life better for kids of all ages. As mentioned, fathers tend to be more comfortable letting kids explore the world beyond the nest, whether that kid is crawling, rolling over, playing with new kids at the park, riding a bike, or sleeping over at a friend's house. They also tend to be more playful and tactile partners. Mothers like to educate through play, while fathers are more willing to settle for delight and discovery. The rough-housing stuff for which fathers are noted helps children develop self-control.[13] These dad-promoted skills seem to be especially appreciated by a child's peers because the child is more socially competent later in life.

The dad-involved child also benefits in other ways, including less likelihood of juvenile justice issues in adolescence, a later age for initial sexual exploration (which means fewer teen pregnancies), resolution of conflict with less aggression and more verbal reasoning, and less-rigid gender stereotyping in interactions with the opposite sex.[14] How this all connects to having an engaged father is less clear, though the paternal style itself seems to generally help kids become better attuned to real-world issues sooner in their lives, easing some of the challenges that are more daunting for kids who do not have a trusted and reliable male presence in their lives.

Educational outcomes also improve for children with involved dads. Such children tend to stay in school longer, do better while they are there, and ultimately enjoy a higher lifetime income. Verbal skills are strengthened for boys and girls, which is somewhat surprising because men have a reputation for being less verbal communicators. Math skills are also stronger among some girls who have had involved fathers, even when those fathers may not be especially gifted mathematical theorists themselves. Maybe the sensitive attention to the whole child—brain, body, temperament—strengthens these developmental achievements. We mention these not because we are convinced there is a direct pass-through of increased measurable cognition in dad-engaged children, but rather to acknowledge the new awareness that fathering can do more for children than just support mom's unique strengths. Dad brings additional strengths of his own.

Emotional maturity is also commonly attributed to kids who've had close paternal connections. A half-century ago, Robert Sears began a study of five-year-olds and their families. After more than two decades, these same children were reevaluated to learn how they functioned as adults, especially in the areas of morality and compassion. The researchers found that the single most powerful predictor of whether those children were empathic adults was their fathers' involvement in their childhood. A decade later, when the subjects were in their early forties, the researchers assessed their social relationships within their families and communities yet again. The paternal warmth they'd experienced differentiated those with successful relationships in adulthood from those with failed relationships.

There is a catch however. Although just "being there" matters a lot, being emotionally available, responsive, and warm matters a whole lot more to children's ultimate well-being. (The same holds true for mothers.) The current version of quality parenting is *intensified parenting*. Parents approach it as a job, even a profession. But parenting is not just a job; it is a vital *relationship*. It isn't just about what you put into it in terms of work and intensity, although that helps. Most important is what you add in terms of sensitivity to your child, how he is feeling, and what he needs every moment of every day. For men, these are new expectations, although vital when we consider the well-being of society. Margaret Mead summarized the issue: "Every known human society rests firmly on the learned nurturing behavior of men."[15]

So, while fathers add to what mothers have always provided, their contributions are both unique and essential. Children thrive when parents ally their values, passions, and talents. Children struggle when they don't. But co-parenting isn't just about what's good for the child; it has to feel right to both partners. And there's the rub. Children don't bean count: witness any child's glee when dad comes home from work, and you know the child has missed his dad all day, and doesn't blame him for having to work longer hours outside the home than mom does. However, spouses often *do* keep track to a greater or lesser extent. When one parent feels he or she is doing the bulk of the family or child care, and he or she had a different understanding or expectation for that care, resentments build. Those smoldering feelings should not get in the way of your marriage or parenting. In the next chapter, we'll say more about avoiding the build-up of negative feelings. For now, it is enough to say that two heads are better than one—two hearts, too.

3

▼

Building a Partnership That Works
The Relationship Is the Solution, Not the Problem

JENNIFER'S HUSBAND FRANK encouraged her to apply for a promotion at work. It was exactly the job she had always wanted, though it meant spending significantly more time in the office and away from their young son, Ben. When the promotion came through, Frank was extremely proud of his wife and pleased that she had "put herself out there" to chase her professional dream. Soon enough, though, he found to his frustration that he couldn't adjust his schedule as he had anticipated to pick up Ben on time from day care. He was constantly juggling his work commitments, trying to figure out how to collect their son and spend a few extra afternoons with him before Jennifer returned home from work on her "late" days.

Although Jennifer agreed it wasn't Frank's fault that things had turned out this way, they got stuck on how to arrange their schedules so that Jennifer wouldn't feel guilty about staying later at work. When Ben asked why she "always works now" and is "never with me anymore," Jennifer broke down in tears and became very angry at Frank.

When Jennifer and Frank discussed this situation with us, Jennifer blamed Frank for Ben's complaint, saying that she felt "unsupported" in her distress, even though she knew they were both stuck in "logistics hell" right now. Frank bridled at being blamed, saying he was "pedaling as fast as I can" to keep schedules and family together, and that he, too, could use more support. We helped them listen to what the other actually needed, having first said how they felt. They collaborated on a schedule revision that worked for Frank; on one of the days that Jennifer worked late, she arranged for a friend to pick Ben up and give him a snack before Frank got him. This took some pressure off Frank at work. He promised to support Jennifer more actively when Ben gave her a hard time. For starters, he had a talk with Ben, telling him that he was proud of mommy for working more to help make money for the family and that it gave him a chance to spend extra time with Ben that he hadn't had before. Frank also made a point of regularly mentioning in front of Ben how great their new schedule was, turning it into a point of pride for the family rather than something to be lamented (because Ben had less time with Jennifer). With a little help, they were able to confront this issue together and solve it as a team, easing the ready blame that can threaten to shut down marital communication.

HAVING TWO NURTURING, competent, and engaged parents benefits children, regardless of whether those parents live together. How they work out their different competencies for the joint benefit of the child and their relationship is the real story, however, because that working out is what makes the difference between happy and unhappy families. Turning parental differences into family strengths is the keystone of healthy family life.

A partnership alliance *between* you and your spouse sets the stage for the quality of life for everyone in the family. Were we to draw a picture, it would look like the diagram on the following page.

The diagram connects mom, dad, and child; many families have more than one child, however. As more lines are added, they take on different significance and power, depending on that particular child and each parent's connection to him. Multiple children are hard on a marriage if

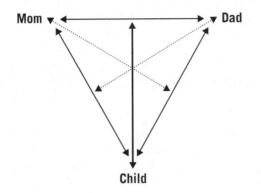

© Kyle D. Pruett, MD

the alliance is shaky to begin with because there is so much stress on the family's main infrastructure—the couple's relationship. But even in families with two or more children, there is a unique basic triangle between each child and his parents. For simplicity, let's focus on one triangle as an example of what is replicated and more complex each time a child is added.

The busiest of the triangle's thoroughfares is the one traveled between mothers and fathers. It is not, however, the only one bearing important two-way traffic. Mother and child have their relationship, and father and child have theirs. And as the dotted lines signify, mom has an impact on dad's relationship with the child, while dad has an impact on the mother-child connection. Each parent can support or undermine the child's relationship with the other parent.

The bold line in the diagram is typically the invisible line, since it is the one least often considered in most discussions of parenting. The majority of parenting books focus on the child, or how one parent (usually the mother) should act to elicit certain kinds of desirable behaviors and attitudes from the child. If only it were so simple. We believe that the parental alliance has the most influence on a child's healthy development.

After the birth of our daughter, Marsha scaled back her work so she could become the primary caretaker, although she continued with her academic research part-time. It was not until our daughter was on her way to toddlerhood that Marsha reentered the world of work in a major way. As she recalls, "I had agreed to give a talk to a large audience of lawyers and psychologists when our daughter was eighteen months old. As I was saying good-bye to her at the door of the conference room, I was wondering why on earth I'd agreed to do this. I didn't feel ready to pull my head out of my parenting and push it into the topic at hand. I had not given a talk like this since before the baby was born, and I wasn't sure I still had it in me.

"As I stood there, lost in self-doubt and ambivalence, increasingly anxious and immobilized, Kyle picked up our daughter and said, 'It's time for Mommy's talk, so give her a big wave and a kiss. You are so lucky to have a Mommy who can help so many people. They came to hear her because she's so good at what she does. Bye, Mommy; do your important work. We'll be waiting for you when you are done.' I had to fight back the tears. I was so moved, but also reassured enough to turn and face all those strangers and do myself proud."

The best working definition of co-parenting encompasses all the arrow traffic in the diagram. At its core, co-parenting is about how the parental relationship shapes the crucial relationship between parents and child first and the world around them second. The key components of a strong co-parenting relationship are:

▼ Being the "kid's team"
▼ Dividing up child care
▼ Caring together, rather than feeling alone
▼ Keeping intimacy alive
▼ Balancing work and family
▼ Managing conflict about your child (the subject of chapter 4)

Co-parenting works best when there is a healthy rapport between parents, and the alliance born of that rapport is nurtured with love and attention. Let's take a detailed look at these components that are essential to building and sustaining a strong, lasting alliance.

Being the "Kid's Team"

What does it mean to be the kid's team? It's sharing a perspective of what makes your particular child tick. For example, say it is New Year's Eve and the plan was for your family of four to attend an early-evening concert. But your four-year-old child's mood turns sour and nasty just as you are preparing to go out. One parent will now have to stay home with him, if your older daughter and one of you are going to have a nice night. It's not at all what you wanted for yourselves or the family, but that's just the way it is, given this child's ability to hold the family hostage when he is over-tired, turning the night miserable. At his stage in development, he must get enough food on time and sufficient sleep in order to function, or he becomes "the family's little monster," as his sister says. He won't be that way forever, but for tonight, he's staying home and so is someone else.

This situation could be viewed competitively: Who has to deal with the unpleasant child versus who gets to go out for a festive evening? But it is really about working together to meet the needs of a deserving, excited sister and an exhausted little guy who doesn't even know he's tired. Mom and dad certainly know and, instead of bickering over who stays home, decide to toss a coin to determine who gets to go out.

Unfortunately, parents don't always agree on how to deal with their child's mood, even when they agree on what makes their child tick. Frank believes that Ben is more flexible and adaptive to long trips and changes in schedules than does Jennifer. Sometimes he goes along with her sense of things; sometime she works on him to accept hers. But their ability to sort through and resolve their differences when they arise is proof that they are working as a team. The stories they share about their son—the funny anecdotes, and cute and embarrassing episodes that have entered family lore—are the narrative they use to keep track of one another and their commitment to put this kid's needs ahead of (most of) theirs.

When you are miles apart in your expectations, however, and spend little to no time trying to reconcile them, co-parenting is not so easy. James McHale's "Families Through Time" study revealed that parents rarely spend *any* time thinking and talking together about co-parenting before the baby's birth. The rule—not the exception—was "not to have spoken about each other's parenting perspectives or ideologies, let alone how they might co-parent together and resolve differences between them once the baby arrived."[1] Room décor, the mother's work schedule, maybe starting a college fund, and the father's active role in feedings and diapering were far more common topics than how the couple actually envisioned raising their child. Of course, they could usually agree on wanting their child to be happy, but what does that mean, especially since the definition changes rapidly along with the development of the child? Those early shared images of family are loving and dreamy, but they do not in and of themselves lead to a plan for how a couple will manage co-parenting from the moment that little being joins them.

It's vital to take time to ensure both you and your partner are on or near the same wavelength regarding the basic values and beliefs you'll rely on to raise your child; this is more important than operating in lock-step on everyday child-rearing tasks. To help get the conversation flowing, we suggest you pick out a few sentences from Phil and Carolyn Cowan's "Ideas About Parenting" questionnaire in appendix A (starting on p. 199), grab a cup of something hot, and do some serious listening to each other.

Some of the statements we find especially evocative for discussion are these:

▼ In general, parents today reason too much with their children.
▼ I sometimes feel I am too involved with my child.
▼ I care less than most parents I know about having my child obey me.
▼ When a child continues to get out of bed after being sent to bed two or three times, he or she should be punished for disobedience.
▼ I like to see a child have opinions and express them even to adults.
▼ Parents should be directly involved in supervising their children's school work.
▼ Fathers have a special knack for raising sons.

Dividing Up Child Care

During the early months of a baby's life, the mother typically does the lioness's share of the infant's physical care, while the father manages the house and family from a peripheral vantage point. What seems to make parents feel best during this time is not that each is doing his or her fair share, but whether the amount and kinds of labor each contribute make sense to them both. For example, while mom is nursing, dad makes dinner. She doesn't mind cleaning up afterwards—it's a nice break from baby time—and dad looks forward to his nightly bonding sessions with the baby. In a few months, when mom is back at work, they can alter this evening schedule so that each parent has time with the baby as well as time to tackle household chores. Again, it is less about time management than it is about shared dreams and visions, so quid pro quo effort-splitting deals aren't going to get you much satisfaction.

For Steve and Judy, it was important to minimize the amount of time Jacob, their four-month-old, spent in day care, sharing the belief that it was "best for him to be raised when he's so little mostly by family." Luckily, they were both able to temporarily reorder their work lives. Judy, who works as a medical technician, is home on Mondays and Tuesdays, while Steve, a social worker, is with Jacob on Fridays, and the weekends are, in their words, "bi-parental." While Judy hopes this will carry them through Jacob's first five years, Steve is less convinced it's "doable or necessary." They agreed to stick with this arrangement until the baby is at least a year old, and then "reconnoiter when he's walking."

Psychologist Jessica Ball and others have shown that it is not whether couples successfully solve and altogether eliminate these problems of divided care; it is whether they feel *heard and respected* in the conflicts that matters more to sustaining marital happiness. When couples keep their common goals in focus, they are working toward a "greater good," even if it sometimes gets lost in the daily grind of too much to do and not enough time in which to do it.[2]

In the popular media, how equally couples split the family work is often equated with how well the couple is working together. Yet couples divide tasks in so many ways, researchers could never count them all. More important is how you and your partner understand this division of labor as part of a larger goal for the well-being of your family. It is worth repeating: How you do it is less important than how you each *feel* about it. To calculate the number of dishes washed or diapers laundered is a parent-centered, anemic view of co-parenting, because it leaves the child's well-being completely out of the equation. The point is to maximize the child's time with parents who are crazy about being with her, not as individuals, but as a team. This is equally true whether you are fighting as a married couple about who gets stuck doing more grocery shopping, or as a divorced couple about whether you get two extra overnights per month.

Caring Together versus Feeling Alone

Joint emotional ownership of the baby and his needs is another cornerstone of co-parenting. It sometimes gets lost in discussions about the physical division of labor. Mutual caring counteracts the common feeling that your spouse is withdrawing. That's the feeling you may get when you're not talking as much, or that the only conversations the two of you have are focused solely on the baby and her needs. Then it feels as if your partner is less available emotionally, asking less often how you are, showing less affection, reaching out less often to check in during the day. Finally, he or she seems physically absent, spending more time at the office or lingering at the gym after a weekly basketball game.

Many spouses first pull away from the other due to fatigue and then later because they feel resentful, isolated, discouraged, incompetent, or ignored. Our own experience with couples has convinced us that the majority of parents typically experience all of these emotions because of the demands of the transition to parenthood, not because they are no longer committed to the marriage.

Most couples expect to be more egalitarian than they actually become, because fifty-fifty splits are not as efficient as developing complementary roles and areas for which each spouse is responsible. Women who stay home with their children feel the loss of their working selves, often reporting that they "have become boring." They feel that friends and acquaintances do not consider them as important as "working mothers." Men feel they've become less essential to their wives sexually and emotionally, as mothers sink all their energies into taking care of the helpless beings who simultaneously need so much while being unable to give much back.

These emotions can be painful, scary, and of course, unwelcome. How couples navigate these tricky waters depends primarily on the partner one chooses. As Yale psychiatrist Stephen Fleck once remarked to Kyle, "Picking a partner means picking a particular set of problems and, if you're lucky, a set of solutions to go along with them." Human nature is such that our vulnerabilities and weaknesses rise to the top when we are spent and confused. These are the very circumstances new parents frequently encounter. But the strengths are usually just below the surface, ready to rise to meet the vulnerabilities, given half a chance.

Caring together means more than just acting like the child's team. It means caring more about the mutuality of your own and your partner's experiences than either one's individually. That is, seeing your *shared* perspectives as more important than either of yours alone. Each parent must clearly communicate to get to this sense of mutual experience. Successful co-parenting couples:

▼ **Minimize the areas of individual isolation, rather than dwell on them or blame them on the relationship itself.**
It can be awfully lonely to get up and nurse a newborn in the middle of the night while your spouse is sleeping peacefully in your bed. Instead of focusing on the fact that he could be giving the baby a bottle, she moves the cradle closer to their bed so she can nurse the infant there when it's time to feed. She can snuggle up to her husband instead of sitting across the room in the rocker. In fact, she manages to snuggle hard enough against dad that he throws his arm around both of them without waking completely.

▼ **See the relationship as the solution, not the problem.**
She really dislikes how he puts his parents and extended family before hers. She is annoyed that he is a bit cowed by his family and doesn't stand up to them. Instead of viewing him as part of the problem and on "their side," she thinks of him as her partner in this dilemma and works with him to understand how they could respond differently so their child can be a more equal part of both families.

▼ **Work at magnifying common beliefs about how family life should feel and evolve.**
Identify three priorities you agree on as a couple for family traditions you want to create and maintain for your child.

▼ **Be mindful of staying connected physically and emotionally at this disorienting time.**
Put at the top of your to-do list something you want to do only with or for your spouse that is separate from your child.

This prescription minimizes the silent spaces, pulls against the withdrawals that follow, and keeps the feeling of aloneness at bay.

With such complex elements, balanced co-parenting takes some effort, because our emotions tend to guide us when we are tired and uncertain about what to do next. In the words of a typical first-time parent, "It's exhausting to know so little about what you are doing, especially when it matters so much that you do it right. I had no clue how hard and beautiful this would be. There's this life and deathness to it that is incredibly scary." These feelings are natural and almost universal. Actively sharing your thoughts and feelings with your partner will help to counteract the fear. So don't underestimate a simple, straightforward act like tenderly taking your partner's face in your hands and saying, "Hi, I remember you. Remember me? We're doing this together, right? I'm right here and so are you." The expression alone is a great first step.

Keeping Intimacy Alive

In our work with new parents, we've heard countless variations of the following: "Who is this person I had this baby with? She is completely different now." "He changed the minute we brought that baby home; I don't know him anymore." These thoughts signal that the co-parenting threshold has been breached. The very relationship that nurtured the desire to have the baby in the first place is headed south; romance, passion, and sex are set adrift like icebergs calved by a retreating glacier. The trusted friendship between these lovers receives little maintenance. The long, cherished conversations and walks are abandoned overnight. And the primary (or only) one who's getting held, stroked, kissed, touched, or receiving adoring looks is the baby.

For partners of both genders, but especially for women, intimacy includes talking about how they feel, positively and negatively. Men typically face many cultural disincentives to being intimate through emotional talk rather than action. They are more often rewarded for being the breadwinner and the maintenance man around the house

Co-parenting Preventive Maintenance Quiz
▼

Rate yourself to see if you are staying connected to your partner. In the past month, how many times have you actually:

TIMES
PER MONTH

____ Made and protected time to be together as a couple?

____ Set up a time and place (when neither is tired) to discuss a difference in how you're parenting your child. It could be anything, such as feeling as if she's cuddling the baby too much, or he's roughhousing too much.

____ Examined your schedules, noted the stress points, and reached out for extra help from a family member, friend, or sitter? If you are the one who makes the call, you get extra credit.

____ Offered to take the baby for three or more hours so your spouse can have a respite from parenting to do something else—shopping, reading, watching a ballgame, exercising, or going out with friends?

____ In the past week, how often have you laughed together about something your child did *and* about something unrelated to your child?

____ TOTAL

What Your Tally Means

0–5 You're on thin ice. Make some changes soon or your relationship might really suffer. Don't rule out getting some professional help.

6–20 You're on track. Be cognizant of how important it is to focus on your spouse as well as your kids.

21–31 You're doing your child a big favor. Keep up the good work.

than for contributing to emotionally laden conversation. Women tend to experience men's "do first, talk later (if at all!)" attitude as emotionally distancing and regularly off-putting.

From the beginnings of relationships with other children, little girls share their secrets and heartfelt emotions as indications of their intimacy and best-friend status. Little boys' friendships depend more on palling around and doing the same kinds of stuff together. So, if men frequently withdraw from conflict or respond with critical or sarcastic remarks, their mates often experience this behavior as a threat to intimacy, leading to a breakdown in communication. Women, in contrast, are prone to pursue the conflict until it is understood and digested. In contrast to men's style of backing off to slow down their physiological response, women want to talk it out right away as proof of their closeness. Bridging this chasm takes work, because it requires sustaining joint attention to the child's *and* the couple's needs. Sometimes the parental alliance needs first dibs to stay healthy.

> Esther, Josiah's and Riva's five-year-old, was so clingy, they rarely went out at night, and only when an extended family member was available to babysit. They were frequently at odds about how much to indulge her demands versus going out themselves to take care of their relationship.

Josiah recounted a time when Esther fell to pieces as they were about to leave on a fancy overnight trip sponsored by his company—a coveted perk for all the good work he had done that year. Riva began to make noise about staying behind rather than all of them being miserable. She couldn't imagine how she could enjoy herself, knowing that Esther would be sullen and unhappy for the next twenty-four hours. Josiah recalls, "I put my foot down, took my wife lovingly and firmly by the shoulders, and said, 'This is just too important to me and for us. I miss you so much. She will survive if we go; I won't if you don't come.'" Riva went, and Esther was fine, of course. Later, both parents told us that they didn't realize how much they needed time to have fun together and refresh their sense of themselves—not as parents—but as a loving, devoted couple.

Balancing Work and Family

> Kyle's grandmother, Winnie, who built and ran a "boys" dormitory at an Oklahoma college, warned her three daughters to delay getting jobs "until your babies are grown up and gone, and your husband has earned enough money so that your having your own money won't scare the pants off him."

There is evidence that prior to World War II, marriages in which both spouses were working were less stable than stay-at-home mom or breadwinning dad families.[3] But today, marital stability is routinely *strengthened* by two-career couples, as long as the mother is happy with her job and each parent supports the other's working.

Still, once the baby has arrived and reality moves in, mothers and fathers start feeling the tug from a host of ambivalences. Mothers can be more ambivalent than they expected about having a very involved father. Although they appreciate the support, on some level they may not want to share this beloved baby's heavenly attentions with anybody—even *him* (a topic we'll return to later on). Furthermore, many high-powered mothers feel surprisingly pained about stepping away from their careers, once the honeymoon period with the newborn passes, and the drudgery of daily life, in a world where most parents go to work, sets in. These feelings can morph into jealousies of a father's "other life."

Dad, for his part, can resent having to work longer hours and spend less time with the baby than he wants. He feels left out of those fleeting moments when the baby first smiles, crawls, or walks. And he misses his spouse's income. He may feel pressure to keep up their standard of living while she's no longer doing her share.

Satisfying both parents means figuring out what minimum each needs to contribute both at home and from a job or career (income, family work, child care, and so on), concentrating on the area that he or she has pulled back from since the baby's birth.

> Take parents Justin and Nancy. Justin is doing more of the income-producing work through his job as a lawyer. Nancy, also a law school graduate, is staying home "for awhile" with their children, ages one and three. She didn't think her life as a trial lawyer fit into her dreams for being a mom. But only three months after resigning from her job, Nancy misses the rush of staying up late, cramming before a trial, and working closely with colleagues. She wants Justin to come home more often and do more of the dishes, the laundry, and other household chores.

Justin's response is to study their finances and suggest they hire a housekeeper two days per week. But Nancy still feels she is missing something, although she deeply loves being a mother. She is always talking to her friends and to Justin—whenever he'll listen—about why this isn't making her as satisfied as she expected.

When the two of them finally sit down and, in Justin's words, "hash it out until we get somewhere," they agree she should find a job in which she can keep her hand in the law (something besides trial work), but limit it to fifteen hours per week. Justin agrees that he needs to be more involved at home as well and rearranges his work schedule to go to work an hour and a half later one day a week, allowing him to spend a few hours with Nancy in her daily routine.

As Justin and Nancy discovered early on in their lives as parents, balancing work and family means checking in with each other to ensure each spouse doesn't feel as if an important part of him- or herself is being

Check-in Questions
▼

- ▼ Are you both satisfied enough with the work for which you are paid so that on balance it is a positive experience?
- ▼ Are you each making enough money at your job so that working doesn't further tax your family economically (for example, needing to pay for child care)?
- ▼ Are you each comfortable with the amount of money the other is making, or do you wish he or she made a different amount?
- ▼ Do either of you feel you are making too big a sacrifice in your career that you may not be able to repair later on in your working life?
- ▼ Do you have enough, and the right kind, of help at home to attend to household chores and the tasks of everyday life that are neglected while you're focused on employment?
- ▼ Can one of your careers tolerate a more flexible work schedule in the short term, while your children are young and love having you around?
- ▼ Is it time for one of you to switch to a different career altogether?
- ▼ Do either of your employers have flextime or job-sharing policies that you could explore?
- ▼ Do you have clear short-term and long-term plans that feel, in aggregate, fair to both of you?
- ▼ Have you made lifestyle compromises for your work-family balance that are exacting a greater toll than you expected or thought they would (such as a difficult commute, long hours, or living in an area you don't particularly like or far from friends or family)?

strangled. It means seeing the big puzzle and how each piece fits, rather than viewing each one—income-producing work, family time, and so on—in isolation. The end goal is a shared one, and if one pathway isn't getting you there, it's time to see if another one will.

Men are often more reluctant to take advantage of such policies, given their (largely unfounded) suspicion that they will be viewed as less seriously productive and ambitious employees.[4] When they are able to balance their family's needs and their work responsibilities, just like working mothers, they report higher satisfaction at home and exhibit higher productivity at work.

The final component of a strong co-parenting relationship is as vexing for most couples as it is inevitable: managing conflict. Why is it so difficult for partners to just get along? We'll tease out some of the dynamics of disagreements in the next chapter.

4
▼

Managing Conflict and Fighting Fair
The Dynamics of Healthy Disagreement

A COUPLE'S DAILY TUSSLES over how to rear their child can seem like verbal jousts over who knows better what the child needs. Consider James and Caryn, the worn-out parents of the adorable but trying four-year-old Marty.

When James complains that Caryn gives in too easily to Marty's "crying act," Caryn retorts that at least she gives him what he needs instead of "ignoring him!" The conflict typically culminates in the designation of one parent as loser, the other as winner. Caryn views herself as the one who really understands Marty, and James as the one who, in her words, "rules from the sidelines without knowing the plays." James views himself as the one shut out, whose opinions get marginalized, reinforcing the family myth that he doesn't know his son as well as his wife does.

Under such conditions, the outcome can never be positive, but if it stops short of outright nastiness—that is, each parent wins some of the time and leaves the loser's ego intact—it can be managed. It is not as optimal as communicating in a way that has no losers, however, with two parents who share their views and agree on how best to proceed. When conflicts continually result in winner and loser positions, with one parent always on top, the problem becomes lethal to all the relationships (mother-child, father-child, and mother-father). The spouse who is designated as the dummy, the out-of-touch parent, or the bad cop (often the father) will begin to assume his expected identity and turn elsewhere for reassurance and acceptance.

As one father plaintively told Marsha: "Before we were married, my wife thought I was funny, smart, and responsible. She used to say she loved how I took care of her. Sure, we had our fights. I was late for dinner when I couldn't get away from work. Or I embarrassed her at a party with something I said. Now we have this baby, and the stakes are so different. She thinks that whenever our daughter gets hurt, it is because I wasn't paying close enough attention to what she was doing, that I cannot make good decisions on her behalf, that I am inept. I even buy the 'wrong' toys." He agonized over how his wife could think such things about him when she loved him. "No matter how hard I try, I can't change her mind about me, and then I begin to feel like the inept boob she makes me out to be. It's no wonder I love being at the office, where they still think I'm the same wonderful, competent guy I always was."

What are the warning signs of mismanaged conflict?

▼ Spending less time at home
▼ Being more argumentative (even aggressive) than usual
▼ Being passive-aggressive (making things difficult though seemingly cooperating)
▼ Not talking much
▼ Projecting a cold, noncommittal tone about whatever goes on between you as a couple.

Mismanaged conflict is sure to lead to a sense of being alone in the relationship. When he withdraws, he could be turning to work, the boys, alcohol, or another lover. She too can withdraw, turning to work, friends, another lover, or burying herself in the children's daily affairs. Not following through on discipline imposed by the other parent can be somewhat less obvious, but still toxic. These relationship problems, once set in motion, can be extremely difficult to reverse, especially without professional help.

Overt conflict is not the only outcome of a weak parenting alliance. Staying silent about decisions or lifestyle choices your partner makes with which you don't agree can be just as lethal. Such silences temporarily dispel anger but create apathy about wanting to work things out. Letting the problem go unrecognized or undiscussed becomes easier. Luckily, Caryn and James recognized that he was beginning to pull away from her and their family, and together they worked on changing the parenting dynamics. Similarly, if Jennifer had not dealt with Frank about her unhappiness regarding the way her job promotion was being supported by him, they might have experienced more serious marital difficulties (see chapter 3).

Managing these conflicts requires parents to communicate openly and assertively but with affection. Whole books have been written about how to communicate. Here is some succinct advice, beginning with this list of do's and don'ts.

Communicating Well
▼

Do
- ▼ Begin statements with "I" and focus on *yourself* rather than on your spouse.
  Example: "I feel angry when you come home late from work" instead of "You are always coming home late."
- ▼ State your feelings, using "emotion" words.
  Example: "I feel angry when you come home late from work because I really need a break from the baby."
- ▼ Ask questions to clarify what your spouse is saying.
  Example: "Do you mean when I am twenty minutes late, or are you talking about when I am very late and don't call to let you know?"
- ▼ Paraphrase your understanding of what your spouse just said to make sure you're both on the same page and you got the important part of the message.
  Example: "It sounds like you feel that I take advantage of you when I am late, and that makes you angry and frustrated."
- ▼ Use body language to help you communicate well.
  Examples: eye contact, an open stance, unclenched hands

Don't

▼ Interrupt your spouse when she or he is talking. Let him or her finish.
▼ Ignore your spouse when he or she is talking. Be open to listening.
▼ Blame your spouse in the middle of the discussion.
   Example: "It's your fault that Juan is grouchy tonight! If you had just shown up on time!"
▼ Insult your spouse or call her or him names.
   Example: "You never come on time. You're so irresponsible!"
▼ Use absolutes or over-generalize.
   Example: "You *never* come on time. I *always* do."
▼ Have the discussion when you're so tired or angry that it's doomed from the start.

Different Kinds of Conflict

There are "before baby" and "after baby" fights, and they differ, according to the researchers who have studied them and to all of us who've had them. Before-baby fights seem to be more about "unpacking the baggage" of hurt feelings, selfishness, and failures to communicate. They are about whether you were paid sufficient attention at a dinner party, or whether he stuck up for you when his mother implied you were too head-strong. After-baby fights seem to be more about "unpacking the blame," lack of respect or regard, and insinuations about who knows what's best for the family. They're about whether he should have introduced the child to Corn Flakes instead of Apple Jacks; whether your toddler should have been allowed to crawl back into your bed in the middle of the night; or whether you even bothered to ask your spouse whether he wanted to have that high-energy, high-maintenance family over to dinner on Sunday night.

Whenever the after-baby fight starts to gain momentum, it does so more on the basis of *how* it is conducted than on *what* the fight is actually about. Does it become a shouting match or does someone make a loud exit—slamming the bedroom door on the way out? Sarcasm, counter-charges, and "you always . . . you never" phrases are what make a fight hurt, not the problem that was the trigger. These are crucial distinctions—especially after the baby—because now there is a new potential victim in the fight and collateral damage is very real. When the arguments get personal and dirty, even young babies can sense that someone important to them is wounding someone else important to them. Consequently, they can become distressed emotionally and physically. The younger the child, the less the distinction there is between the mind and the body. They both hurt, as such events are not easily forgotten or neutralized.

The golden co-parenting rule: No fighting in the presence of the baby; keep it this way until the baby is at least four years old, and has plenty of language and fighting skills of her own. Even then, keep it clean.

Does better management of conflicts really matter that much to relationships? The answer is yes. In an intriguing international telephone survey of 28,000 men ranging in age from twenty to seventy-five, respondents ranked the most important factors in their lives as being in good health, having a harmonious family life, and being in a good relationship with their partner. A satisfying sex life was a top priority for just 2 percent.[1]

The Gender Wars

Men and women tend to have different communication styles when marital conflict intensifies. Marital researchers John Gottman and Bob Levenson found that men are more likely than women to feel the intense, negative, bodily sensations of emotional "flooding" (rapid heart and breathing rate, reddening face) in response to the emotional arousal of an argument, particularly when they're feeling blamed or criticized.[2] They are likely to respond by withdrawing from the conflict to manage their physiological upset. Alternatively, these events can lead them to respond loudly when upset and seem more menacing than usual. Men need to be aware of this predisposition and to consciously manage the reactions behaviorally: learning to slow and deepen their breathing, literally counting to ten, consciously relaxing muscle groups, and envisioning tranquil places.

Women, on the other hand, tend to emote, actively expressing their feelings by getting angry or whining. They are also more likely to withhold affection. Some women say that these reactions, while negative, are preferable to no reaction at all. Men tend to disagree. But it is what they have in common that is most destructive: Research has shown that one predictor of a marriage that won't last is that, when engaged in conflict, neither partner takes responsibility for diffusing the tension or lessening the intensity of the battle.[3]

The Four Negative Reactions

The Gottmans delineate four common types of negative responses partners have to each other during conflict: contempt, criticism, defensiveness, and stonewalling.[4] The other partner feels even the most tepid versions of these reactions as disrespectful at best, infuriating at worst. Let's take a closer look at each.

Contempt

"Great timing. Way to give the kid a sugar high before bed!"

We discuss this first because it can be a bold—and bald—indicator of serious trouble. When Frank was at his most contemptuous, he would dryly ask Jennifer if their son Benjamin really needed all the coddling she gave him, or whether she needed it for herself as a way to prove she was a better mother than her mother had been. Sarcastic and disrespectful, contempt erodes self-esteem and relationships with incredible speed and efficiency. Eye-rolling insults hurled with righteous indignation make it nearly impossible for your partner to defend himself.

Contempt can leap out at some dark, unguarded moment even among the good-hearted and loving. It is best neutralized by admiration and appreciation, expressed early and often. Realizing the viciousness of his remarks, Frank quickly added that he was just jealous because Jennifer didn't coddle him that way anymore. In fact, he continued, she was a wonderful mother, and he appreciated the way she made Ben feel loved and secure. He just wanted to get in line.

Once the angry moment passes, identifying together the source of such contempt is important. Frank realized he was competing with his son for his wife's affections. Before the baby was born, Jennifer was understandably much more attentive and demonstrative; he missed that a lot. If Frank expressed these feelings more directly, chances are she would be more sympathetic and respond in kind.

If Frank hadn't identified his own anger and contempt, Jennifer might have identified it for him, but he would have felt the sting as well. This is one time where apologies help but cannot be the only balm. If you see yourself in Frank, you might ask: *What am I so angry about? Is my partner really deserving of this level of disregard? Why am I acting this way when I don't really want to?* Using this kind of behavior with anyone so central in your life puts you at risk for doing it with others too. Your child, as he acts provocatively, could be next. And that is somewhere you don't want to go.

Criticism

"Why is it always my job to make sure there are extra diapers in the bag?"

Criticisms usually start over seemingly small issues, such as, "Why do you always leave the wet towel on the floor after you bathe the baby?" and "Why don't you burp him again before you put him to sleep? You leave him with gas pains." These are the "you always/never" javelins hurled at a partner's vulnerabilities. Words or thoughts like "slob," "cheat," "selfish," and "lazy" announce the criticism's intended target.

You can avoid criticism wounds by using the classic "I" statements, turning the attack into a complaint originating in one parent's needs, not the defects of the other. In these situations, you could calmly say, "I'm upset that I always have to clean the floor when you are done bathing our daughter," or "I appreciate your giving him the bottle, he loves that, but I am worried that he's uncomfortable when you don't burp him one last time." These kinds of statements draw less blood and evoke less defensiveness, yet deliver the message. Then, it's back to co-parenting as usual, provided that you aren't expressing disappointment to the exclusion of more positive emotions like appreciation, respect, and affection. Practice saying three positive things per day to your spouse that you wouldn't normally bother to say—even if you thought them—and watch how it works in both your favors.

Defensiveness

"Well, someone has to be the parent around here!"

Defensiveness is the knee-jerk reaction to criticism. You tell your young child, "Don't touch," and she says, "No!" after she jerks her hand away. You tell your spouse she is headed for trouble by letting the baby fall asleep on her chest at nap time, and she doesn't say, "Hmmm, you could be right." Instead, she feels criticized, a bit hurt, and begins to explain her behavior. Resisting your own defensiveness is best done by owning up quickly: "It's not helping her learn to sleep on her own, is it? It's so hard for me to put her down. Maybe you can help me." Countering your spouse's defensiveness means offering a sensitive comment that sides with the spouse for a moment, such as, "He's so beautiful; it's really hard to let go of him, isn't it?" Often it's over quickly and the tension is diffused.

Typically, defensiveness emerges when mom brings up some complaint, since women tend to start these difficult conversations. She says, "Last night when you came home from work, you really got the baby overstimulated. It took me forever to calm her down!" Dad immediately feels criticized and responds with his own defensive criticism: "And as long as we're talking about things I am doing that you don't like, I wanted to tell you the other day that when you corrected me in front of our friends, I was pissed." Mom becomes frustrated that when she does finally bring up an issue, it gets parlayed back into a problem dad has with her. So she feels damned if she does and damned if she doesn't bring up the issue.

In any conversation in which you feel defensive, begin by just listening. Then respond to your partner's complaint and try to acknowledge the behavior she is upset with: "OK, I guess I did get him revved up at bedtime, and it took you longer to get him settled. I wasn't thinking about what you needed, was I?" She is relieved you understand and accepts your apology.

After some resolution has occurred, you might tell her you have some issues, too, and would like time to raise them now or perhaps later. Together you can choose whether you have enough stamina for round two.

Rules for a Fair Fight
▼

- ▼ The person who has the problem is responsible for bringing it up as soon as possible. Before you raise the issue, think it through in your own mind.
- ▼ State the problem to your partner clearly and concretely. ("I am feeling [*angry*] because of [*the way you put me down at your parents' house*].")
- ▼ It is important that you both understand the problem. The partner who is on the receiving end should reflect back what was said. "I hear you saying that you feel [*pissed off*] because of [*my travel schedule this month*]." After reflecting back what was said, ask clarifying questions so you know exactly what your partner meant. For example, "Describe." "Tell me." "What is it that upsets you?"
- ▼ When both partners agree on what is being said, the first partner continues to talk.
- ▼ The partner who brings up the problem takes first responsibility for offering a possible solution that requires changes from *both* people. ("I can make sure you know what I want. I would like to suggest that I [*take the baby to my parents this weekend, so you can have a night to yourself*].")
- ▼ This solution can be discussed, and then your partner may offer a counterproposal. The solution should involve changes *both* of you can make.
- ▼ Discuss several options until you agree that one resolution is the most *workable*. Not right vs. wrong, but workable.
- ▼ Once you have agreed on an idea, proceed to talk about how you will put it into action. This means being able to clearly answer the questions: Who will do what, when, and how?
- ▼ Once everything has been worked out, think about what could happen to undermine the agreement and how realistic it is.
- ▼ Working through conflict stirs up a lot of feelings because it means you had to give up something. Congratulate each other for the willingness to compromise.
- ▼ Agree to come back to this problem after some specific period of time to reassess how the agreement is working. You may need to change it or fine-tune part of it.

Stonewalling

"I'm so done talking about this."

She is trying to pursue the conversation further; he says, "I don't want to talk anymore about this right now," and walks out of the room. She follows him into the kitchen, and he stares at her silently over his coffee or beer.

Favored by men more than women, this response to conflict can be as frustrating and maddening as it is effective. No "you always/nevers" or eye-rolling, just stillness in the face of *agita*. This helps men avoid the high pitch of emotion they experience when facing tension, but it infuriates the stonewalled partner who is effectively rendered invisible. Instead of imploding, it is easier on both partners to stay present, keep breathing, and do their best to listen. Ask questions for clarification, reach for the other's hand while listening, look into each other's eyes directly even if you aren't going to say anything just then. But don't look away, at least for long.

If you are the woman, hold your spouse's hand and say nothing. If he pulls away, follow him but sit quietly at the end of the couch. Say something like, "I know you aren't ready to talk just now, but I'm not giving up on you. I'll just be right here." Then when you see his body relax a little, say quietly that you want to talk and listen if he can stand it. Try to insert some humor; men will respond positively to it most of the time.

For the man, you can look away and even walk away if you must, but tell your spouse, "I'll be back in a few minutes. I need to cool off." Letting her know this is a temporary break in the action rather than the end to the conversation is reassuring and effective.

Beyond Gender

Not all conflict-prone differences are based on gender, of course. Some are simply due to different personality styles and predilections. For example, is one of you a list maker?

> Marsha is an organizer who loves making lists and checking off the items one by one. It's therapeutic for her. She also makes lists for Kyle, if not actual ones, then in her head. She reads his to him just as she does her own, proud that she's helping both of us stay organized.

Kyle sighs silently, as such lists seem like just one more thing to keep him from focusing on what he was already set to accomplish. Now he wonders whether Marsha is really just asking him to squeeze in one more thing. "Whose list is this anyway?" he ponders. He winds up feeling like he doesn't need another mother, and Marsha winds up feeling bewildered that mothering would even come into the picture. Efficiency morphs into resentment.

Sound familiar? Given almost every couple's differences in communication styles and conflict resolution, along with the decline in a couple's satisfaction following childbirth, it makes sense to discuss with your partner soon what you each really expect of the parenting experience itself. In chapter 3 we introduced the work of researchers Carolyn and Phil Cowan who codified many of the issues couples face as new parents in their "Ideas About Parenting" survey. (See appendix A.) The entire questionnaire about parents' personal belief systems is meant to trigger useful and open-minded discussion —so important in keeping the fight "fair"—about what each parent thinks is good for the kids. It initiates those hard-to-have discussions about such topics as spoiling, discipline, punishment, coddling, babying, co-sleeping, at what age are babysitters OK, Mama's boys and Daddy's girls, how soon to pick up a crying infant, among others. In another study, the Cowans asked couples to complete the "Ideas About Parenting" form and then predict how their partners might respond. The majority of parents found the task quite challenging and their predictions of their spouse's ratings were wrong at least as often as (or more often than) they were right. Why not flip to appendix A and take a crack at the questionnaire yourselves?

The differences in one partner's predictions of the other's ideas about parenting arise because what's important to us in the abstract is not always how we act. Knowing what we value is critical, because couples who have similar values are more satisfied with their relationships. But just because we share certain values or ideas about parenting doesn't mean unconscious notions don't hold sway over us.

Putting It All Together

How do couples deal with value differences when they erupt in conflict? Let's take a look:

> Jill and Paul are on the way to their children's sports event, and their two kids, ages five and seven, suddenly start fighting in the backseat. Things escalate quickly, and the children start slapping at each other, adding in a few kicks intended to annoy rather than harm, but they are quickly getting out of control.
>
> Paul, who is driving, pulls the car off the road and opens each rear passenger door successively, sticks his head close to each child, and says, firmly and loudly, "Slapping or hitting

of any kind is never permitted and not acceptable in this family. It is abusive, and it's how wars start. And it will not happen again." Then Paul returns to his seat. A moment of stunned silence follows on the children's part, and Paul starts to drive again. Jill turns to the children and says angrily, "What on earth could have been important enough to cause you to act like that?" The children start up again, arguing just as vigorously as before Paul's dictum about whose fault it was, with each giving his/her version and shouting it out louder than the other.

Paul calmly turns to his wife and says, "Hon, it didn't matter who did what. Hitting and kicking is just plain wrong, and there was no reason to talk about it. All you did is invite them to fight again and avoid taking responsibility for their own behavior." Jill, feeling reprimanded and not willing to let Paul's harsh words be the end of it, says, "I just wanted to hear what made them erupt, so I could explain that even that wasn't a good enough reason to kick or hit."

Later on, when the couple had a quiet moment together, they talked about what had happened. Paul thought it was another example of how Jill encouraged talk in a way that often led the children into blaming, rationalizing, or arguing with their parents. It brought out an adversarial, lawyerly response from two verbal children who thought it was their day in court to plead their cases. Paul's take is that sometimes "less is more" in the explaining realm. Moreover, he felt undercut by his wife for opening up the argument again, when he felt he had literally closed the door on the issue, undermining the very lesson he thought he had effectively driven home moments before.

As they discussed it, both understood the other's perspective, and Jill admitted her discussion opener hadn't been effective "this time," emphasizing that in general she still preferred her method. Paul's more common male response—less talk, more action—stood in contrast to Jill's more habitual inclination to talk things through. In addition, Jill came from a family where yelling was scary, because both her parents raised their voices often and loudly. Returning loud arguing with more loud arguing didn't ever seem like an appropriate option. Paul's experience of a mother who didn't have an adequate sense of her own authority and a father who wasn't present for many of the battles left him feeling that swift, forceful clarity reigns supreme. Without the further discussion, Jill would have withdrawn into her feeling of "here we go again with him telling me what I do wrong," and the feelings would have festered. By having a discussion about parenting differences based on gender and experience, they could each see the benefit of the other's perspective. They could agree about which method was effective in this circumstance, leaving the door open to Jill's preferred method for other teachable moments.

In this situation, as in many others, the eventual resolution was not about crowning a victor, but talking effectively about "perpetual issues,"[5] the ones that keep coming up in your marriage time and again. They may have to do with the values where you differ the most, or behavioral differences (such as he is punctual, and she is habitually tardy; he favors more structured family activities, while she likes unplanned time). As parents, the point is to deal quickly with the children's behavior. As partnership parents, make your point without undermining the other person insofar as possible. Later, the two of you can rehash the scene and discuss motivations, outcomes, and potential ways to do it differently next time. Or just concede the point (admittedly, that's not always so easy to do) and learn something from each other.

Try seeing the situation from your spouse's perspective. Fathers, especially those whose wives are doing the bulk of the hands-on parenting, should try to take most of their cues from their mates. And mothers should use a lighter touch when bringing up their concerns to their spouses. This helps mitigate their mates' more intense reactions—the emotional "flooding" that can exacerbate the conflict.

Jackie and Hal had just moved from another state into a university-based neighborhood. They worked hard to find a house in the area because it had the best public schools, and they expected that their almost-kindergartener would go there. But then they went to look at the private school around the corner. The classes were smaller; the kids were involved in very creative endeavors. Jackie immediately decided this was the school for their five-year-old son, Josh. Thus began a protracted discussion.

Hal wanted Josh to try the public school for a year and see how it went. "After all," Hal argued, "isn't that what we have always said we'd do? How can you give up our values so quickly? It's only kindergarten. It will be very expensive to consider years of private school." Jackie, with her degree in early education, disagreed vehemently. She told Hal, "Kindergarten sets you up—for good or bad—for the rest of your educational life. Of course we believe in public school, but this is Josh's life, not some political compromise!"

Jackie became increasingly infuriated with Hal when they discussed kindergarten options. Whenever she brought it up, Hal became caustic, pointing out it was the money he was making that she was spending, and that she didn't seem to care about the added economic pressure he would have to bear. In the face of his sarcasm, she would wind up yelling at him. He then withdrew and refused to discuss anything further, turning his attention back to his computer or the football game on TV, irritating her even more. Someone had to break the pattern, and Jackie figured it might as well be her.

One Sunday morning after breakfast, while Josh was in the adjoining room preoccupied with his train set, Jackie tried a different approach. "Hal," she began, "I need to talk out this school thing for Josh, and I don't want it to get out of hand as it did last time. I haven't always listened patiently, and I really want to understand what you are feeling beyond what we've already talked about. Is this an okay time?" Warily, Hal nodded, refilled his coffee mug, and then joined her at the kitchen table. Jackie listened patiently while Hal talked about his economic concerns (yet again) and also his fear that they were slipping down a snobby slope that was in conflict with the value he thought they both placed on supporting the local neighborhood public school. He talked about his parents' values and how important it was to them to send him to a public school. Then he ended by acknowledging that Jackie was knowledgeable about this subject because of her training as an educator, and that she knew a lot more about what kinds of activities Josh was doing at home that were linked to school readiness.

Feeling more supported and respected, Jackie opened up about her fears that the No Child Left Behind Act had changed the public schools for the worse, resulting in too many work sheets and decreased teacher initiative. She worried about what other neighbors were choosing and how this would affect Josh's friendships over time. Jackie discussed some ideas she had for part-time work she could do from home that would bring in some additional income without changing her availability to Josh when he wasn't in school.

After talking further, they agreed to spend a day together at each school and then make their decision. They also agreed to have a small get-together with their neighbors to discuss the choices other parents were considering. That way, the men could be a part of the conversations that to date had occurred mainly among the women. Hal realized he didn't quite trust Jackie's spin on things because she was so invested in the outcome. As each felt more open to the other's ideas, they agreed that, no matter what they decided, they each needed to support the final decision. They also discussed how they could decide just for this year and not consider it a final decision for the next eight years. They ended the conversation, and Jackie piled onto Hal's lap and held tight to his neck. Hal chuckled, "The air seems clearer in here and I can breathe again."

As Jackie and Hal's story illustrates, some conflicts are not always about how one person behaves, but about making decisions concerning a child's life over time, with less than optimal choices. These conflicts occur by the hundreds during a child's first six years of life, and even happy couples find it difficult to make decisions without it getting personal, precisely because the stakes seem so high. Conflicts are often not about each other, but about how to make a decision in circumstances that pull on competing values. Try using the following communication techniques, keeping in mind your goal of a strong co-parenting alliance:

1. Define the conflict as a mutual concern.
2. Discuss common goals.
3. Find creative agreements that are mutually acceptable compromises.
4. Understand your own needs and express them forthrightly.
5. Make sure that both partners are on equal footing, that you have access to the same information and opportunities to be heard.
6. Use open, honest, and accurate communication of your own needs, goals, and position.
7. Express anger and hurt in order to clear the air and be able to move ahead cooperatively.
8. Explore both similarities and differences in your positions so that you can find common ground from which to begin resolving the conflict or difference in attitude or opinion.

To keep the co-parenting relationship strong, try not to focus on any one of these techniques at the expense of the others. The small gestures of appreciation, affection, and humor bring and keep couples close. There are times when logistics and/or the kids are out of control, and we hardly touch, much less spend time in the same room or finish a conversation. However, most failures or screw-ups can be quickly forgiven and forgotten with a silly pun, a surprise caress of a thigh, or a whispered, "You're just the best." The kids seem to notice these moments of grace, and their foolishness often stops sooner rather than later. Sometimes we catch them smiling at us, or even trying something just as sweet with each other. That's because the emotional traffic around the relationship triangle flows in both directions. If you nurture and develop your co-parenting relationship with the effort you put into your child, the honeymoon can and will last a very long time.

5
▼

Valuing Your Spouse's Contribution
So Glad I Chose You

ULTIMATELY, THE STRENGTH of your co-parenting commitment depends on how you and your spouse feel about each other as your child's
other parent. Is there mutual regard, doubt, competition, envy, pride, disappointment, jealousy, anxiety, or joy in everyday life together? Do you
agree about the work and family choices you each made, or are making,
in order to get this baby off to a good start? Were you looking for your
child to revitalize your relationship?

Differences in strengths and perspective—what's seen as funny; what
scares you; what you're sure of; what seems natural; what you can hear
in the baby's cry, but your spouse can't—may, in fact, be your salvation.
Those distinct responses to the children, the situation, or you as a couple
are all grounded in a unique character and personality. Maybe your

spouse is on the shy side but becomes a children's entertainer when telling bedtime stories. Marsha tends to stir things up, and Kyle is more conciliatory. Each of you knows your own attributes; they don't change much over time. Whether you call these habits, quirks, traits, or perpetual issues, they are part of being couples that can make trouble in your roles as parents. Yet, it's a good thing there are two of you caring for the child and that you both are not feeling the same way at exactly the same time. In this chapter, we'll look at how your differences can be appreciated and even celebrated.

The Givens

The unchangeable attributes of your personalities may be quite familiar, but not always appreciated. It's enlightening and amusing to do an audit and write them down. They make a lot of solutions and problems possible. The ranges for the most common attributes are:

▼ Organized vs. goes with the flow
▼ Needs more couple time vs. wants time alone
▼ Wants time together as a family vs. being alone as a couple
▼ Prefers ritual vs. likes spontaneity
▼ Spends vs. saves
▼ Seeks religion or spirituality vs. is agnostic or atheist
▼ Is ambitious vs. is mellow
▼ Is punctual vs. is casual about time
▼ A discipline enforcer vs. an explainer
▼ Is neat vs. is sloppy
▼ Prefers spending time with extended family vs. chooses peers
▼ Is playful vs. is pensive or serious
▼ Likes sex for intimacy vs. chooses sex for comfort
▼ Responds intellectually vs. responds intuitively

These differences play out in thousands of ways. Children notice and prefer a particular parent for whatever they think the differences will mean for them. For example, as a young child, Marsha would periodically wet her bed. She would have to stand and wait while her mother changed the sheets, making a nice clean bed for her daughter even in the middle of the night. If it was her father's turn, he would fold a towel into thirds, stick it under her, and put her right back to bed. Marsha still remembers her mother admonishing him for not making their child more comfortable. Yet Marsha preferred her father's solution; it was fast and easy, and she'd be back in bed in no time.

Consider some other common examples of preferences from the child's perspective:

▼ Joy chooses Dad's lap over Mom's because it is bigger and cozier.
▼ Abraham chooses Mom at bedtime because she is snuggly and smells "sweeter."
▼ Bernardo prefers to talk to Dad about science because he gets more of his facts correct.
▼ Emily talks to Mom about what happened on the playground because she "cares about the stuff that happens between the kids."
▼ Anna, who worries if Mommy is happy, doesn't worry so much about Dad because "he always seems okay."
▼ Wylie likes Daddy to give him a bath because he is allowed to splash more.
▼ Jenna likes to go grocery shopping with Dad because they get more "fun foods," but Albert prefers Mommy because she knows more of the brands he likes.
▼ Rob says Dad is more fun to cook with because Mom wants to get it done right, while Dad likes to go a little crazy and lets him help more.
▼ Alan likes when Daddy comes home because he throws him up in the air, and he likes when Mommy hugs him.

These differences offer the kids two perspectives on how to live in a world with two different people who love them. But do they polarize kids' relationships with their parents by turning child rearing into a gender-specific series of activities? Not necessarily. Kids think of these differences fondly—more as family lore than right-versus-wrong parenting behavior by a feminine mom and a masculine dad. See if you can recall a few of these preferences from your own childhood.

But when a child chooses sides according to his knowledge of his parents' differing styles, emotions can roil. In the cases of Joy and Abraham, their parents think that the children's preferences for snuggling are amusing, as they are based on their physical differences. But Anna's parents worry about why their daughter is focused on her mother's happiness; is this something the child is sensing, or is this just a mother's burden? Is it a reflection of Anna's state of mind? Should they seek professional guidance? Her father is greatly concerned that his wife has allowed their daughter to become preoccupied with her moods. He is often angry at his wife about this very thing.

What about the parents' perspectives? Sometimes being the parent the child doesn't prefer can be just fine; if ice skating isn't your thing, you're grateful your spouse is happy to pile on the layers and head out to the rink with your eager six-year-old. Sometimes it can be annoying when your spouse and child gang up, such as when he allows more splashing than you think is good for the bathroom floor, or your efforts to correct your rambunctious four-year-old's bad habits go unheeded by the two of them. In any case, it's important to work together routinely to understand, if not enjoy, these differences.

Bernardo likes to talk to his dad about science. Valerie, his mom, doesn't mind. She loves how the two of them have bonded over the topic, but she is concerned about how Bernardo is developing socially. She thinks he needs to interact more with kids his own age, a feeling not shared by her husband, Jonathan. She worries about whether their child is left out in certain social situations. Both parents have witnessed the times when Bernardo plays by himself off to the side, instead of with the other children his age, or at birthday parties when he has to scramble to find a place to sit.

Jonathan does notice and care about these fleeting moments in their child's social life, but he places a different value on those dynamics. He thinks that in the end Bernardo will find his way, so why spend much time and energy worrying about it now? For Valerie, each moment is a building block for their child's self-esteem, competence, or popularity. In the end, Bernardo has a mother who looks out for him socially but doesn't get too anxious about it, thanks to his father's moderating perspective. Yet, his mother is there to listen when Bernardo needs an extra boost of confidence. Valerie and Jonathan have learned to balance each other and talk enough to know what is occurring in their son's life; it works for all of them.

Kids' perceptions can fuel conflict, especially if they play into one parent's preconceptions about the other. As we've learned, Jennifer has long harbored the feeling that Frank is not doing his fair share of the parenting. It didn't help when Ben started noticing some differences too:

▼ Ben knows his mother has the snacks ready for the car trips. Dad often forgets, so they wind up stopping at the convenience store. Cool!
▼ Dad doesn't care if Ben goes to school in unmatched or even unwashed clothing, as long as it doesn't have visible stains on it. Jennifer is embarrassed by this.
▼ Dad doesn't care so much if Ben eats cold cereal three times a day, as long as it has milk and fruit in it and not (too) much sugar.

As expected, conflict ensues. Sometimes Jennifer feels jealous that Ben perceives Frank as the more laid-back parent. If she tries to be laid back herself, she winds up angry at Ben for a behavior she feels is unacceptable. If she jumps in and tries to guide his behavior, he becomes angry with her. She in turn becomes angry at her husband for standing there and not backing her up. Over time, Frank has learned that certain directed looks from his wife mean he'd better take her side on this one, or else. He has risen to the challenge of making sure Ben knows he agrees with his mother in more instances than not.

These differences are actually your *assets* as a couple. Of course, they can cause consternation and, when combined with stress, trouble in relationships. What is the best way to cope with your partner's troubling traits? Next we offer separate advice for moms and for dads.

For Moms: Letting Go a Little

Because a mother is usually the parent who spends more time with the kids, while assuming the bulk of responsibility for the coordination of their care, she often has additional information and authority where the children are concerned. That can make her prone to "gatekeeping." Even when mothers and fathers are equally involved in raising children, mothers may feel a sense of ownership of the children compared to fathers. This results from some combination of the biological role (a mother incubates and therefore *owns* the fetus) and the social roles adopted by many parents (reinforced by societal expectations), all of which sanction mothers over fathers as primary caretakers of children, regardless of family logistics.

What Is Gatekeeping?

A gatekeeper is someone who supervises and maintains boundaries for a person or place. "Maternal gatekeeping" refers to a mother's protective beliefs concerning the father's involvement in their child's life, and the behaviors that either facilitate or hinder the parents' collaborative child rearing.

Gatekeeping in and of itself is not a bad thing, but when a mother wields it in a controlling manner, it can adversely affect the marriage and a father's relationship to his children. Psychologist Michael Lamb studied new parents in the nursery and gave a task to fathers related to the care of their new infants. When mothers were present, fathers looked at their spouses before doing the task, as if seeking confirmation: "Is it okay that I am doing this, and am I doing it correctly?" When the spouses were not present, the fathers performed the tasks more efficiently and competently, according to the researcher's assessment, suggesting that the mothers' presence as gatekeepers was a hindrance to the fathers' competence and confidence.[1]

Although mothers are typically the gatekeepers of young children, fathers can be as well, especially when they are the children's primary caretakers. But because mothers are usually in charge, we'll talk about them as the gatekeepers here. Gatekeeping can occur regardless of whether parents are married, divorced, or never married, and regardless of the parents' satisfaction with their relationship as a couple.

Mothers who fall prey to gatekeeping have definite ideas about how involved fathers should be and strong opinions of how competent their mates are as fathers. This plays out in a mother's behavior: how she speaks about her mate in the children's presence; to what extent she updates the father on the children's health, schooling, or social lives; and to what extent she implies that she knows what is best for the children and the correct way to do things, all the while implying that the father does not, and sees no particular reason to bring him into the loop.

A gatekeeping mother in charge might say:

▼ "Honey, would you dress the children, and *make sure* . . ."
▼ "Could you please watch your language in front of our child? He may pick up on it."
▼ "I'm sorry. I forgot to tell you about the note that came home from school yesterday letting us know he's been sad at school."
▼ "Did you make him brush his teeth for the whole two minutes?"

The motivations for maternal gatekeeping vary widely, depending on the circumstances. Mothers may have a difficult time even temporarily relinquishing their authority and their desire to be the primary parent. They may strongly identify as, or feel pressure to be, the perfect mother and enjoy the recognition and kudos received for their maternal or feminine contributions to the family. They may feel possessive of their children; after all, they know them best, right? In the worst-case scenario, a mother may fairly or unfairly view the father as incompetent, problematic, or even dangerous to the child. Furthermore, she may be protective of her child, purely as a function of his age. If the youngster is not old enough to verbalize his own needs and desires, his mother may feel qualified to make decisions and judgments for him, becoming the monitor, supervisor, permission grantor, and controller of all others' involvement with the child, including (maybe even especially) the father's.

Studies show that when mothers perceive their partners as motivated and competent to engage in child-care responsibilities, fathers are more involved in child care.[2] The father-child relationship is thus based on the triangle (introduced in chapter 3) that includes father, child, and mother. A mother's feelings about the father's competence as a father strongly influence his relationship with his child. In research on divorced parents, positive gatekeeping (that which supports shared parenting) is linked to the mother's belief that the father's involvement is important, and that it's her duty to help facilitate it. The father's positive gatekeeping response is linked to his acknowledgment that the mother's role in his relationship to his child is a valid and central one.[3] When fathers find that the gatekeeping actions of their spouses constantly hinder or block their access to their kids, the ability of the children to benefit from co-parenting and the unique attributes of each parent is undermined. Gatekeeping can damage the father-child relationship and the parents' ability to cooperate and to minimize their conflicts. As discussed in chapter 2, children with less involved fathers experience academic, behavioral, and social difficulties in the short and long term. Rigid maternal gatekeeping therefore can pose a combined powerful threat to the vitality of the father-child relationship and the overall well-being of the child.

How can you tell if this kind of behavior is going on in your home? If you are the mother, ask yourself:

1. Do I ever:
   ▼ forget or fail to tell my husband information about our child that I've received from people outside the family?
   ▼ insist (quietly or otherwise) that we do things my way with our child?
   ▼ present my husband with alternatives for spending time with our child that are more about what I want than what our child really needs?
   ▼ criticize the way he does things, even when it's not that important?
2. How often do I do any of these things?
3. Do I do it more when I'm angry or feeling protective, or is it just a habit most of the time? Do I even recognize when I'm doing it?
4. Does my husband notice when I am being overprotective? Does he think this behavior is problematic?
5. How would I feel if things were reversed?

If you are the father and not in the gatekeeping role most of the time, ask yourself:

1. How often is my wife controlling when we are doing something together with our child, or giving me instructions about our child's care?

2. How does it make me feel?
3. Are there times she is justified? Am I paying too little attention to what I'm doing, or insisting I know something about our child that I really don't? Am I not noticing when he is upset about something I am doing or not doing for him?

Are you being honest with yourselves? Here's a pop quiz for gate-keeping mothers.

Gatekeeper Quiz for Moms[4]
▼

Circle the answer that best describes how you feel.

1. It is part of my job as a parent to positively influence my child's relationship with his/her father.

   False   Somewhat False   Neutral   Somewhat True   True

2. It is my job to help my spouse be the best parent that he can be for our child.

   False   Somewhat False   Neutral   Somewhat True   True

3. My spouse tries to be a good parent but doesn't know enough about parenting to be the kind of parent my child needs.

   False   Somewhat False   Neutral   Somewhat True   True

4. In order to best take care of my child, it is important for me to positively influence my child's relationship with his father.

   False   Somewhat False   Neutral   Somewhat True   True

5. My spouse does a pretty good job being involved with our child, but he does not have a good understanding of who our child is and what he/she needs.

   False   Somewhat False   Neutral   Somewhat True   True

6. My child benefits from the time he/she spends with his/her father.

   False   Somewhat False   Neutral   Somewhat True   True

7. It helps my child's self-esteem to have a good relationship with his/her father.

   False   Somewhat False   Neutral   Somewhat True   True

8. Our child would be better off seeing less of his/her father and more of another father figure.

False   Somewhat False   Neutral   Somewhat True   True

9. My own parenting is more central to how my child's feels about him- or herself than is my spouse's parenting.

False   Somewhat False   Neutral   Somewhat True   True

10. My husband is loving, but he often needs me to tell him what to do or how to do it so he doesn't offend or disappoint our child.

False   Somewhat False   Neutral   Somewhat True   True

If you circled "Somewhat False" or "False" to statements 1, 2, 4, 6, and 7, and "Somewhat True" or "True" to answers to statements 3, 5, 8, 9, and 10, then you are probably gatekeeping in unhelpful ways when co-parenting; you are not supporting the child's other parent in your behaviors or attitudes. It is time to talk to your spouse seriously about your co-parenting partnership.

For starters, think about specific situations in which you believe you acted in reasonable ways, versus situations in which you were a bit unfair. Now consider one of the unfair instances and think about what it would take for you to do it differently next time.

Ingrid and Eddie have three children under the age of six, two boys and a girl. Life is, of course, hectic, and Ingrid has gotten into the habit of leaving Eddie notes with detailed instructions about how to handle his Tuesday and Friday afternoons with the children. On those days, he comes home early and she goes to work until after the children are in bed. Lately, they have been having a fight every week, or at least it seems that way. Last week, Ingrid finally understood Eddie's exasperation after he blurted out in front of the children, "If you want to be a single parent, then go for it. But if you don't, back off!"

We asked Ingrid to write down how she thought she was being protective and how she was being unfair. She made this list:

Protective: I am making sure that Eddie takes enough diapers and wipes so the baby won't be uncomfortable.

Unfair: If he does run out, he can just go to the store and get more. And if she's miserably uncomfortable, he won't do that again.

It's just that I'd feel more comfortable if I knew he'd packed a diaper bag before he left, just in case. He just doesn't think of these things. I suppose I could ask him if he needs help packing the bag, or if he has it covered instead of writing a note about what to do. That assumes he knows what to do, but might need help reminding.

If you sometimes act like Ingrid, pick a day when the family is spending a lot of time together, and make mental notes of the instances when you catch yourself micromanaging your mate. Ask your husband if he notices anything about your gatekeeping behavior. How often is it happening? Do you do it more often in private or in public; what are you thinking/feeling at those moments? Many gatekeepers aren't really conscious of their actions. Are there any particular things your spouse does or does not do that triggers your behavior? You might begin the conversation by saying,

"I've noticed that when we're both with the kids I have a tendency to be kind of bossy and make decisions without consulting you. Agreed?"

"Today, when we were at the park, I decided when it was time for them to come out of the sprinkler and called them out while you were in the middle of a game. I didn't check with you first, or give you a chance to check with the kids. Do you think I do this a lot?"

"Have you been angry about this?"

"How does it make you feel? More distant from me or the children? That I'm being a jerk?"

"Can you tell me when I'm doing it so I can learn to stop?"

Here's another way to get the conversation going with your partner. Look at this cartoon together. What makes it especially funny or not so funny to each of you?

Now, pay attention to how many times you and your spouse are discussing something, and one of you says, "Yes, but . . ." The following anecdote shows how this can be a real communication killer.

> Shawn was on his way to do some errands with their infant, Brandi. His wife, Cindy, was heading out the door for some much-needed time at the gym. As they were leaving, she called out, "Don't forget to have her back by 1:00 for her nap. And did you take a bottle? I don't think you warmed it up."
>
> Shawn answered, "I know when nap time is, and I just figured we'd be back in time for the bottle."
>
> Cindy responded "Yes, but what if she gets hungry earlier?"
>
> "Then I'll come home early," Shawn growled.
>
> "Yes, but she'll be hollering by then."
>
> "She'll live."
>
> "Suit yourself."
>
> *Try replacing the "Yes, but . . ." with a "Yes, and . . ." and see how different the exchange feels:* "Yes, and sometimes she gets hungry early, and it's no fun to hear her yell."

Although the mother is giving advice in both examples, the second response feels more helpful and less full of insinuation and blame.

Frank and Jennifer understand this all too well. Frank reported to us that he'd once proudly told his wife that he'd done a load of laundry because the baby had spit up after a meal. Jennifer's response: "Did you use the hypoallergenic soap?" Using the correct soap is important, but Jennifer's response turned a positive moment into one of confrontation.

Try relying on this metaphor to see your relationship in a new light. You and your spouse are mountain climbers roped together for mutual safety. Each takes a turn in the lead, allowing the other one to rest, maximizing the other's strength and endurance. Each person moves up only when the other one does; if one stumbles, the other's progress is hindered, and vice versa. There is no place for competition when climbing a mountain. You climb as a team and reach the summit together or not at all.[5]

For Dads: Stepping Up to the Plate

As with everything else in the co-parenting relationship, mothers cannot (and should not) do it alone. Fathers need to step up to the plate. When a mother exercises decision-making power about a child's whereabouts and relationships, including possibly monitoring the child's relationship with his dad, a dad fathers best by being an involved and valued team player. So, if you're a father, ask yourself:

1. Do I know all I can about my child's personality, preferences, needs, and habits? When does he eat, sleep, get grumpy, or want to be social?
2. Do I know where my child's things are kept—the diapers, blankies, clean outfits, and extra pair of mittens?
3. When I tell my wife that I will handle a situation, do I follow through?
4. Am I sensitive to my spouse as well as our child? Do I reassure her when I know she does something very differently from me?
5. Do I recognize and acknowledge verbally all that my wife does to keep things running smoothly? Do I remember to compliment her?
6. Equally important, do I know when to take my wife's advice and direction, without withdrawing into self-pity at her lack of appreciation for me?
7. Do I truly recognize that she is, in fact, keeping almost everything together, and that sometimes I make it harder when I come barreling in with my own ideas on how to do things?

Doing it your own way is quite different from doing it your own way *within* the partnership. The former negates what else is happening around you and will surely lead to more restrictive gatekeeping on your spouse's part. The latter takes into account your role on a team as an active member who is not always in the lead. It requires viewing yourself as an equal; after all, a shortstop is as much a part of the team as the pitcher. You take responsibility for sharing the work and knowing how the game is played.

You could ask your spouse, for example, "Hon, what do you usually take to the park for food, just in case?" Or, maybe you hadn't thought about food: "Is there anything you usually do with her that I should know about?" When she starts telling you what to do with *your* time with your child, you might try responding humorously, "I thought you wanted a husband, not a nanny." Or, "Anything else I can do for you, dear, to ensure that you don't worry about us one iota while you are at the gym?" If you are really irritated, you might even say something like, "I must really be a boob. You don't seem to think I'll get it right at all! I promise to sign a contract." If humor works, you are back on the path to partnership parenting. If it sparks anger or hostility, consider it a warning sign that the two of you have some work to do.

It's crucial that both parents successfully manage their separate authority within your relationship because of the high cost to kids when one parent withdraws. When parents help each other control their emotions and behavior in the midst of turmoil—and don't simply cover for one another—the kids are appreciative and feel nurtured when they need it most, and by *both* parents.

6

▼

Assumptions and Actions
What Grown-ups Do and Don't Know About Raising Kids

I can't believe I actually said it: "Why can't you just do
what you're told the first time—like your sister?"

I'd heard the very same question from my mother
most of my childhood. I disliked how it made me feel so much
that I swore that particular question would never come
out of my mouth if I ever had kids. And here it was!
I really thought that if I tried hard to parent without
being as judgmental as my parents were,
it would just go better, naturally.

—Jean

DESPITE MORE THAN 5,000 YEARS of parenting advice and experience, it's amazing how little of it comes as second nature even though many of us may feel quite confident about parenting a child of a certain age or developmental stage. What parents think—together and apart—about their parenting job is a topic often covered in national polls. One of the most influential and wide-ranging was the landmark national survey in 2000, "What Grown-Ups Understand About Child Development," conducted for Civitas, Brio, and Zero to Three: National Center for Infants, Toddlers and Families.[1] The survey was based on interviews with 3,000 American adult women *and* men, over a third of whom were parents of children under six. Rarely has such a detailed picture been taken of what parents know and don't know about child development. We include this information because a better understanding of a child's development can help you and your partner raise your young children more sensitively and skillfully *together*.

First, both of you should take a few minutes to complete the parts of the survey that we have adapted here (the answers are given in appendix B). Then you can see how your answers compare to a random sample of Americans on either of two websites; www.civitas.org or www.zerotothree.org. We'll also look at how this information affects you and your spouse as you face the challenges posed by your growing child, from babyhood to preschool.

Your Parenting Profile
▼

Part A: Development

_____ 1. At what age do you think a parent can begin to have a significant impact on a child's brain development, for example, affect the child's ability to learn?

_____ 2. At what age do you think an infant or young child begins to really take in and react to the world around them?

_____ 3. Some people say that a child's experiences in the first year of life have a major impact on their performance in school many years later. Others say babies twelve months and younger are too young for their experiences to really help or hurt their ability to learn in school later in life. Which do you agree with more?

_____ 4. At what age do you think a baby or young child can begin to sense whether or not his parent is depressed or angry, and can be affected by his parent's mood?

_____ 5. Following are two statements about children. Decide whether each one is definitely true or false or probably true or false:
   a. Children's capacity for learning is pretty much set from birth and cannot be greatly increased or decreased by how the parents interact with them.
   b. In terms of learning about language, children get an equal benefit from hearing someone talk on TV versus hearing a person in the same room talking to them.

_____ 6. This question relates to how important it is for children of different ages to spend time playing. For a five-year-old, how important do you think playing is for that child's healthy development? Use a 1 to 10 scale, where a 1 means playing is *not* at all important to the child's development, and a 10 means playing is *crucial* to the child's development. Use any number in between.

_____ 7. Here are different forms of play. Use a 1 to 10 scale to rate each of the following play activities, where a 1 means the activity is not at all effective in helping a child become a better learner, and a 10 means the activity is extremely effective in helping a child become a better learner. Use any number in *between*.

    _____ a. A six-month-old exploring and banging blocks

    _____ b. A twelve-month-old rolling a ball back and forth with her parent

    _____ c. A two-year-old playing a computer activity

    _____ d. A two-year-old having a pretend tea party with her mom

    _____ e. A four-year-old making artwork using a computer art program

    _____ f. A four-year-old memorizing flash cards

    _____ g. A four-year-old collecting and sorting leaves in the yard

    _____ h. A four-year-old making an art project with art supplies

    _____ i. A six-year-old and his friends playing pretend firemen

    _____ j. A six-year-old playing cards with his dad

_____ 8. Suppose a twelve-month-old goes up to the TV and begins to turn it on and off repeatedly while her parents are trying to watch it. It's impossible to know exactly why the child is doing this; however, for each of the following reasons, how likely do you believe that explanation is?

    _____ a. The child wants to get her parents' attention.

    _____ b. The child enjoys learning about what happens when buttons are pressed.

    _____ c. The child is angry at her parents for some reason, so she is trying to get back at them.

_____ 9. In this case of a twelve-month-old child turning the TV on and off, would you say that the child is misbehaving, or not?

_____ 10. Suppose the cries of a three-month-old are frequently *not* responded to by her parents and caregivers. In this case, how likely is it that the following is happening: very likely, somewhat likely, or not likely at all:

    _____ a. The baby's self-esteem will be negatively affected.

    _____ b. The baby will learn to be independent.

    _____ c. The baby's brain development will be negatively affected.

    _____ d. The baby will learn good coping skills.

Part B: Expectations

_____ 11. Should a fifteen-month-old baby be expected to share her toys with other children, or is she too young to be expected to share?

_____ 12. Should a three-year-old child be expected to sit quietly for an hour or so, be it in church or in a restaurant, or is three years old too young for a child to sit quietly for an hour?

_____ 13. Suppose a six-year-old points a gun at a classmate and shoots him. Do you think it is possible that this six-year-old could have fully understood the results of his actions, meaning, could understand that the classmate might die and never come back, or do you think that a six-year-old simply cannot understand these consequences?

Part C: Spoiling

_____ 14. Some people say that a six-month-old, because he is so young, cannot be spoiled, no matter how much attention his parents give him. Others say that a six-month-old can be spoiled. Which do you agree with more?

_____ 15. Rate the following behavior, on the part of a parent or caregiver, as appropriate or as something that will likely spoil a child _if done too often_:

_____ a. Picking up a three-month-old every time she cries

_____ b. Rocking a one-year-old to sleep every night because the child will protest if this is not done

_____ c. Letting a two-year-old get down from the dinner table to play before the rest of the family has finished their meal

_____ d. Letting a six-year-old choose what to wear to school every day

Part D: Discipline

_____ 16. At what age is it appropriate to spank a child as a regular form of punishment, or do you think it is never appropriate to spank a child?

_____ 17. True or false: Children who are spanked as a regular form of punishment are more likely to deal with their own anger by being physically aggressive.

_____ 18. Here's a situation: A baby enjoys crawling to a set of stairs. Suppose the parent consistently says no, calmly but clearly, every time the baby wants to crawl up the stairs, and then moves the infant away from the stairs. At what age should this infant be expected to know _not_ to climb the stairs and be able to stop herself from doing so without being reminded by her parents?

Part E: Relationships

_____ 19. True or false: Children usually have stronger bonds with parents who do not work and stay home than they do with parents who work full time outside the home.

_____ 20. True or false: Children with fathers who are active in their lives tend to develop more self-confidence than children who lack an active father in their lives.

_____ 21. True or false: Children with fathers who are active in their lives tend to be better problem solvers than children who lack an active father in their lives.

Now check your answers with those of the child experts (see appendix B). What age and stage do you know most about? Where are the gaps? Do they overlap with your spouse?

Survey Results

Although most of the parents surveyed had a lot of information about child development, clearly there were important gaps in their knowledge base, and some of those gaps were not unimportant to how children turn out.

Awareness and Moods

Parents of young children and other adults interviewed for the survey often underestimated young children's awareness about what is going on around them. The grown-ups were unsure whether a child was reacting to or taking in important events in the family or the broader world.

Even babies can be quite distressed by parents who, for whatever reason, compete for the infant's attention, not an uncommon occurrence with new parents. For example, even the youngest babies can react to dysfunctional play. First, the mother plays with the baby, then the father. Each one points out how much the child responds to his or her attempts to capture her attention. While the baby laughs and gurgles at first, soon she begins to cry, leaving both parents confused about what's just happened. They don't realize how their complex moving in and out of play—in what was to them a friendly one-upmanship to make their baby respond—was too overstimulating for the child to absorb, much less enjoy.

As co-parents, it is important for each of you to delight in watching the other, but be sure to give your young child time to disconnect from one parent before she begins interacting with the other. Parents must be aware of their impact on the child both individually and as a couple. The twosome can be a powerful force that occasionally overwhelms, as when one parent disciplines the child and the other one chimes in to be supportive, but ends up making the child feel that they are ganging up on him.

Many, if not most, of the adults surveyed were confused about when a young child is aware of the moods of others, including themselves. They think this awareness comes much later in life than it actually does. Babies can be aware of others' moods in the first three months of life.

Before age four, obvious parental disagreements can be quite upsetting to a child. Even after a child is four, the disagreements she witnesses should be minor, with resolutions that are more behavioral than verbal occurring immediately—for example, parents hugging each other after a tiff is more reassuring than simply hearing them apologize. At this age, children are still young enough to need to see the relationship heal, as in the case of five-year-old Robert.

> After Robert's parents had a brief quarrel, the child watched his parents hug and kiss. Then he jumped up from his child-sized chair and ran over to the couple, smooshing their faces close to each other and yelling, "Kiss, kiss. Oooh . . . happy ever after!" He needed to see that co-parenting alliance repaired right in front of his eyes.

In addition, most surveyed adults did not understand that babies as young as six months can be depressed; most respondents said thirty-six months was the youngest age. And they were unaware that infants can be deeply affected by witnessing parental conflict and violence. Even when a baby cannot recall what he has seen, his body will react to signals of conflict and anger with a spike in physiologic responsiveness, such as increased breathing and heart rates and increased muscle tension.

Importance of Play

The same group of adults was confused about the role of play in children's lives; they felt that young children's play is more entertainment and diversion than it is learning. That's just wrong. For children, play is their research and development part of the day. That's why one of the more popular teaching tools in preschool is the dress-up corner. Here children learn about role playing, empathy, taking turns, how boys respond versus how girls do, and so on.

The respondents also felt that flash cards were more intellectually useful to young children than play (wrong again). Developmental science has shown repeatedly that play, especially playful learning, serves as the best cognitive foundation for developing language and problem-solving and thinking skills from the early months of life.

Just under half the surveyed group felt that for kids three years old and younger, the more stimulation, the better. Not so. Infants are easily agitated and disorganized by overstimulation. Averting their gaze, putting their hands over their faces, arching their backs, and tensing their muscles are the baby's way of telling you, "enough already." In the example we gave earlier, the baby was overstimulated both by the intensity of the encounters with her parents and by the subtle social implications of what was occurring between her parents.

Behavior Expectations

Respondents often had expectations about moral behavior that are inappropriate for young children. The adults felt that most eighteen-month-olds push the buttons on the household media remotes to get back at grown-ups, when at that age the child's actions basically stem from curiosity. That kind of retaliatory behavior isn't expected until a child is closer to three. As for question 13, they also believed that a six-year-old who shot and killed a classmate would fully understand the ramifications of his actions, when, in truth, to the average six-year-old, death is something that comes like sleep, is reversible, and passes in time. Cause-and-effect reasoning of this kind is more typical of eight- or nine-year-olds. Finally, a third of parents of young children expected a fifteen-month-old child to share her toys with other kids. While most parents are understandably eager to teach their children to share, a child shouldn't be developmentally expected to share until at least age two-and-a-half.

Darlene was so embarrassed by fifteen-month-old Josie's refusal to share her toys at a play date with her neighborhood mothers' group. Josie was yelling, and even tried hitting, to get another child away from her precious stuffed animals and blinking-eyes toy robot. Darlene, fearful that the other mothers would think badly about her own parenting skills and her daughter, was surprised and relieved to hear from us that Josie was acting appropriately for her age and that she would begin to share more consistently (but no guarantee) after she turned two. Still, Darlene should plan for many "slipups" well into kindergarten, depending on who was asking Josie to share and if she was worried about her favorite toy being badly treated or appropriated for too long. Interestingly, Josie's dad laughed when Darlene told him about the incident; he reassured his wife that every kid he ever knew went through this at her age.

Josie may have been acting her age, but the results of the survey make it clear that many of the parents' expectations about discipline are at odds with what research suggests about most young children's emotional needs and abilities. While most parents consider spanking to be part of an overall method of discipline, they also know that it encourages children to be more physically aggressive when they are angry—that is, they do it despite knowing it neither works nor leads to better self-control. A smaller, but significant portion of parents of young children (one-third) felt that it was appropriate to spank children age two or younger as a regular form of discipline. This seems counterproductive at best; toddlers are likely to be especially confused by this kind of adult behavior. Why would a grown-up hit you when they are trying to teach you to get your own impulses under control—telling you to "use your words" or "keep your hands to yourself."

In terms of expectations about self-control, a fourth of the young children's parents in the survey expected that a three-year-old would be able to sit quietly for an hour. In their dreams! Four-year-olds *might* be able to pull it off and then only occasionally, given their limited attention span and appetite for action and social engagement.

Development Potential

A third of surveyed adults, whether or not they were parents, were also surprisingly certain that every baby's potential is mostly set at birth. However, development can be very heavily influenced by the family and the environment in which that baby is raised. How nature is nurtured is the key to healthy development, not just choosing the right parents. (After all, you wouldn't want just anyone to raise your child, right?) A nurturing home environment is critical though; as the child develops, each milestone he reaches becomes a stepping stone to his next achievement. That's why it's just easier for two parents to raise a child. It is, of course, not the only way, but it is more efficient and stacks the deck in your child's favor: You have two heads, hearts, and sets of experiences—doubling the knowledge, patience, stamina, and understanding.

Despite knowing that regular reading and talking with young children are good for their intellectual development, two-thirds of parents and other adults rated educational TV and solitary play on the computer as "very beneficial." These activities may be a little helpful in passing time and even periodically entertaining, but they are far from being intellectually very beneficial. While many studies have been done, each having slightly different findings, overall they support the notion that most TV is not great for kids' intellectual development, even educational, noncommercial TV, which is far better than most.[2]

For example, Baby Einstein might actually reduce your toddler's vocabulary,[3] while *Sesame Street, Read Between the Lions, Pinky Dinky Doo*, and shows that stimulate the imagination (e.g., *Dragon Tales*) teach important skills and lessons, though they still are screen time rather than hands-on play.

Spoiling

Expectations about spoiling were especially striking: Slightly less than one-half of parents of young children felt that picking up a three-month-old every time he cries will spoil the infant. But years of pediatric research from Canada argues the opposite: Picking up the very young *reduces* their crying at that moment and later as well.[4] Tiffany Field, an international expert on touch and child development, conducted very convincing research in this area: She found that touching and holding distressed infants is more effective in comforting them than merely using words and is an essential building block in the formation of trust between infant and caregiver.[5]

In addition, one-third of parents of young children believe (incorrectly) that letting a six-year-old choose her own school clothes is spoiling her. And just under half of parents of young children believe that letting a two-year-old leave the table before the rest of the family has finished is also spoiling him. In reality, it doesn't hurt the child's manners in the long run, and it can make for precious adult quality time.

The Effects of Paid Employment

Most respondents to the survey knew that close, sensitive relationships with loving caregivers were a key bedrock experience from early on. But a large percentage believed that working parents cannot develop an attachment to their children that is as strong and durable as that of parents who stay at home. Work and family research shows the opposite. Long-term data published by the National Institute of Child Health and Human Development indicate that whether mothers are working or nonworking is not the issue in child attachment; rather, maternal sensitivity and responsiveness are the keys, not overall time logged on the job. Otherwise, parents who work more outside the home or travel for business would be less close to their children than parents with nine-to-five jobs, right? University of Minnesota's Alan Sroufe argues that one positive feature of working mothers with children in child care is that, while children experience repeated separations, they also learn that their parents always return. Separations become predictable and of a reliably short duration.[6]

In Good Company

If you have concerns about how ready you are to do this parenting job, this survey might help you see just how common these concerns and knowledge gaps are. The survey respondents who were not parents felt the "vast majority of today's parents were not at all prepared when they had their first child," a "no confidence" vote. Among those who were already parents, general preparation for parenthood broke down this way: one-third of parents felt "very" or "extremely well-prepared" for parenthood. Another third of parents felt "somewhat" prepared, and the final third felt "very unprepared" for parenthood. Interestingly, there were no gender differences in how prepared people felt; it was more a function of education, with more educated parents feeling better prepared.

> Two young moms, a social worker and an elementary school teacher, were talking about their favorite topic on the playground—motherhood. Both were wonderful at working with other people's children, and they could handle many difficult situations that arose. Katie commented, "Given all I know about working with mothers and their infants, I couldn't believe how helpless I felt the first time my son wailed in the early evening for about an hour. I tried everything to get him to stop crying. It was eerie, how he fell apart every day at that time. I know kids do that, and I was still surprised when it happened to me.
>
> Mindy responded, "And after all my comments about how parents spoil their five- and six-year olds, I cannot believe how often I find myself not only changing my mind and giving in, but then second-guessing myself. And I should know better."

As these mothers' comments illustrate, knowledge is one thing, but being prepared for parenting is another. Sometimes the two go together, and sometimes they don't. That's what makes this whole enterprise so complicated, and why it is a relief to have two of you working together at it.

The future parents surveyed—those childless adults who plan to have a child in the next few years—showed a worrisome lack of knowledge in many areas of child development. They were more confused than parents or grandparents in terms of what children need or could do. They also tended to believe that they were well prepared for parenthood, when their answers indicated that they were just the opposite. A portion of those future parents, however, are often quite keen to get educated. They start paying attention to parenting literature, talking with other parents, and checking out appropriate websites. They'll learn the most, however, from the on-the-job training that is parenthood.

When parents were asked about the areas of child development in which they felt most confident about their knowledge, they listed motor and physical milestones first, intellectual milestones second, social milestones third, and their children's emotional development last. Parents were then asked how to rate the areas in which they felt they made their most important contributions to their children's development. Supporting their children's emotional well-being topped their lists routinely—outdistancing social growth, personal safety, and intellectual growth.

The most interesting finding in these last responses is the gap between what parents feel is their most important job—supporting and stimulating the emotional well-being of their children—and the parenting competencies they feel they are most lacking—understanding their children's feelings and what they need. Little wonder, then, that they find it hard to "know how to handle difficult situations." The bottom line is if a parent doesn't understand what his or her child feels or needs, of course it is going to be hard to know how to handle difficult situations.

You'll find helpful approaches to understanding more about the development of your child's inner world of feelings in chapter 8. Time alone with your child at any age, in which you focus on being emotionally available to them in the moment, will teach you the most about who are they becoming, how they feel, and what they need from you.

Reading the Numbers

When it comes to understanding the basics of child development, all these survey results show us is that mothers and fathers are more often than not on the same page. Fathers, who made up slightly less than half of all parental respondents, were less certain of the role of pretend play in strengthening young children's cognitive abilities, and they had somewhat less general information overall about children's behavioral milestones. But they had a better understanding of their own contributions to their child's development than did the mothers. The vast majority of those insights are as useful to fathers as to mothers. They are further evidence that the involvement of both parents is essential to the child's well-being.

Leveling this playing field of expectations is very important to strengthening the parenting partnership. Parents who are anxious about their ability to work together effectively on behalf of their children (based on what they don't understand about each other's and their child's needs) probably have more reason to worry than those whose own parents were poor collaborators. As James McHale concluded from his co-parenting research, how the current couple works together and feels about parenting together is more influential than where each parent came from in terms of how their own parents did or did not work together as co-parents. Once again, nature is a part of the picture, but nurture trumps it. He summarized, "It isn't where you come from, but where you currently are that matters most [in strengthening the co-parenting alliance]."[7]

Fathers do in fact know as much as mothers, at least among those folks who respond to such surveys. Many parents of both genders have gaps in their knowledge of their child's growth and development. Gate-keepers, take note: Neither parent is likely to be significantly right more often than the other. They need each other to get information, figure out how it applies to *their* child, and decide what they will do about it in a world that is very different from the one in which their parents raised them. Nonetheless, the survey also showed that mothers will continue getting information from their mothers, and fathers will seek it from their own and their spouse's mothers.

Growing Pains

Informed by this macro view of American parenting, let's take a closer look at the most common challenges mothers and fathers face as together they parent their developing child. We now move to specifics.

Babyhood

Bill and Julie were all organized for their new family. When their son was born, they both changed to part-time work so that they could raise their firstborn on their own. They stepped back from their active social lives and "nested with a vengeance," to quote Bill. The sleeping and nurturing rhythms of infancy seemed to suit them just fine. There was always a fire crackling away in the fireplace, sweet lullabies played on their docked iPod, and a pot of herbal something sat on the trivet under the tea cozy.

Bill and Julie had made a conscious effort to keep father Bill and baby John close to each other. But in our interview with them of who was doing what for John, Julie was surprised to hear how much credit Bill took for "taking a pretty healthy share of child-care labor." Bill was equally surprised to hear that Julie took offense at his reporting of his involvement in "such a positive light."

We were interested in this struggle over "fair-share parenting," as Julie called it, but more intrigued by the fact that this close and loving couple had never shared this particular frustration with each other until the moment of the interview! Why hadn't they talked about this before?

> Bill told us, "I thought she was quietly appreciating that I was a hell of a lot more involved with John than her father had ever been with her growing up." Julie said, "I didn't think he needed extra credit from me for doing what he promised, and said he wanted, to do—being close to John is its own reward."

Once this issue was put on the table, the other under-the-table issues made their debut. Good-naturedly, they began to talk about some of their other concerns.

> Bill was not, after all, all that sure that carrying six-month-old John all day was such a good idea. In the new father's view, "Nobody but John gets your attention, and besides, he needs to learn to sit up sooner or later. It's not good for your back, and I miss my wife."
>
> Letting John "cry it out" on his own was the position toward which Bill leaned, while Julie was quicker to pick up her son. She asked, "We know about all that stress hormone stuff. Doesn't it bother you to think we could fix it faster then he can himself, and we're consciously choosing not to?" Bill teased Julie about her "Moms just know everything" attitude. While affectionate, an edge was present in this exchange. Bill said, in closing, that he loved raising John with Julie, but he wished she gave him more credit for what he brought to parenting that differed from what she brought. While he acknowledged all that he had learned from watching Julie take care of their son, Bill admitted that, at times, it felt almost as if she was "managing" him. "It makes me want to back off the whole father-baby thing. Not cool," he added.

These discussions are typical of parents during the first year of their child's life. Mothers feel "so responsible so often" for the baby, in contrast to the father's "being responsible when I ask him to be, or when he feels like it." One mother summed it up this way: "That he [her spouse] devotes so much energy to having fun with the baby makes me happy, but what I need more of with the kids is help, not entertainment." But compared to the developmental challenge coming next, these issues remain small potatoes. What's coming is . . .

Toddlerhood

Toddlerhood is something else altogether. With "No!" and walking under his belt, the young child is not just ready to roll, he's ready to rule. Some parents take a shine to their child's challenging swashbuckling ways, while others find it worrisome or just profoundly annoying. As for its effect on co-parenting, there is a lot more complexity to consider than there was during infancy.

Listen to Brian and Amanda, proud but exhausted parents of twenty-three-month-old Seth:

Amanda: "He used to be so sweet—smiling, humming cute little jingles, going to sleep on a dime—but now he is hellboy. From what he wants to wear in the morning to what he eats for dinner, it is one uninterrupted argument! I had this nightmare that he'd turned into this saber-toothed tiger—I guess it was because he'd been biting both me and Brian. He has three words that he just screams when things don't go his way: 'no,' 'mine,' and 'goway.' Don't get me wrong; he's smart, cuddly, and adorable the rest of the time, but it is heartbreaking to go from loving him so completely to being pissed at him so often. When he was an infant, it was unimaginable to me that this would ever come to pass, even though I'd heard about it from my sister."

Brian: "When Seth started to stand up and cruise around the furniture, he had this kind of manic laugh, like he was saying, 'I'm up on my own now, and I'm coming after you.' At first, I was kind of proud of this feistiness, but not for long. He seemed determined to upset everyone and everything. He bit the dog and his mother. He'd fling his arms, clean-sweeping any flat surface in the house that he could reach—desks, coffee tables, breakfast nook, my workbench, the dog's bed. He'd spank his mother when she wasn't looking—sometimes days after he'd gotten a spanking from her—like he'd been planning revenge all along. I still love the kid, of course. He's a ton of fun, smart as a whip, and incredibly curious. I just can't wait 'til he rejoins civilization."

Meanwhile, how are Brian and Amanda doing together in dealing with "Seth the Disabler"? Terribly. They are feeling more overwhelmed as a couple than as individuals.

Brian: "I've never seen Amanda so angry about anything in her life, and I'm not much better. She's an only child, but I've got brothers and learned young to give as good as I got. But honestly, we are both having a hard time managing our tempers. I find my-self erupting at least once a week; I'm sure it's scary to them both. And it's probably not fair to blame Seth, but his behavior makes me feel out of control."

Amanda: "As upset as I am with Seth some of the time, I'm more upset with Brian. He's yelling bloody murder, practically throwing Seth into his room for a time-out with no explanation, and swooping in to 'problem solve,' as he calls it, just when I'm starting to get somewhere with Seth."

With healthy, normal toddlerhood arrives a tsunami of emotion, started by the earthquake of new autonomy and "do it my*self*" arrogance. Hardly any co-parenting alliance is ready for the full force of it. Remember the parents from the survey who were "uncertain how to handle difficult situations" because they are equally "uncertain about understanding young children's feelings and needs"? When these two immovable forces meet, tectonic plates must shift to relieve the building pressure as that tsunami sweeps into the nursery, kitchen, bathroom, or bedroom. One of the bigger challenges to the co-parenting rapport over time is to help each other stay upright in the face of this powerful force of nature.

Our advice to Brian and Amanda is to get everything breakable out of reach and find an area in the house that can be just Seth's to mess up. Give him noisy toys that are the real thing (like pots and pans), so he has a safe place to be a tsunami. Then Brian and Amanda have to decide who will deal with him when. Because Seth is so labor intensive, they should do more one-on-one parenting to give each other a break at regular intervals. Most important, they need a way to tell each other, rather than Seth, when they are angry at him, so the parent who is less angry at that moment can take control for awhile, while the other parent cools off.

Often during toddlerhood, feelings run high for the first time about the other partner's lack of consistency in dealing with the child's outrageous behavior. Parental views on time-outs, yelling, ignoring, and the use of shame or even spanking are challenged on the spot, and charges of erratic caving in or "you're undermining me" start to fly. The idea of the tag team goes out the window. Tempers flare, individuals retreat from the partnership, and they begin to harbor their own fears that there is something wrong with their toddler, their partner, and maybe even their marriage, accompanied by the emotional withdrawal we discussed earlier.

There's a more troublesome co-parenting issue that typically arises at this time: parents' competing values. Should our child be taught to fear strangers, or the dark, or Halloween? What's OK or not about the TV or computer use, or running naked through the house? Is it OK to call adults by their first names, play with toy guns or Barbie dolls, reference God?

Many of these values wars owe their existence to powerful family-of-origin experiences—positive and negative. When raising their own child, the parents now view these value-teaching opportunities as a chance to get it right this time around. For example, a parent who was taught to "look out for yourself first" may feel strongly that his child must learn the more egalitarian lesson to "do unto others." Consequently, it can be infuriating to see your partner teach what you feel is exactly the opposite value. Getting entangled in this kind of conflict can be disturbing to the child, because he sees it ultimately as his fault, as in, "If I wasn't afraid of the dark, Mommy and Daddy wouldn't be arguing about how to help me go to sleep."

While such differences are more common than not, toddlerhood has a way of making them feel especially dangerous to the parents. Balancing their toddler's headlong drive to be "me, myself, and I" in the context of trying to meet the needs of the whole family is challenging. It helps if parents can address this conflict in values in terms of personally held convictions; start by using "I" statements instead of accusatory "you always" statements. For example, rather than saying to your partner, "You always clean up after the kids! How are they ever going to learn to take care of themselves?" you might phrase it this way, "I believe kids learn from their mistakes, so they should have a chance to make a few and learn from the consequences. Do you disagree with that?"

Such comments often slip out at moments of hurt or to justify an angry accusation. But by talking with your mate about these important differences in perspective, and the justifications behind them, you can build, rather than erode, your parenting alliance over time. On the other hand, if you feel permanently stuck, which is common, getting professional help is a good idea. How do you know if you're in this place? Ask yourself: Even when we try to talk together about the kid's needs, does it usually degenerate into a heated argument, leaving us both hurt?

Any help you seek at such moments should be competent, experienced, and informed in matters of family, child development and co-parenting. Relationship help at the right time is likely to be more effective, and certainly cheaper emotionally and financially, than putting it off. Our years as clinicians have taught us that when even a simple question leads to trouble, then the trouble needs to be addressed sooner rather than later to get a couple back on track, and avoiding painful travel down the wrong—often dead end—road.

But for most co-parenting alliances, patiently supporting your mate in the face of toddler eruptions, having frequent conversations about values, keeping it light whenever possible, and working actively to manage your frustrations will succeed. Bill and Julie have some work to do before their toddler tsunami hits, especially given how they felt about each other's roles in their infant's first year. Now is the time to refresh their friendship by articulating their love and admiration for one another, turning toward each other whenever the baby pulls them away, and spending more time together as a couple of interesting adults, not simply joint baby-minders. (Refer to the co-parenting preventive maintenance quiz on p. 44 for more guidance.)

Preschoolhood

Once toddlerhood eases into preschoolhood, things get calmer for co-parenting. The arrival of more useful, communicative language helps parents enormously, reducing the guesswork of what the children need daily. Kids' raw emotions begin to mature, and some useful new emotions arrive developmentally. Shame and pride provide parents a new ally in the struggle against impulsiveness. Wanting to be a "big" girl or boy is a cogent new argument for why one shouldn't put ketchup on the cat. Other developing emotions help parents out too; empathy, embarrassment, and generosity[8] all help the child become a more civil member of the family and therefore less challenging to the co-parenting alliance. Of course, going forward, children—aided by rapidly growing vocabularies and a growing sense of cause and effect—will start to say the darnedest things about their parents. We include some of our favorite quotes from children we've encountered over the years that show how important it is to them that Mom and Dad develop and maintain good co-parenting rapport.

> "I like when Mom and Dad aren't so tired and stressed out that they can really listen to me. They do that better when they are both with me."
>
> "I like when Mom takes half the day off and Dad takes the other half off when I'm sick. That way they can both take turns looking after me."
>
> "Sometimes Mommy says no and Daddy says yes. I like it best when they say the same thing. No one gets mad."
>
> "I love when Mommy hugs me good night and Daddy holds me tight. Daddy hugs are just different."
>
> "When Mommy and Daddy are angry at each other about me, my stomach hurts, and so does my heart. I get scared they're going to divorce."
>
> "When Daddy is around, Mommy is happier. She just is. Me, too."

"My Mommy's smart in some ways and my Daddy is smart in other ways." (Question: "What about you?") "I get to be smart like both."

"When Daddy gives me ice cream at night and Mommy finds out, she says, 'Oh, Steve.' Daddy rolls his eyes and Mommy looks mad. But I love ice cream and I'm glad Daddy does it. (Question: "Was Mommy really mad?") Child giggles. "Uh uh. I think sometimes she thinks it's funny."

"I'm less scared when Daddy checks for monsters. He's bigger and stronger than Mom and he'll make 'em leave. Monsters run away from Daddy, especially when Mom is behind him."

"Daddy fixes things like chairs. Mommy fixes my toys. Together they fix my baby brother's screaming. . . . I hate when he screams."

Children know and deeply appreciate when parents show each other respect, positive attitudes, and affection for each other over ire—even when they disagree. That teaches kids that differences are not deficiencies. And as children grow older, they feel proud to have bits and pieces of both parents inside them to count on.

PART
II

7

▼

Discipline
"Wait 'til Your Father Gets Home!"

"When [my husband] is mad, he gets right in our son's face
and just cuts off the behavior. Not me—I get down on his level and
talk to him. Sometimes [my husband] is right because it stops
the behavior midstream, and sometimes I'm right because
he's just too much in our son's face and it makes him so upset.
That makes the behavior worse."

—*Mother of a seven-year-old daughter and a five-year-old son*

WE DON'T HEAR THE PHRASE—*"Wait 'til your father gets home!"*—much
anymore, but it touches us instantly. It is one of those enduring parenting
mantras. In fact, fathers and mothers may be most at odds when it comes
to discipline and setting limits. In this chapter, we explore the effects of
those differences, and why they are useful to co-parenting families.

Moms vs. Dads: Behaving with Authority

Kids have certain preferences for a particular parent when they want to
get their needs met. In general, children tend toward their mothers if
they need comfort when exhausted, sick, or just plain miserable. They
tend toward their fathers when they need physical protection or want

something to be fixed, or are in the hunt for adventure, fun, or games. Children of both genders show such tendencies equally. According to leading gender researcher Eleanor Maccoby; "Boys and girls have not been found to differ in the quality of their attachment to either of their parents. Boys do not appear to be more interested in their fathers than girls are, nor are girls more likely than boys to seek closeness to their mothers than their fathers."[1] But does the same equanimity hold when a child needs discipline? Maybe not, says Maccoby. The time-honored stereotype waiting until dad gets home no longer applies:

▼ Fathers tend to spend less time reasoning, explaining, or rationalizing why a child needs to be disciplined.
▼ Fathers tend to use fewer words and less time to set a limit and expect compliance, whether or not it is granted by the child.
▼ Fathers tend to use less reciprocal bargaining with an errant child and significantly more imperatives ("just get in your room—now") than do most mothers, who tend to rely on more relationship-based socialization techniques ("do it because I told you to and I'm your mother").
▼ Fathers tend to be more willing than mothers to confront their children and enforce discipline, leaving their children with the impression that they in fact *have* more authority.

Fathers tend to *behave* more authoritatively when it comes to disciplining their children than do most mothers. This "acting with authority" can surprise many mothers, who are called on more frequently to discipline the child because, in general, they log more parenting hours than do their spouses. Nevertheless, this authority appears to be the reasoning behind "wait 'til your father . . .". Invoking a father's authority has the appearance of being effective, at least in the short run, which can be frustrating for many mothers.

Sandra was a stay-at-home mom who also spent fifteen hours a week doing at-home work for her father's web design firm. She and Dan considered themselves to be successfully co-parenting their toddler and preschooler, despite her husband's forty-eight-hour workweek. Since the recent economic downturn, he had added a graveyard shift as a supervisor two nights a week to make more money, but was still able to "cover the kids" while Sandra worked in their over-the-garage office.

Sandra commented, "One thing that sticks in my craw about his parenting is how cocky he is when it comes to his ability to set effective limits with our kids. He says 'stop' once and they actually do! With me, if they stop at all, it'll take three or more times and then I have to raise my voice anyway. I just don't get it. I'm with them two or three times as much time as he is. I know when they are about to act up, and I intervene pretty fast, I think. Shouldn't they listen better to me than to him?"

Sandra's children might appear to be less responsive to her limit setting for a couple of reasons: One, her tendency to reason makes the kids (and possibly her) think she has to *convince* them why they should stop pounding on each other. Second, they may have gotten too familiar with, or deaf to, her resolution tactics over time. Dan, who is a little less familiar in general, and more likely to loom menacingly than to reason about stuff, gives the impression that he's neither interested in nor open to negotiations. This may add up to the sense that he "means it the first time" and that he is more "effective" than Sandra, particularly with kids of this young age. Over the long run, this authority may not hold up. The more worrisome issue facing this couple, however, is Sandra's perception that Dan is being "cocky" about the effectiveness of his discipline compared to hers, indicating that he's got some repair work to do on this tag team's co-parenting rapport.

Feeling competitive about who is the more respected parent is as common as it is troublesome for couples. But the children's bestowal of this honor is fleeting; their choice of whom to listen to frequently changes for reasons that have nothing to do with which parent is deserving. A mother's view may hold sway on the "why can't we have ice cream for dessert" issue because she means no when she says it; the father says no screen time on school nights and means it, but the mother lets the children watch or play when she has something she needs to do.

Before we take on some common challenges in typical disciplinary co-parenting, we need to explore one thing that can influence effective limit setting: parental style.

Parenting Styles

Two generations ago, University of California-Berkeley developmental psychologist Diana Baumrind described a general parenting style that she deemed to be especially effective in setting limits with kids. She mapped out this style, which she titled authoritative parenting, along with two other, less effective styles: authoritarian and permissive.[2]

Authoritarian parents have a controlling and detached style with relatively little expression of warmth, compared to other parents. For example, a child complains that she wants a snack, and her parent says,

"No, it's too close to dinner." "But I'm h-u-u-u-n-n-gry, I didn't get much lunch," whines the child. An authoritarian parent might then simply say, "You won't starve. You should've eaten more at lunch."

On the other end of the spectrum, permissive parents are "non-controlling, non-demanding, and relatively warm." Take the same scenario. The passive parent might respond to her child, "You can take a snack if you need to—anything you'd like."

Authoritative parents maintain control, while exhibiting warmth and being receptive to their children's communication. Again, consider the same scenario. The authoritative parent responds, "I'll bet you're hungry; you didn't eat much. Some fruit can hold you until dinner, but I don't want you to ruin one of your favorite meals, so let's see what you can do to take your mind off food while I finish cooking."

Baumrind found that the children of authoritarian parents were relatively withdrawn, discontent, and distrustful, and children of permissive parents were the "least self-reliant, explorative, and self-controlled,"[3] while children of authoritative parents were explorative, self-reliant, and the most content of all the children studied in her middle-class sample. Your child will respond much more readily to your discipline over time if you adopt the more authoritative style. Stick to your guns but recognize your child's feelings may be different from your decision, give a brief explanation for your rationale if appropriate, and maintain your loving, affectionate stance. Do not equate being firm with being cold, tough, or harsh.

As helpful as this research is, it is only part of a preamble to the discussion on how such parenting styles fit into the work of strengthening your co-parenting alliance. It's not just one parent's authoritative style that serves your child well; it is likely that authoritative co-parenting is best for the well-being of the family as a whole—marriage, co-parenting, and each parent-child relationship.

So how do we move from thinking about individual parenting styles to co-parenting? Clearly our parenting choices are the products of personal style and biases, influenced by powerful family traditions and cultures. Having observed many families, however, we are struck by how often men and women discipline in a way that is associated with their gender: a mother's "negotiable-sociable" style and a father's "imperative–move on" style. It is personal parenting style and preferences, family experience, and gender that must be negotiated and balanced *within the couple* to create the best mixture of discipline as authority and support for your child. We examine this process of becoming an authoritative *couple* in the rest of this chapter, as we consider the most common behavioral challenges children create for their parents to solve together.

When the Kids Are Acting Up

Figuring out when to intervene is the precursor of any disciplinary effort. When kids are very young (not yet talking), it's an easier decision, and most mothers and fathers tend to view these situations similarly. We decide based on what we see, since infants and pretoddlers don't hide much. If safety is a concern, neither parent is likely to hold back very long, although mothers might move more quickly to intervene based on what their (typically greater) experience tells them about the extent of a potential behavioral meltdown. If the kids are exhausted, they'll need help sooner than usual to stay safe and not fling the kitchen implements or themselves about, especially if younger siblings are on the scene.

Although simpler when children are quite young, it's isn't always easier. Most first-time mothers and fathers are pretty reluctant disciplinarians. Responding to each teachable moment to cobble together a moral consciousness around issues such as no biting, hitting, or spitting, not to mention waiting one's turn, sharing, and thinking about others is a hair-raisingly complex issue compared to the sweet rhythms of infant care and feeding.

Are you risking some of your limited supply of parental capital every time you discipline a child and she gets mad at you for it? If you're one of those parents who feels like the bad cop every time you have to discipline your child, remember this: Though in the heat of the moment he may react negatively, imagine what kind of person he'll become if he never hears the word no.

Let's look at how mothers and fathers react in a typical parenting scenario.

Jennifer and Frank were back for more advice. Jennifer explained that things were going well, but they had hit a new pothole. Shortly after Ben turned four, Jennifer and Frank had a second child, Rose. Rose was now crawling and getting into Ben's cherished stuff in his room. Last night, she swiped his perfectly ordered Thomas the Tank Engine collection right off the train table. Ben thought she did it on purpose and tripped her. She howled.

Frank rushed in and yelled at Ben, telling him he couldn't play with the trains for a whole day. Now Ben was howling too. Jennifer was furious at Frank, "I know he can't trip her, but she did mess up his room, and they are both too little to understand." Frank disagreed. "There is no reason for an almost five-year-old to hit a one-year-old, who obviously doesn't understand what she's doing."

Jennifer wanted to explain things to Ben, to teach him that he behaved badly because he was angry, but his behavior really hurt his little sister: "Is that really what he wanted to do when he stopped and thought about it?" She didn't want to just stop Ben's behavior. She wanted to give his feelings some words.

Frank was worried Ben could hurt Rose since she was so little; he didn't think words were the right choice of discipline: "It is important to just cut these aggressive behaviors off. She's only going to be more trouble when she begins walking." Frank felt they could discuss Ben's feelings some other time, when heads were cooler.

So who is right, Jennifer or Frank? They both have valid points. That's what makes this stuff so tricky. Beyond the timing of when to step into the disciplinary arena is the whole topic of what you want to accomplish once you are there. Here, mothers and fathers often chart slightly different courses, just as we see with Frank and Jennifer. Ben is likely to tell his mother he did in fact mean to hurt his little sister. Why not, when she hurt him (that is, his precious stuff) first? Jennifer opened the door for that in a way that won't help Ben much. Frank's impulse to cut off the behavior and say it is never right to hurt her is necessary. It would also be helpful to Ben to acknowledge that he was angry. But the message is that while feeling angry is OK, tripping or hitting isn't. One part of what each parent did, combined, would be the better response. Together, they could give a message that is structured and helps their child control his anger, but also gives credibility to his feelings: an authoritative response.

When it comes to disciplining their children, fathers and mothers generally do not share identical socialization goals for their kids. And this can negatively affect their co-parenting rapport, if not gently managed. As we see in this example, both goals are valid and important. The trick is not to take turns but to integrate the two perspectives into one that incorporates important elements from both and blends them into a better response than either parent may have given alone. Let's look at two perspectives, influenced in large part by typical gendered responses. As we learned in chapter 5, mothers and fathers feel strongly about their jobs in preparing their children for life outside the family. It shows up particularly in the area of discipline. Mothers tend to feel it is their job to teach their unruly or noncompliant kids (at any age) that disobedience has consequences that can hurt the parent-child relationship, such as:

▼ When you hurt your sister, I am upset with you (that is, you risk changing our relationship for the worse).

▼ Your behavior makes me feel unsympathetic and, for the time being, less close to you.

▼ I withdraw to show you that not listening to me has its negative consequences. In fact, it has negative consequences for your present and future relationship with me and your sister. So please stop lashing out.

Fathers tend to feel it is their job to teach that same unruly child that disobedience doesn't just cost you interpersonally; it also costs you a choice place at the real-world's table. They feel that it is crucial to get across the idea that noncompliance with adult wishes will cost you respect and the benefit of the doubt from the world outside the family.

▼ When you don't listen to me and act like you can't control yourself, you're headed for trouble out *there*.

▼ Tripping your sister can lead to tripping someone else, and that isn't cute. You'll get into trouble at school. Maybe someone will just get up and push you back.

▼ Listening to me will help you stay well liked and safe. So knock it off and listen better—now.

Recognize yourself in these examples? Wondering which is right for you and your child? Let's examine another gender or role trend before we resolve the issue.

Shame: The Great Humanizer

At the end of a child's second year, a new emotion arrives developmentally, and just in the nick of time: shame. It's as powerful an emotion as any a young child will encounter, short of blind rage or pee-in-your-pants delight. Without it, parents who strive to be effective disciplinarians would be lost. By age two, distraction has exhausted its usefulness as a technique—the kids are just too smart now to fall for it very often, unless you are a trained illusionist. Reasoning shows promise, but their language skills are not quite up to the rhetorical argument stage.

Shame arrives on the scene to help children control their impulses. It works now—as opposed to when they were younger—because the child's growing moral sense and self-awareness combine, rendering her capable of figuring out embarrassment and, more importantly, its causes and effects. Before this happens, it's pretty pointless to argue with a pretoddler about how she wants to be a "big girl" and should not scream bloody murder when she loses a race to her older cousin, because she couldn't care less about the rules of embarrassment: "There's the race, I want to win, and you should let me." But once a child is able to feel and recognize embarrassment, *voila*, she now *wants* to be that big girl and race as fast as she can for the sheer joy of running like the wind and finishing the race, just like the other big kids whom she emulates.

But like all developmental gifts, shame needs to be evoked in moderation. Depending on the child, it can be easily over- or underdone. The youngest of our four children, our son J.D.—smart, sweet, and rowdy— currently has a quick sensitivity to feeling shamed. Many behavioral scientists would not find that too surprising, given that boys may be a bit more easily embarrassed in settings where their autonomy, size, or competence receive insufficient respect at the moment.[4]

As J.D.'s mother, Marsha sometimes comments on his hair standing straight up or his clothes being dirty, even though we are walking out the door to go somewhere "nice." She hopes the shame will lead him to comb his hair or offer to change his shirt. No such luck. It triggers a loud "Mom, I have no clothes I like that fit" [not true!]. "Mom, now I'm not going with you because you embarrassed me." Forget about telling him there is a simple solution; he doesn't see it that way. Now we're getting later by the minute, and Marsha is in a dead-end tug-of-war with J.D. about whether he'll look clean or not.

As J.D.'s dad, Kyle understands the fragile male ego Marsha has unwittingly stepped on and weighs in with a comment that emphasizes J.D.'s autonomy, "Why don't you keep your shirt on as you are, and we'll bring another in case you change your mind when you see the other kids" [which he usually does]. J.D. accepts the solution (or the cover it gives him), glares at his mother for a second, and is off, as Marsha and Kyle share a private, knowing glance.

The effects of shame help a mother make her "relationship consequences to misbehavior" point and help a father make his "real-world consequences to misbehavior" point. For most children, shame does its job pretty efficiently without a lot of help from either parent. So be glad it's part of the scene, but don't let it hog the spotlight; it doesn't wear well as emotions go.

Discipline and Learning

What does discipline really mean? Its usage as a label for punishment has come to overpower its more moderate origins. The root of the word is *disciple*, which denotes one who learns or apprentices himself for the purpose of learning. In short, effective discipline should be about a *learning* experience for the child, not getting spanked or punished. Next we examine some methods of discipline, including spanking and bribery, along with more positive approaches.

Spanking

In the Civitas survey we discussed in the previous chapter, 67 percent of parents of young children felt that spanking was an appropriate part of an overall discipline approach. However, most experts now concur[5] that spanking is a way of shaming, more akin to bullying than to disciplining. There is really never a good reason to do it. It leads children to feel anger and shame and to act aggressively. While spanking may temporarily stop the misbehavior for which it was intended, you will likely see bigger misbehaviors and bigger problems emerge if you continue to use physical punishment as a strategy for discipline in place of true teaching. It basically teaches kids to avoid getting *caught* by parents when they are "bad," not to avoid being bad in the first place. If you and your spouse disagree on spanking, take as much time and as many discussions as it takes to sort this out between you. Your relationship with your kids and each other is worth the trouble.

Bribery

On the other side of the shame continuum is another behavior-reinforcing technique often used for toddlers through kindergarteners—the bribe. It's not usually where either parent begins philosophically, hoping that they will not need to stoop to rewarding acceptable behavior with ice cream, candy, or toys. Their children will honor their deep and abiding love for them, respect them, and simply do as they are told out of like-minded adoration and regard.

Then, something *really* important gets complicated, such as potty training, or sleeping in one's own bed, or the like. Things were going along OK, a little progress here and there and then—nothing! The child's progress is off the track. Parents quickly get frustrated, and desperation forces the issue. That's when the bribe starts to look attractive. Media messages support it. The super-nannies and super-moms on TV and in the magazines and the bloggers all use reward systems of points, stars, chips, money, no nap, or extra time with mom, dad, the computer, or the dog. And many of these bribes appear to work—for a while.

Why don't bribes work in the long run? When we offer kids M&Ms in order to get them to eat their broccoli, they understand instantly that you are asking them to do something inherently unpleasant to get whatever goody you proffer. What if the kid might have eaten the broccoli anyway? Many of them actually do, at least they are willing to give it a go. But once you add the M&Ms as dessert or reward for eating broccoli, a child's motivation to eat his greens—minus the goodie—is dead in the water.

Classic research by Stanford University's Mark Lepper and David Greene shows us why we should be skeptical of giving kids seemingly harmless rewards.[6] In their study, a group of preschoolers were supplied with some flashy new markers, without explanation. The children who responded most obviously to the markers were invited to play separately with the researcher. The first one-third of the group was told that if they drew with the new markers (which they had already been doing with delight), they would receive the "good player award." The second one-third was asked to draw with the new markers and then was simply surprised with an award when they did. The final one-third received mild praise—the same dose as the first two groups—but received no award. Two weeks later, the researchers added up how much time each child now used the markers. "The results were surprising: the first group (the ones promised the "good player award") showed only 42 percent of the interest in the markers as the "no award" and the "surprise award" groups. It's as though the kids knew the rewards were a kind of counterfeit praise. Messing about with fancy new markers was its own reward; no adult tricks or treats required.

In *Kids Are Worth It*, Barbara Coloroso argues strenuously that rewards and bribes are ultimately as ineffective as spanking and threats.[7] So what's a parent to do? Luckily, there's a middle of the road response that will make even the most truculent young child feel supported.

Positive Reinforcement

One way to encourage children to behave in a positive, pro-social manner is to use positive reinforcements. A positive reinforcement is something the child enjoys that you use to show your pride and support after he accomplishes the desired behavior. You do not hold the token out as the reason to behave positively in the first place. Our favorite "reinforcer" of desirable behavior and extinguisher of nondesirable behavior is the surprise bonus. This is the unpromised, unexpected goody. The child feels great getting it and sees it as generous, as opposed to the earned reward, for which he is just doing what's expected at the close of the contract. With the promised earned reward, he winds up feeling that it is just accounting, not the unanticipated affirmation of his essential worthiness for being or doing something you—and he—value a lot.

Values

There are, of course, important human behaviors that even surprise bonuses can't teach or promote, like empathy or the golden rule ("do unto others as you would have them do unto you"). Those values you learn in your own skin, in your own family. No treats of any caliber will get you there any faster if you can't find them on your own. Your child watches and copies your behavior all the time. The best way to teach values is to live by them. Your child quickly comes to know which values you just talk about and which ones you actually live by. Teaching by example helps the most, but ultimately it's the child's embrace of these values that makes them stick, not the parent's appreciation of them. Getting values to stick comes by watching and then by doing. Involve your children in your own good deeds and positive actions. For example, if you've agreed to feed your neighbor's cat, have your kids fill its water bowl. Or at the dinner table, make sure you mention that you spent the afternoon helping your elderly neighbor clean out her garage; it's even better if the kids can help you finish the job on the weekend.

In using reinforcers, as long as you and your partner both agree with each other's values and intended outcomes, then the only and mostly internal struggle is to be fair, consistent, and true to what you believe in while your values are being tested daily. Co-parenting involves being open with each other about each of your strengths and weaknesses, and then helping each other to be the best parent you can be, especially when it is difficult. Your differences don't matter here, but your alliance does. You are being the reinforcer for the other, when he or she falters. This means making sure the kids do help the elderly neighbor. It means putting a hand on your spouse's arm (out of earshot or behind the kid's back) and saying, "You don't really mean that, honey, do you? I'm not sure you'll get what you want from doing *that*. Try this?"

Gender differences may not matter as much with the next disciplinary technique: getting kids to behave through reasoning or arguing.

Arguments with Your Child
Let's look again at the earlier example of Marsha's trying to get J.D. to change his dirty shirt before going out. A typical scenario between moms and sons might go like this:

Child: My shirt isn't really dirty because I just wore it for a few hours.
Mom: But it has a stain on it.
Child: That isn't a new stain. That's always there. That won't come out. It's not actually dirty.
And so on.

In general, fathers tend to be somewhat critical of mothers for arguing with the misbehaving child, not so much with the *why* of the argument, but rather with the *way* the argument goes down.

Bart, a thirty-one-year-old short-haul truck driver and jazz pianist father of two sons, a preschooler and a first-grader, says, "Sally is a fantastically creative mother in every way with our kids, except one. She argues with them about getting dressed, brushing their teeth, getting ready for bed, their manners, coming to dinner when called—all the same way. It's not about what she needs them to be doing at the moment; it's about why they aren't listening to her. They get confused, shut down, do zip, and she argues even more. I try to sort things out for them—you know— translating kind of—but that just pisses her off more."

Mothers will say that they are trying to educate their kids to *listen* to their parents first and *comply* second, because it's good for overall family functioning; but then they feel immensely frustrated when it so rarely works. Many fathers will not cotton to arguing, period, relying instead on their authority, as discussed earlier. But for fathers who do feel there is a place for arguing in their overall disciplinary schema, they tend to encourage a different kind of argument than do mothers. It tends to be less about arguing passionately for compliance in behaving and listening and more about arguing through persuasion and reason.

Jay Heinrichs, an author and philosopher, proposed in a *Wondertime* magazine article that kids should be encouraged to argue with a purpose.[8] Since they are going to argue anyway, how about helping *them* win occasionally for the good of the family and their own self-regard? His thesis is that arguments should reflect reason rather than passion.

Heinrichs explains that his kind of arguing can teach decision making ("We're going to do something outside this morning; shall we play soccer or go swimming?") by helping children to think through their options and then persuade others to follow. He also encourages emphasizing the future; "What's a good way to make sure that the toys get picked up?" is preferable to "Who made this huge mess?" He suggests deflecting the screaming, whining, and the drama by not engaging with anything other than, "Oh, come on now, sweetie. You can do better than that." He cries "foul," whenever a child stomps out of the room, shouts someone down, or recounts a previous atrocity by an aggrieved party, and then summarily chooses the opposite side. Finally, and to our mind especially useful, he ensures that kids win periodically. When they present a good argument, it should carry the day—maybe even earn one of those surprise bonuses we discussed earlier.

On a recent Sunday afternoon, our seven-year-old begged us to ignore his older sister, who was agitating for yet another activity. At first she said we should all go out, to which he replied we shouldn't, and an argument destined to separate winner from loser was at hand. He further argued we should stay home instead "for tea and cocoa in front of the fireplace," since we were all "tired and feeling a little weird." And so we did. His sister later gave him a squeeze and said, "Good idea, little buddy."

Heinrichs's point is that a good argument is always preferable to a good fight. Persuading another to agree with you, or at least lay down arms and negotiate, is good preparation for success in the real world. Teaching kids to think about what motivates the audience is a crucial aspect of this educational approach. Kids rarely fight just for the thrill of it. They want their way, to be sure, but they'd rather have you value their efforts at winning than dismiss them. Finally, they need to hear often that it's in *their* best interest to keep *you* happy with *them*. It's like the pesky but memorable little sign at the dentist's office: "You don't have to floss all your teeth, just the ones you want to keep."

Arguments with Your Spouse

So, let's figure out how you can argue fairly rather than fight with your spouse, as well. Mothers and fathers need to exercise the art of persuasion. Mothers, instead of withdrawing or pouting just a little, and fathers, instead of leaving the room or yelling, put your back into getting your spouse to agree with you. Give a good, honest reason for why you see things differently. If she doesn't buy it, find a better one. Also, make sure he feels that he too can win some of the time. Give in when he least expects it, just for the chance to see the surprise on his face. Appreciate how good it feels to see her get what she wants. And remind him how truly affable you are when you're happy. Pleasing your spouse should not be a chore; it is a pleasure for which you are highly motivated because everyone gains.

With your spouse and child, it is best to know when not to argue and when it is OK to be convincing. Sometimes it is important to just let the issue go—the wordless capitulation to a child or the simple shrug to your spouse. Choosing your arguments is every bit as important as choosing your battles.

Spoiling

Mom: "Oh honey, you didn't get him another Red Sox shirt, did you? He already has enough; he's just asking because he knows it makes you happy to see him like your team. So let him please you, but not with more sports paraphernalia."

Having heard the case for disciplined argument, let's consider the opposite, less disciplined end of the parental spectrum: caving or spoiling.

Now, in the first decade of the twenty-first century, the short-lived (now distant) legacy of the affluent nineties has been playing itself out. The nineties generation of parents prided itself on providing every advantage for their kids, primarily because they could and secondarily because at the end of a long day at work (usually for both parents), capitulation buys peace.

Packaged Facts market researchers tracked $54 billion spent on preschoolers to middle-schoolers in 2004—up $17.6 billion over the 1997 numbers. Teenagers were even worse (better?); they spent $175 billion on themselves in 2004, up $53 billion from seven years previously.[9] It's interesting to speculate how often those kids had to ask for something before their parents caved. Providing at will may generate more attitude than gratitude. That certainly is what advertisers fervently hope; having begets wanting, which begets consumption, not appreciation.

Here's the problem with kids who have known too few limits on their appetites or opportunities. Overindulged kids who have received too much too soon learn entitlement, not useful coping strategies for life's coming disappointments. The disappointments inevitably come. These are the kids who are surprised at how vulnerable they feel when the gravy train jumps the track. Stanford University's Center on Adolescence researcher William Damon describes how such children as teenagers spend "large amounts of their time feeling anxious and scared, instead of sorting out what they can do to have a life that matters."

The co-parenting angle comes into play here. Generally, parents don't approach this complex game of discipline identically, anymore than they have identical socialization goals for their kids. Whether gender itself plays a distinct role in how parents set limits is practically impossible to prove. The fact that two different adults have to administer these mostly unsuccessful bribery or capitulation schemes practically guarantees trouble in the parental relationship when facing their children's appetites and impulses.

Steps for Co-parenting and Discipline

Lose the time-honored "wait 'til your father gets home" for "wait 'til your parents have talked about this together." Then you wait to have that conversation with each other about what happened, how it felt to you, what the kid(s) said during testimony (one of you will have already debriefed the perpetrator), and finally what you want them to *learn* and how you want them to *feel* from this limit-setting, teaching moment. *Talk together, using the "we" pronoun five times for every "you," keeping it short, about this event only—not the person—end it, and move on feeling better.* If this sounds time consuming, you're right, but only in the short run. When the tag team is calm and prepped, the match doesn't start nearly as often, so in the long run, this is a huge time saver. The other side will eventually learn that resistance is futile.

Abraham Lincoln said it best in another context: "A house divided against itself cannot stand." Complete agreement about what to say is nice, but rare. A negotiated settlement or agreement is more common and equally effective, as long as the parties agree on the content and timing of the talk. If the parents are just too far apart to talk to the child together, then the parent who was present during the infraction should probably deliver the solution that suits the needs of the kids. Then the tag team sorts out why both parents couldn't get it together this time for the child's sake. This last step is critical and totally worth the trouble if you want that stronger co-parenting rapport to emerge.

Encourage a healthy, but joint disregard for materialism (or cynicism about materialism): "How long did that ____ actually make you happy?" As parents, you both have to walk the walk here, or your kids will brand you sooner or later with the scarlet *H* (for hypocrisy). Why do we emphasize a disregard for materialism? Because, increasingly, parents give in on the gadgets and electronics and then find they need to discipline *about* those same gadgets.

Practice preventive discipline as partners. When all you do is say no, why bother listening to you, right? Here are some ways to help each other say yes, so that when either or both of you do say no, it will matter more.

▼ Children adore being heard. They thrive and delight when they have you by the ears. So, if you are talking *at* them more then you are listening *to* them, back off and close your mouth. It's the best way to teach them to listen. Besides, they can say the darnedest things.

▼ Demonstrate your care for them by remembering the things that matter to them: the names of their softies; friends (imaginary and real); the funny, clever, and loving things they've done in the last few days; and how you shared their most recent accomplishment with your spouse.

▼ Acknowledge regularly what they bring to the family that is unique — absolutely theirs alone—and how perfect it is in the family treasury. If you have to think long and hard about this, it's a sure sign that you need to look and listen more.

▼ Share their excitement about whatever they are turned on to (nonmaterial pleasures preferred)—music, books, friends, sporting event, pet, food, silly thing at school. Then tell them what you have learned about them and their passion. It will bring you closer, which helps in future arguments.

▼ Use your parental magic trio, the three things that always help when your child is down: humor (jokes welcome), music (the singing or humming parent—tuneful or tuneless), and the vastly underappreciated back rub. These are magical because they make you feel better too.

As co-parents, make sure you are engaged in these preventive discipline principles *together*. Does only one parent know about these principles, or are you sharing ideas as you go along? If only one parent, probably the mother, has this information, she will more likely be the gatekeeper and tell her husband how to do what she has learned. Have him read or learn about this stuff for himself; or share your ideas while you read, and discuss with him later. But neither of you should be the sole disciplinarian. If you recognize typically male ways of disciplining or techniques you are not likely to use because "he" or "she" does, try switching places. Our kids call this "having an opposite day." Try to be more like each other, which can be great fun, surprise and delight your child, and help you two develop empathy and appreciation for each other's position and opposition.

Kids from toddlerhood through adolescence need to know the limits of acceptable behavior because it helps them feel safer and more secure when they know what their parents expect of them. As grownups, we generally take offense when someone tells us what to do; we feel belittled and disrespected. Less so for our kids. They may bridle a bit, but ultimately they are happy to have directions when they feel lost. That's how they develop self-control and self-esteem, feeling secure about where they can go and who they can be when mom and dad are not hovering overheard. That place in the world—without mom and dad—will, of course, be where they will spend most of their lives and the place for which they need the most preparation. Knowing that their parents feel and act differently, but that they will support each other on all the big issues and expect certain behavior, helps your child feel prepared for the world out there.

8

Care and Feeding
Keeping Your Child Healthy in Body and Mind

MOMENTS AFTER A BABY is brought home from the hospital or birthing center and parents are on their own for the first time, the pressure begins to do the next thing just right, whatever that may be—to hold her, swaddle her, provide for her needs. It's at that precise moment when co-parenting enters reality. Say mom is breast-feeding, and she is focused on feeding the baby; dad may be focused on that too, but mom is wondering about getting the infant latched on, and dad is wondering about how to prop mom up so she's comfortable and able to provide. Already and by force of nature, mom and dad begin on slightly different journeys to their destination of raising a healthy child.

Mothers and fathers feel differently about their roles in caring for their baby's body and mind from day one. For a mother, things that happen to the baby (physically and emotionally) early in newborn life seem to affect her as well, just as in pregnancy when that cord was ferrying supplies for their shared life. The baby is hungry, mom feels peckish; the baby is tired, mom is beat; the baby is cranky, mom's on edge. For a father, things that happen to the baby need to be figured out, fixed, savored, or managed, but they are not happening in the same way to him and *his* body; there is no umbilical history to recall.

This categorical difference between mothering and fathering is the foundation for certain differences in the ways that mothers and fathers approach their children's overall health, from infant care and responses to crying to diet, nutrition, and emotional development, which we'll explore in the rest of this chapter.

The Basics

From the beginning, caring for your child is caring for his or her body. Both parents learn how to do this best on the job, but their preparation for that job is usually vastly different. Mothers typically have had more experience than dads with the bodies of other people's babies sometime in their lives. Nurses, midwives, and other women in her circle offer her advice, ranging from handling gas pains, shortcuts for dressing, to strategies for bathing tiny, slippery bodies. But the cultural and social expectation is that she'll have maternal instincts that will guide her, such as knowing intuitively when the baby is sick or discriminating between the hungry and tired cries.

Dads typically have had little to no experience managing other people's babies and it's generally not been expected that they should. This frequent discrepancy between a mother's and father's preparation (or lack thereof) for this part of parenting is what makes early infant care such a potential hot button for co-parenting conflict. Professionals will vary widely in their expectations and willingness to help dad learn how to handle the infant's physical needs, especially if he does not ask for help. Asking for help is in the category of asking for directions when lost, and is a tired excuse.

What should a father do to prepare for the birth of his baby? The *second* most important thing is to ask for help in learning how to care for *their* infant. But the top priority for dads is to devote the necessary hours to talking with their pregnant partner about how they want to raise their child and why, so that co-parenting has a better-than-even chance of working from the outset (as discussed in chapter 3). Almost every hospital or birthing center offers classes to help new parents practice the basic skills they'll need to take care of their newborn; in addition, there are many nursing and pediatric reference books and websites full of good information.

In Bernie Dorsey's "Conscious Fathering" program,[1] the *cycle of care* involves learning five essential infant-care skills. It is targeted to new dads, but not exclusive of mothers, who also need to master these skills. The five skills are:

▼ **Feed.** Most babies feed on demand, so they call the shots about when to feed them expressed breast milk or formula, as you, the mother, and the pediatrician have already discussed. Hold your baby close and support her head (weak neck muscles are an evolutionary design flaw) with a cradle between your index finger and extended thumb. Before the birth, practice with dolls until this is second nature.

▼ **Burp.** Babies swallow air as part of feeding, especially after a big feeding. The air needs to be helped back out by holding the baby upright with gentle pressure on the abdomen. That's why when you hold his tummy against your shoulder and give rhythmic, gentle, back pats with your free hand, the air comes out.

▼ **Comfort.** Frequent diaper changes protect skin, provide comfort, and allow for social interaction time. Have everything on hand, and never leave the baby on the changing table for a second. For girls, wipe front to back (top to bottom on a baby lying on her back), and for boys, keep a cloth diaper at hand to protect the wallpaper and your shirt. If the skin looks OK and isn't chapped, you're doing great.

▼ **Rest.** Most new parents are stunned at how much their babies need to sleep. In their first three months, the average is fourteen to twenty hours a day. Soothing and comforting a baby to sleep takes time and quiet. Whenever possible, feel free to join the baby in dreamland to slow the advance of your own sleep deprivation.

▼ **Deal with the baby's crying.** Babies need to cry just as we need to talk. There is no magic solution. Soothing is a process of eliminating the usual suspects—hunger, fatigue, being overwhelmed, a tight or full diaper, being overheated or cold, or nothing in particular. Don't hand the baby over to your partner until you've tried everything, or you've absolutely had it. Shaking babies can mortally wound them; therefore it is simply *never* an option.

These five essential skills will make you a player-partner in the game. Your child is rooting for you to get good at it.

For dads, it's poor co-parenting form to undermine your commitment to your child's well-being by implying, "I don't do diapers; I'm a guy." Learning the skills to manage your baby's physical care from the beginning greatly improves the odds that the incredibly joyful and impor-tant nurturing moments with your baby will happen with you, too, rather than only with your spouse. Men hate to feel inept. So, get prepared and get in there. There is nothing else in your life like the all-encompassing love that comes from this connection. Getting involved now gives a particular boost emotionally, physically, and neurobiologically to your child, not to mention that your partner may find it incredibly sexy.

What's your job when she's breast-feeding? Breast-feeding is such a good health idea for the baby, but how do you keep from drifting off the field of play while this incredibly intimate thing goes down? You can man-age your baby between feedings, diaper when the gastro-colic reflex kicks in (with the fresh onesie at hand), and do the heavy lifting when transport is required. If your wife is pumping breast milk so she can get some sleep or wants you in the rotation, give the occasional bottle. When you actively participate in caring for your baby, your marriage and your relationship with your child will benefit in a multitude of ways. Whether you succeed is only partially a function of your competence; it has more to do with the *why* you do it. You do it for your marriage *and* your baby. Your partner *really* needs to feel cared for at this time, when all she's doing is taking care of someone else. Waiting nearby, ready to do small things for her—even if it's just sitting next to her—is a loving way of being around and being part of the early days.

The Tender Touch

The way we handle our children physically is crucial to their developing self-esteem. We convey our children's inestimable value through the ways we touch and deal with their bodies—and their feelings—minute by minute. As important as words are to this enterprise over time, the *way we are* with them from the beginning matters more than what we say.

Tiffany Field, the infant psychologist whose work we discussed in chapter 6, is worth revisiting here just to re-emphasize the efficacy of physical over verbal comfort as the best way to calm upset infants and young children.[2] Physical forms of comfort bested verbal ten to one, proving that a good cuddle beats a good talk hands down, from infancy to prepubescence. In adolescence, cuddling obviously gets more compli-cated, depending on who's doing the cuddling and the adolescent's mood toward the cuddler at the moment.

In addition to the value of a loving touch, we parent best when we stay emotionally available and warm with our children. When we are able to sustain this availability as a constant through our "parental tone"—through feeding, bathing, dressing (when they are babies), meals, limit settings, awakenings, and bedding down for older children—it helps us stay responsive to our children's cues. That's why it's best to pick up those crying babies in the first six months of life and see what the problem might be, no matter how many times you have done it before. Or go put your arm around the pouting toddler to say, "I'm right here—what do you need?" If you are lucky enough to figure it out, the baby or toddler will respond instantly, and if you're not, at least you've shared a good, if noisy, cuddle in the meantime. There is no harm done in showing him you are there for him and you cared enough to try.

Remember a big lesson from the survey in chapter 6? You cannot spoil infants by responding to their distress; all you can do is reinforce their trust in you. The success of their future relationships with others is built on this very trust between them and you. You can begin worrying about spoiling later in the first year of life.

Being emotionally available may be harder for fathers because of the lack of experience they bring to the changing table, in addition to their feelings of separateness, never having shared the same body with their child. In our experience, this is especially true when you are trying to figure out if your child is overstimulated in his interactions with you. Petey's parents often banged heads over this question of how much stimulation was good for him and when.

> One thing Petey's parents disagreed about most often was whether Simon's frenzied play sometimes pushed Petey beyond his comfort zone. Marilyn thought it did; Simon was less sure. Marilyn thought Petey's wild giggles meant he was a little scared, and Simon thought they meant he was "lovin' being on the edge."

How to tell? When babies have had enough handling, playing, or feeding, they start putting their fists up in front of their face, looking away from your eyes and face to something more bland visually, really crinkling up their forehead (mild furrows typically mean "I'm interested"), or pushing away whatever it is you are offering. They have also maxed out their attention abilities when their back starts to arch, and they start to really fuss and make their "it's not just gas" cry. Fathers particularly need to learn that when this is the signal, don't force the baby to look at you by getting your mug back in their field of vision, don't try to match the intensity of the emotion-shifting superball, or don't reposition her so that she *has* to deal with you no matter what. This may be quality time for you, but you are missing the message that it's not working for the baby. When she's had it, don't up the ante. She wants out of the game, not more cards.

Mothers need to learn the same cues. Maybe you have learned them and are annoyed that your partner hasn't. What you don't want to do is brusquely tell him the baby has had it, because he then feels you are telling him what to do, a sign of unease and a vote of no confidence. That can make your partner stubborn, increasing instead of decreasing his intensity. Or he might listen to you, and slink away thinking, "Fine, then do it yourself; he's all yours." This too is just what you don't want to happen.

So, how can you help the baby reset his sensors to engage with you in more useful ways? No permanent damage is done in these miscues, whether they happen on dad's or mom's watch. In fact, a reasonable number of miscues might just be boot camp for coping and adaptation for the other times when no one seems to meet the child's needs. But in the short run, here's how to help the baby reboot: Let him call "time" to look or turn away and suck on something awhile, as you back away and lower the pitch and volume of your voice. Usually, you'll see the arched back relax, and the baby's breathing regularize and the facial muscles soften. You are ready to reconnect when the baby looks for you again, "Oh yay! . . . It's you!"

Try the same thing with your spouse. Back away. Soften your voice and point out what the baby is doing, and let him recalibrate in his own time and way. Then he's ready to reconnect with you and/or the baby.

Calming and Comforting

A top concern new fathers have is how to competently calm their fussy newborn. Kyle came across an old calming and comforting technique that has special appeal to new dads because it works most of the time and involves practice, tools, and action. In his first-year medical school class on child development, he showed the swaddling and soothing technique for fussing babies that is featured in pediatrician Harvey Karp's DVD, *The Happiest Baby on the Block*.[3] To Kyle's surprise, nearly a third (more male than female) of the class asked for extra time to review the tape and practice the technique. The comforting technique combines the snug swaddling of the infant, followed by a holding and rocking sequence that stimulates the infant's innate calming and self-quieting reflexes.

Figuring out good ways of holding and comforting your newborn is vital, because neurobiological ("brain growth") and psychological ("mind growth") advantages result when a child is consistently dealt with warmly, sensitively, and responsively. Being in "sync" with the baby keeps her central nervous system's stress hormones at low levels. This permits longer periods of uninterrupted growth and integration of experience within the brain. Brain-tissue growth and neuron interconnectedness occur at the fastest rates in the early months and years of life. Harvard's Jack Shonkoff, co-author of the influential "Neurons to Neighborhoods" report mentioned in chapter 2, has said that a child's "early experience is the architect of the brain." Why not give that architect the best tools to do a sensational job? If you have older children, you need not despair over this accelerated early life timetable of development, concerned that they might have missed out on some critical period of brain growth. The brain is a remarkably plastic organ and can adapt with agile creativity to life's slings and arrows well into adulthood.

Married life has its parallels. Getting the tone right from the beginning (prenatal) leads to strong roots for years of more stressful conditions, such as (emotional) drought or life's stressors. Patience, marital affection, and intimacy are lower on the food chain, now that a new baby has depleted the water and nutrients from the family soil. Such intimacies are harder to sustain when they were not there from the beginning, just as with growing children. Co-parenting can substantially support the young child's development—through clear communication, expression of affection, tolerance, patience, humor, and matching what you want to give to the needs of the baby and your spouse. As a divorce consultant, Marsha sees that many couples are not aligned on this crucial last point: one partner thought he was giving a lot, but it wasn't what the other partner wanted from him or needed at that point. So a lot of wasted effort results in feeling underappreciated: "Why didn't she notice all that I did?" "Why did he do so little of what I needed?" As you and your spouse learn to find the right balance of stimulation and comfort for your baby, you'll also be matching each other's needs for this same balance, creating a reciprocal universe that ultimately benefits the family at all levels. We explore more hands-on ways to create these healthy parallels in the marriage, in particular, in chapter 12.

ON A CONCRETE LEVEL, there are three intimately connected areas of care for the young child that can become potential co-parenting hot buttons for couples: diet and nutrition, emotional development, and social development.

Diet and Nutrition

We've already discussed breast-feeding in the first year. It is straight-forward from a diet and nutrition standpoint; an infant benefits, especially for the first six to eight months of life, if she is breast-fed. However, breast-feeding maintains an imbalance within the marital relationship, since one parent is clearly favored, given what mom has to offer that dad doesn't.

Sometimes parents disagree about when the breast-feeding should end. Dad wants to be more involved, mom wants to be freer to do what she wants, or the lack of sleep is taking its toll on one or both of the parents. A formula-fed baby makes for a fuller baby who will sleep longer.

A mother may long for the freedom part, but she also knows that cutting back on breast-feeding will likely lead to a reduced supply of milk, forcing a more complete halt to the feeding earlier than either parent intended. Whose needs does she give priority to: hers, her infant's, or her husband's?

Certainly in the first six months to a year of the baby's life, the baby's needs come first. After that, it is time for negotiation. Here are some questions for discussion.

▼ How often should Dad feed the baby? If breast-feeding, this involves planning and pumping ahead or agreeing about when you will begin to substitute formula for breast milk and how often thereafter you will do so.

Pros: When dad feeds the baby, he feels more connected to the child, mom gets a rest, and the child learns to use a bottle.

Cons: For dad to feed the baby, a bottle is necessary, which means mom must pump and freeze the milk or use it soon. Not pumping can lead to discomfort or becoming engorged.

▼ What night-time schedule will we as a couple work out? Many couples prefer that dad do a feeding during the night, if the baby is getting up often to feed. But maybe a feeding right after he returns home from work is better.

Pros: If dad gets up at night, mom gets a longer period of rest; the nights can be lonely, and mom might appreciate the support during those long, dark hours.

Cons: If dad is maintaining a long day at work, having him more tired when he cannot rest during the day might be hard on him and not good for his productivity at work.

▼ When should mom go back to work, or should she quit her job? If she's been working fewer hours since the baby was born, should she continue with this schedule or increase her hours? Whatever choice is made has economic and well-being implications for both parents, so both need to think this through.

Pros: Mom might be able to bring some needed income to the family; she can return sooner to a job she enjoyed, making it more likely she will lose less ground in her career; she may enjoy the juggling of time at home and time at paid work if she can balance them with equanimity.

Cons: Juggling paid work and breast-feeding can be difficult, depending on the environment in which mom works; sometimes going back to paid work heralds the end of breast-feeding before mom is emotionally ready; internal conflict about balancing work and family, and stresses that emanate from trying to do it all can negatively affect the working parent's patience and feelings about parenting, employment, and even the marriage.

▼ When should breast-feeding cease altogether? Sometimes the child decides when she is done, but often parents will have to make the decision and see that it happens gradually but progressively.

Pros: Finishing breast-feeding gives mom more freedom in her schedule; it gives her more choice about how to spend her time—at work and at home; it evens out the playing field for mom and dad to give bottles on a more equal basis; it may free mom up to expend more time, energy, and sexual interest toward her spouse.

Cons: Many women cherish this delicious time of parenting and are ambivalent about giving it up; some babies give up breast-feeding easier than others. If yours persists, it is stressful to change before the baby is ready.

By the beginning of the second year, a *toddler* is usually ready to share mealtimes with the family, in a safe high chair and a carefully aligned nap and appetite schedule. It's then time for another co-parenting conversation with each other about your individual experiences with food as nutrition, social occasion, love, and reward. Some conversation starters are:

▼ Do you think kids are born with a sweet tooth or do we foster it?
▼ Should we push solids so we can get some sleep?
▼ How important is it to you that we eat together as a family? How often?
▼ Does it make you feel like a good parent when our child eats well? Why/why not?
▼ Do you believe in using food to reward good behavior? Ever/always?
▼ Which foods might be OK to use as rewards? Does it matter if they are healthy foods?
▼ How do you want to handle fights over eating? What he should be eating, how much, and when?
▼ What should you do about total food boycotts?

Why do this now? Because you can sort out your agreements and disagreements about food and eating before the dramas start; your toddler will drag both of you through them all by the hair—later.

The trick to feeding toddlers lies in bringing very low expectations to the table. A varied diet of fresh veggies, fruits, grains, and dairy are as sophisticated as you need to be. Try to hold your creative culinary talents in check or for use with grown-ups only. Exercising such talents will only set you up for disappointment if you try to cook fancy for a toddler. Let them eat their fill of plain and healthy food, and they only need to stay at the table until they are no longer hungry. Then they need to "gey dow." Though you and your mate may not agree on what to feed, how to feed (OK to let him use a spoon, even though he makes a royal mess of himself and the kitchen?), and when to let him have it his way, even if he hasn't gotten much nutrition this meal, it will be far easier on your marriage if you agree about the important issues and who will manage the eating and when (for example, dad does breakfast and mom does dinner). If they get more food *in* them than *on* them, it has been a successful meal. Anyway, that's what multivitamins are for (check with your pediatrician, of course).

At this age, manners (often a favorite of mothers) are for another time and place, and staying at the table until he is done or eaten all those carrots (often a favorite of fathers) are other lost causes for now. Keep your powder dry—both of you—for other, more winnable, battles. Besides, you're more likely to win both these battles later when he or she is older and more aware of the power of social acceptance. Right now, your child could care less what you think of his eating habits, but his preoccupation with things other than his parents' wishes is not personal. It's just a periodic rehearsal with real food, some of which he needs to keep growing, while proving that he is not necessarily civilized or lovable. It's just food, and whenever the meal is over for him, it's over.

The *preschool gourmand* is only a little different. She will typically enjoy having her own regular place at the table and will want to pour her own milk (from a small plastic pitcher), and feed herself with her own utensils. A preschooler can and will typically stay at the table longer than a toddler will, but if not, let her go and tell her it was nice to have her at the table for a while.

Her appetite is bigger, so use the chance to increase her tastes for new foods, unless, of course, she is passing through one of those "white foods only, please" phases (noodles, rice, bread, cereals, pasta, milk). Then it is best to serve her just what she'll eat and wait her out. Fussy periods are usually about control and, as such, they always pass. Letting it pass may be harder for one parent, usually the dad. According to our pediatrician colleagues, it's harder for fathers because it seems the kid's "asking for more than their share" of special attention and it's "just not good to always give in to it." In general, the less energy put into this struggle the better, because it is one of those developmental dead ends and simply not worth going to the mat over.

Arguing with your spouse about your preschooler's eating habits is never fruitful. This phase will pass, and your child will be healthy when it's over. So don't waste a lot of energy fighting over these periods that pass more quickly than the residue of anger in your marriage. Whether your child has a more balanced diet this week, she will be fine and less fussy in a few months. Some of it can be humorous, if approached that way. The child who would only eat Ritz crackers three weeks ago now won't touch them: "I just don't like them anymore." Just as suddenly, and not because of anything you have or have not done, she will reacquire her taste for them.

When you feel the tension rising between your partner and you, try these opening questions:

▼ When she's fussy and nothing is working, what do you think our bottom line should be, and what are you willing to let go? Is it OK if I do it differently than you would have, or are you going to be frustrated with me too?
▼ How do you think we should handle it when he throws his spaghetti or turns over his cereal bowl?
▼ At what age should we insist that she try new foods, or stay at the table until finished eating, or stay seated through most of the meal (versus dancing around the room or leaving and returning frequently), or eat what we make for her (versus changing her mind as soon as the food is on the high chair or table)? If age isn't to be our guideline, what should be?
▼ What time of day is easiest for you to manage these things without being upset? Are there meals you'd prefer to supervise?

By the time kids are in *kindergarten*, they know pretty well how much and when they need to eat, when they are full, and whether they like a food or not. Once again, foods clamored for one day can get the "yuck" treatment the next. When they tolerate something new, it's worth some hoopla. When they want to spit it out, help them tell you why. They can't be expected to like every single vegetable. Amounts consumed can also vary a lot. Some parents get upset about how much food is wasted: "He asked for an egg and now he doesn't even want to eat it; he can leave the table hungry or eat it." Do your best to keep your mealtimes pleasant for all the folks at the table. It won't kill a kid's nutrition to eat too much cold cereal. Let kids eat to fullness and then let them go, and then (at least one of you can) enjoy your decaf.

After laying out some behavioral ground rules on eating, we offer some ways to improve the likelihood that kids will eat healthy and enjoy it, so that mealtimes are the fruition of something that both mom and dad value, regardless of who cooks and who cleans up. Here are some of our favorite, healthy, co-parenting approved, nutrition goals.

▼ **Fats.** Kids need them. Babies should get one-half their calories from fats, and toddlers about one-third. We try to steer our kids to foods with olive and canola oil (pastas, noodles, and so on), with occasional nuts and avocados. Omega-rich fish (as long as it is low in mercury; see National Research Center for Women and Families' safe-fish list at www.center4research.org) and certified organic eggs and meats (trimmed and skinned of fat, broiled, not fried or ground) are favorites too. Since plaque in arteries starts to show up in ten- and eleven-year-olds—depending on who your grandparents are—this is not just about nutrition and obesity prevention. It's about longevity.

▼ **Snacks.** Kids need a lot of snacks because of the energy requirements inherent in growing relatively quickly. Junk food is not going away, so try to make peace with it by considering it a very occasional item (not daily). If kids simply must eat the occasional potato chip, rebag the whole bag into handful portions. Kids are just as inept as grown-ups when it comes to portion control. An alternative is to spend time with the kids making some hummus and then dipping foods that make noise (carrots, snap peas, celery, and whole-grain crackers or tortilla chips). If you don't have ten minutes to do that, offer freeze-dried fruits, which have chewy appeal, or low-fat yogurt (but watch the processed sugar content).

▼ **Sweets.** Real sugar in sensible amounts (pinches, not heaping spoonfuls) always does the trick as a sweetener. It's far more nutritious than diet soda can ever pretend to be. Doughnuts belong on the dessert cart, not masquerading as snacks or breakfast food. If your child has already developed a sweet tooth with your help (yes, you or someone close to him probably introduced him to sweets and/or the "necessity" of regular desserts), low-sugar cocoa in a large glass of milk will often do the trick. A couple of cookies with real milk will do nicely most of the time, but reserve the place of honor for fruits—the fresher the better.

Gardening with young kids is another area where both parents can be involved together or separately. Growing stuff that you can actually eat is inherently magical to kids; there is simply no downside to it. It teaches the vital connection our bodies have to the natural world in which we, and the things we love, live and die. It is where caregiving, nutrition, and wonder converge. All you need are a few deep pots (clay preferred), soil (organic is worth the extra cost), and a sunny nook somewhere. No machinery is needed beyond a small trowel and watering can. Seedlings from a local nursery or farmer's market tip the odds of success in your favor. Begin with tomatoes, green beans, and lettuce. We love the metaphor of harvesting what the other sowed, and it will not be lost on your kids.

Emotional Development

The second area that challenges co-parenting is working together to promote your child's emotional development. As we saw in the survey discussed in chapter 5, it can be more difficult to anticipate your children's emotional milestones than their physical ones, simply because they are less obvious. This area of development is further complicated by parents' tendency to ascribe their children's emotional openness—or the opposite—to their gender rather than their temperament and the nature and proclivities with which they were born. For example, it's well known that as boys get older, parents stop talking or inquiring as much about their feelings, such as, "How is my sweetie feeling this morning?" This is particularly true when dealing with the most troubling of emotions for mothers and fathers: anger. It is tempting to think that more anger and its behavior sidekick, aggression, comes from boys and is more of a parental concern, but California researcher Eleanor Maccoby has shown that most parents don't much like aggressive speech or behavior directed at themselves or at peers by either sons or daughters.[4] However, fathers, unlike mothers, tend to allow it, because they encourage their sons to defend themselves physically, but fathers less frequently allow aggressive talk from their daughters. Fathers may tell their daughters, "Hey, that's not how we talk to other children, even if they do take our toys"; to their boys, they might add, "If he takes your toy from you, tell him to give it back. You had it first."

Similarly, research by New Zealand psychologist Robyn Fivush looked closely at mothers' attitudes toward strong emotion and found that mothers more readily tolerated anger and retaliation in their sons than their daughters.[5] Reestablishing harmony between the child and others was more typical of mother-daughter interchanges. Does this sound familiar? These are the same behaviors we mentioned earlier, in our discussion about mothers' and fathers' tendencies as co-parents. It suggests that learning to connect emotion and behavior through verbal communication may be part of the power of the "mother tongue" to indoctrinate children (and future parents) as to when to *hold* their tongues and when to let 'em rip. Remember (from chapter 4) psychologist John Gottman's research on the emotional flooding that makes it hard for dad to talk about his distress when he feels confronted directly by his spouse? And mom's desire to talk sooner rather than later about her distress? It all begins to take shape now, as parents begin the socialization process with their own children early in those children's lives, despite their best intentions and values not to treat their different-gender children differently.

When we look for the very beginnings of this differential behavior, we see that both parents are more likely to talk about emotions with daughters than with sons. Judith Dunn's evidence shows that parents are more likely to actively suppress emotional displays in boys than in their daughters early on.[6] A mother's use of "emotion talk" with eighteen-month-olds was only two-thirds as frequent with sons as with daughters. By the time the child was twenty-four-months-old, the difference is twofold. Interestingly, the girls were also more likely than boys to initiate "emotion talk" by age two ("Sally happy, Mommy!"). Complementary research by Robert Buck into nonverbal communication explains why mothers can more easily read a daughter's emotional state than a son's by age six.[7]

Dads typically could use some help communicating more naturally with their kids about the emotional issues in their daily lives, given the critical role that emotional awareness plays in our overall mental health. Before kids have much expressive language, the best kind of emotion talk is for the dad to talk about *his* feelings—the pleasant ones—that accompany his life with a young child:

> "I love the smile you give me when your bath is over—it makes me feel just great—squeaky clean, too!"
> "I really miss you when I have to go to work."

Once your son starts to talk, all he'll talk about is himself, and that's fine. "Me, myself, and I"[8] are his favorite topics, because it is hard work to find the right place for himself in this world of busy grown-ups, and talking about himself is a good way to figure out where he belongs. Around age two-and-a-half, children begin to get the idea that not everyone feels the same way they do all the time. That's when we heard our son narrating his every movement for ten to fifteen minutes at a time: "J.D. up in chair—eat ceweal" . . . "J.D. hugging Livy (his sister)" . . . "J.D. gowin' ou'side." His audience was him, rehearsing for the big event coming soon, if unknown to him, the accurate use of the personal pronoun "I." Then, emotional talk really matters, because it's about *their* feelings, not anyone or everyone else's.

When boys or girls can and do talk about their feelings, they are popular with the adults caring for them. Teachers love when a child tells them he's "sad because . . ." or he "is fwustuated." At toddlerhood and beyond, it's especially important to start talking with more intentionality with your children about *their* simple, everyday experiences. Eleanor Maccoby suggests that mothers may be more interested in doing this than dads.[9] Here's some advice—aimed slightly more at dads, but just as appropriate for moms—to help you connect with your child.

▼ Pick an experience you've recently shared, the details of which are clear in your mind—the visit of or to a grandparent, bringing home the puppy, trip to the park, etc.
▼ Get down to the child's eye perspective—physically and emotionally—to see what might seem important from down there.
▼ Gently ask him about who went, how he got there, what happened, and how he felt about what happened (excited, sad, happy, scared). There are no right questions or wrong answers, just details at this point.
▼ If he says he doesn't remember or know, offer a prompt and see if he joins in. If you are really listening (not multitasking), odds are good he'll be seduced and off the story goes. If not, give it a rest. He's not in the mood today.
▼ This is not homework; it is something to take delight in. If it's not fun, you are working too hard at it. Parents have their best luck in the car or bus on short errands, or walks for hot chocolate or frozen yogurt.

This is the stuff of which emotional lives and memories are made. Such communication from both parents strengthens children's sense of themselves as unique and bolsters adaptation, literacy, and, ultimately, problem-solving skills.[10]

Social Development

We turn to the third area: How co-parenting nurtures kids' social skill development. For young children, "social" means making friends. This appetite, too, emerges early in life: from the end of the second year, children pick sides and groups according to gender, whether the other kids are familiar to them or not. The task of moving from parallel play—just being next to someone of your choosing, while you each do your thing in your own space—to learning socially acceptable behavior is tough for children this young. Sharing, taking turns, and occasionally capitulating do not come naturally. And it's all made more complex by the loosely defined code of "Toddler Property Laws": "It's mine if I've ever touched it or wanted to touch it."

By age three, children from many differing cultures show preferences for same-sex playmates, as though being with one's own makes the task go more smoothly. By ages four to five, they spend the bulk of their play-time with children of their own gender.[11] Boys are quicker to make and unmake friends, while girls make more intense relationships and have an early and lasting sense of their hierarchy.

How mothers and fathers feel about their children's social adeptness is often closely aligned to their own childhood experiences, both positive and negative. Did you have plenty of like-minded peers with whom to play? Were they formally in school or play groups or informally in the neighborhood? Was there a neighborhood? Were there siblings around to play or fight with? How open were your parents to letting you play with kids from diverse backgrounds? Socially, did you as kids feel more often like winners or losers?

Common parental stereotypes pit mothers against fathers in the "socialize the girls" and "toughen up the boys" tradition. Other typical stereotypes minimize the father's interest in helping his daughter handle competition, social intimidation, and bullying. Mothers, on the other hand, are supposed to pay closer attention to the social hierarchies (Which friend is the flavor of the week? Who is excluding our child this week?) that exist just under the surface of children's (and adults') relationships. And stereotypical mothers are supposed to be committed to helping their children have a powerful position in those peer pecking orders. Fathers are prone to thinking much of this focus is futile, as they feel less conflicted about going their own way in social situations, if it suits them to do so.

Maintaining a strong parenting partnership provides your children the freedom to explore their friendships, unencumbered by stereotypical, gender-based behaviors. Again, the key to this good rapport is open and frequent communication about how kids' friendships are evolving. Sometimes it means one parent jumps in to distract preschoolers' play from getting too violent, when the other parent is reluctant to do so because he or she wants the "kids to learn to sort this out on their own, despite the tears and bruises." Sometimes it means holding back when your spouse wishes for a lighter touch, because the other child's parents are our good friends, so, "we don't want to be too stern with each other's kids." Often it means just intervening and then talking about it later to sort out if that approach was *really* so bad and if another approach would have been better.

The physical, emotional, and social arenas that parents negotiate with and for their children are the very same ones they negotiate together in their social and work spheres. If they cannot do it with and for each other, they will have a harder time selling it to their children.

> Frank and Jennifer described a dinner party with four other couples, all of whom had children around the same age. One of the couples makes Jennifer feel very uncomfortable. "She is just 'fancy,' like she has a fancier house than the rest of us and she has a high-profile job that she somehow manages while handling her three kids, and she always looks like she's in control of everything. I feel intimidated around her." Frank laughed. "I'm sure she has it together no better than the rest of us. She does make it look good, but that's important to her; it's not important to us." He put his arm around his wife, "You always look good to me," he adds. Jennifer gives him a smile but sighs, "I am just not that confident as a woman or as a mother, maybe."
>
> They then recount how Ben got into a tussle with this other couple's son, and the son said something to Ben that made him cry. "This always happens with them," Jennifer fumes. "I really like being part of this social group, but it always makes me feel tense because my kid always winds up getting his feelings hurt."

Clearly, Jennifer is seeing or attributing the same kinds of feelings to Ben that she is having. We talked quite a bit longer about how Frank could help in those situations. Next time, he will be the one to intervene when Ben's feelings are hurt. Also, he will decide what to say, if anything, to the father of the other child. We suggested to Jennifer that she ignore the situation to minimize it, focusing instead on the other three couples at the dinner. This takes the pressure off her and her interpretations of the situation. And it allows Frank to be a safety valve for her.

Here are a few other examples when couples have to negotiate with each other in order to also act as role models for their children:

1. If mom is angry at dad for leaving work later than planned, making him late for dinner, she seethes quietly about it. She won't be as effective at calming her children's predinner hour mania when they get riled up, because she too will be riled up.
2. If mom is uncomfortable at dad's company holiday party and feels shy in crowds, it may be harder for her to help her child feel less shy about going to a birthday party where there are a lot of unfamiliar children and social chaos.

3. If dad and mom cannot create a regular mealtime most days, their toddler or preschooler is not likely to sit at the table and honor the dinner hour.

4. If mom or dad is a "picker" who tastes with her or his fingers while setting the table for a meal, neither will get far talking to their child about manners.

5. If one parent has a tendency to express anxiety as a way to work out a problem (such as making the kids aware how late the family is to go somewhere because one parent is typically late getting ready), the kids are going to feel more anxious about where they are going.

None of these behaviors are problems in and of themselves; we all have habits we wish we didn't have. But when one spouse's habit conflicts with what another wants or needs for herself/himself or the children, then the parents have to work it out first, before the children are likely to get it "right." If they don't, don't blame them or your spouse. Look first to what you can change yourself, then, what you want to discuss with your spouse, and what you want to live with—in yourselves and your children. If parents can count on their differences to curb their own excesses—if they can accept sharing and not getting their way all the time and needing everyone else to be just like them—they will provide their marriage and their children a rock-solid foundation on which to build a great life.

9

Co-parenting and Sleeping Children
Learning to Be on One's Own

MOMMY, I HAD A SCARY DREAM. I can't go back to sleep. Daddy, can I come in your bed?"

You have three options:

1. "Okay, son, let's go. I'll take you back to bed and stay with you a few minutes."
2. "Hop on in, honey."
3. Mickey is accustomed to bringing his blankie and "stuffy" with him, knowing you'll probably let him curl up on the floor next to your bed. He's not really expecting you to let him in your bed, but he's also sure that you won't send him back to his room.

Which one did you choose? Do you both agree on the answer? Does it depend on the particular night?

How about when he was younger? At what age did he stop sleeping in a bassinet or crib in your room? How long was he in your bed? How did you handle his howling in the night until you caved and came back to his room?

Sleep—the one-word lullaby—is so simple, welcome, and healthy. Just looking at your sleeping child safe in the arms of Morpheus is a calming salve. No wonder lullabies are the most common form of sung music around the globe. Sleep in sufficient quantities is as essential to the physical and mental health of adults as it is to children. The problem is that sleep isn't actually so simple a task; we rarely get enough of it in this part of the world, and for children, just learning to sleep alone is not easy. However, because it is one of the thorniest issues in early parenthood, it qualifies as one of the thorniest in the co-parenting world.

Sleep as Transition: Theirs and Yours

What makes sleep complex are the transitions—*getting* to sleep, getting into it, staying asleep, and, finally, easing out of it. These can be harrowing for a baby and for her first-time, sleep-deprived parents. Once you learn the facts about sleep, they will enable you to figure out how to help your child (and yourself) develop healthy sleep habits.

First, sleep is not a constant state for children of any age. Sleep may start quietly and, for most children, move relatively quickly from drowsiness through light sleep into the first deep-sleep phase. But there are alternating, more-active cycles that repeat several times throughout sleep. Active sleep (dreaming) is called REM for "rapid eye movement." You can see the eyes darting back and forth under the shut eyelids, sometimes accompanied by small, random muscle twitches and more shallow and rapid breathing. Although it looks anything but peaceful, it is an essential component of regular, restorative sleep. Deep sleep—the kind photographers and parents like—tends to alternate every hour with shorter periods of REM sleep, and then back again. It's worth knowing about this rhythm because the transitions between these stages of sleep are often marked by brief awakenings. These awakenings are usually private moments, and every other one seems to be slightly more intense, explaining why every three to four hours one or both of you may hear a short cry or movement from the crib. The majority of children under the age of two will typically return to sleep without parental intervention, learning to comfort themselves.

Before we take a closer look at how both parents can help children of various ages to sleep well, we want to acknowledge that most parents know that there is more to sleep than R&R; there is *separation*. In your bed or not (more on this later), children have to sleep in their own skins, not yours. And they must leave you and your attention, adoration, and safekeeping to *go*—go *to* sleep—and that means leaving you. We must literally *let* our children go, to sleep. For many parents and children, this is the first and one of the hardest separations, as Emily, a new mother, discovered.

> Emily told us, "When I finally got home with Priscilla, I was so happy to have some privacy with her. There were so many nurses, visitors, friends, and family at the hospital. So I was shocked at how sad I felt when she went to sleep after her first nursing in my own bed. I wasn't done with her! Of course she needed her sleep and so did I, but I got all hung up on feeling lonely after she fell asleep from feeding. Now she was asleep and I was wide awake. I wanted to wake her up to make sure she knew I was there for her and have a few more moments of awake time together."

For many parents, letting a child go to sleep is the first small step on the path that eventually draws the child into the world outside the family. Not surprisingly, mothers and fathers often experience this separation process quite differently. The parent's own birth order, the child's gender, the strength of the co-parental alliance, and the number of children in the family all have some influence on how this separation process plays out.

- ▼ **Birth order and number.** Parents who were firstborns are more used to parental tolerance for sleeping. Parents who were second, third, or later had parents who were firmer and less inclined to give in to their cries. They had heard it all before. Similarly, the more children you have, the easier it gets to stick to routines for bedtime and sleep.
- ▼ **Gender.** Mothers sometimes hang onto daughters just a tad longer than their sons. That goes for sleep times as well.
- ▼ **Co-parenting alliance.** The happier the couple, the more inclined they are to work together to solve the dilemma, and the more motivated they are to have the kids sleep in their own beds as soon as possible.

When Babies Wake During the Night

Here's how these influences play out in combination:

> Doug and Sheila called themselves "older parents" (both were thirty-six), who were quite accustomed to just knowing how to

handle things—at work, at home, wherever. Their six-month-old child, Susie, started to stir up trouble with her "sleep issues." Before this, she'd been a "natural" when it came to sleep. She took two two-hour naps a day and had been a "through-the-nighter" since the age of roughly four months. But now, for the first time, she had trouble settling down and was raising "hell" about going to sleep. Sheila said, "She's so turned on by her day, she can't turn off."

The parents found themselves carping at each other around the baby's bedtime regarding whose job it would be to "deal with the sleep gremlins" that night. They were both surprised at, in their words, "how much of a jerk [the other one] was being about this."

To compound the problem, they each dealt with it quite differently. Sheila thought it worked best to rock Susie back to sleep in her rocker, wait until she had passed through her REM cycle into a deeper sleep, and then put her down in her crib. Doug, one of five children, thought that took too long. His mother counseled that he just go in, reassure Susie that he was there in the house, and leave. And don't go back in—even if she cried. For the first time in their marriage, Doug and Sheila started going to sleep at different times so they would be fresh to deal with Susie when she awoke.

After an impromptu joint conversation with Sheila's older sister, they agreed to try a different bedtime ritual. One parent would give Susie a warm bath and a back massage, and then Doug, who had the better voice, would sing her a lullaby while he was sitting in the rocking chair with her. Sheila would then nurse her to set the mood for bed and lay her down. This worked about half the time. The rest of the time, Sheila continued to rock Susie to sleep. When it took "too long," she just took Susie into their bed so that "we can all get some sleep." Doug resented Sheila's "weakness," though he thought she had a point, given that they were now both extremely tired all the time. Yet he feared it would be, in his words, "setting a dangerous precedent. Besides, the pediatrician said that by six months, she has to be out of our bed, or she'll never leave."

Sheila called their nurse practitioner who wisely invited them *both* in for a talk. The nurse understood that having a conversation about sleep issues with just one parent is a waste of everyone's time; with both there, it would be a much more productive conversation. (It's time to change the widespread and ineffective practice in nursing and pediatrics of just talking with the mother because she is "the only one that matters.")

Doug and Sheila first shared their frustrations, to which the nurse respectfully listened, and then agreed on the following ritual: After the feeding, one parent would put Susie down in her crib while still awake. The parent on duty would then stroke and kiss her head, whisper, "Goodnight, sweetie," and then leave the room. The nurse explained that she agreed in part with Doug's mother that the "going down awake part" is important for helping the baby learn to fall asleep on her own. When Susie cries, the bedding-down parent is to stay the course—but out of the room.

If she's still crying after five minutes (they agreed to use a timer since their "inner clocks" differed considerably), either parent could come back in, leave the lights off, do the head rub and kiss again, then leave after a minute, without picking Susie up to comfort her (the hardest part for Sheila). If it's a bad night and she is still crying, the parent should stay out a little longer, and then repeat the same "visiting ritual." The baby's diaper should be changed only if necessary, with no talking or singing allowed (to keep it boring), and then leave. Hard as this may sound, having a kid who can't get herself back to sleep in the middle of the night without your help for the next five to six years is exponentially harder.

Sometimes parents worry that their baby is fussing because he's hungry. In the rare event that you are sure of this (for example, he refused his last feeding), it's OK, to feed him, but again keep it *boring*. You don't want to teach your child that there will always be food, fun, and mom or dad right there in the middle of any night, ready to party whenever he awakens. Parents worry that this approach seems too strict, but a baby's crying session almost always feels longer to parents than it really is. Remember, it's the middle of *your* night too, and your coping, reality testing, and patience aren't at their peak. This kind of crying doesn't damage children, and your protective feelings *and* frustrations are absolutely understandable. Babies trust you when you are calm, loving, and doing what's best for them—though it may be hard for them to act calm about it at that particular moment.

Sheila said the thing that surprised her most about this plan was when the nurse told her to keep the feeding "boring." Doug piped up immediately, "I knew that would bug you, but it was right-on advice. You love that warm, fuzzy intimacy of Susie's middle-of-the-night stuff. I do, too, but it's not so good for her to get turned on by us and what we enjoy when she's supposed to be asleep."

Sheila admitted, "It's hard when I've been away from her in the day to pass up these particular times to comfort her, but I guess you're right. She needs to know that we're there, not the diversion." Children who are trying to learn how to be alone need to trust that their relationships remain steadfast. Sheila raised another issue: that "Doug doesn't always hear Susie's cries as often as I do, if at all."

In our experience, this is more rule than exception. Research on parents' different responses to infant cries shows that, while fathers are as responsive physiologically to baby cries as mothers, what happens next is the real issue. Maternal responsiveness results in hormonal triggers that promote caregiving behaviors and emotions, while fathers' testosterone levels go up, triggering more protective and vigilant behaviors than nurturing ones.[1] When this happens, fathers are prone to check that the baby is safe (there are no strange noises or smells emanating from her room, for example), while mothers are primed to rely on their own intuition or emotions to determine what the crying is about and what is needed to fix it.

We are not saying that men shouldn't be expected to feed and comfort their children in the night. In fact, many pediatricians and nurses actively encourage men to alternate the nocturnal changing-feeding-comforting rotations with their spouses, not just to cut down on fatigue, but because infants and toddlers may find it easier to settle back to sleep after daddy comforts them than mommy. According to renowned pediatrician Dr. T. Berry Brazelton, "The father's body doesn't mean 'food' in the same way hers does, even when bottles are used. It's also easier for children to separate from this guy whose body they were never part of in the first place."[2]

The ritual proposed to Doug and Sheila was not just a suggestion to save them time and emotion. Nor was it just about getting two parents to agree to do child maintenance in a reasonably sane and predictable fashion. Children of all ages feel more comfortable and safe when routines are followed and traditions respected. Feeding, diapering, dressing, and leaving for the first day of elementary school (all the way through college) all feel less upsetting when kids know what's coming next because someone they love and trust said to them calmly and confidently, "This is the way we do this," and then went and did it. These rituals work like anchors in a rising sea, holding fast when life gets choppy.

This sounds good, in theory. The co-parenting problems arise when we look at the general attitudes of mothers and fathers toward the rituals of sleep. The mother rarely complains that these nightly routines are taking too long or that a firmer hand is needed. More often, a mother will tell us that *not* going to her crying child makes her feel as if she isn't being a good parent, and she worries that the baby will not know she is really present emotionally and physically. Fathers tend to get less upset about the crying and don't usually make assumptions about what their nocturnal absence signals to the child. This matter-of-fact attitude can lead to mothers doing more of the nighttime work of getting the child back to sleep. She may resent that she is doing more, especially if both parents are employed. In turn, it can lead to a father feeling that the mother isn't putting the same emphasis on their couple time that he is, and that she is being overly solicitous of their child. One father said to Marsha, "Once the baby is down for the night, it's grown-up time as far as I'm concerned. Our baby has had my wife all day; I want her back just for a little while, even if all we're doing is sleeping together." Next we offer some solutions to this perennial struggle of new parents.

The Family That Sleeps Together . . . Stays Together?

> "I just came from my pediatrician's office. I told him Lauren still sleeps in our bed and he said that isn't good for the child after she's six months old. Am I screwing her up?"

So often this kind of universal advice from child experts in whom parents put their faith serves only to make parents feel bad when they don't toe the line or can't get their kid to conform. That's why there isn't one magical age that should ever be used as anything other than a guideline for a child sleeping alone. It depends on the child, her parents, their cultural norms, even their living conditions. You want your child to learn how to put herself to sleep because it is good for her to do so, not just to make your life easier. If you don't do it by six months of age, it is harder to make it happen later. However, regularly having your children in your bed can be a major point of marital contention when mom and dad feel differently about when it should end, and/or when one of them isn't getting enough sleep because of it. Here are a few co-parenting guidelines.

- ▼ Sleeping all together feels wonderful for many people and won't necessarily hurt your child if it extends for longer than many child experts recommend (six months).[3]
- ▼ In general, your child will have a harder time learning to fall asleep and stay asleep if he is still sharing your bed when he's age two and three. This important skill will help him feel rested and have confidence

in his ability to handle those dark, active moments during the night. Recovering from being scared takes a little longer and may require parental reassurance, but it can be worked out from the child's own bed.

▼ Many parents use as a rule of thumb: "when they are no longer getting a good night's sleep themselves." At some point, your toddler —without waking—kicks, turns sideways in bed, pulls the covers, and so on, leaving parents who sleep less soundly tired and annoyed.

▼ Parents know that nighttime can be the loneliest part of the day. New mothers who are breast-feeding often feel lonely when they are up and their spouse is sleeping. Many of us remember feeling scared of the dark. The primitive mood of nighttime pulls on all of us to be physically close and connected. Here's another time to comfort your child without assuming your experience is the same as hers, and without feeling you have to fix what development will eventually take care of for you. Parents can inadvertently pass on their fears and vulnerabilities to their children. Turn to your partner instead of your child. If you can't find your own comfort there, it's time to look at how your co-parenting and couple life overlap. (We suggest periodic maintenance for this issue in chapter 12.)

▼ Parents have different tolerances for privacy, sleeping near each other, and waking up during the night, so work this out with your mate. Don't let your child take over this aspect of your time together, whether it is a quiet moment of talking, cuddling, reading, or having sex, without being in agreement. Depending on your lifestyle, make sure having a group bed doesn't eclipse other needs as a couple that are eclipsed during this family period. Somewhere that peaceful respite and intimacy have to be preserved.

Talk together about what you each feel and how you want to handle the situation (as described in chapter 4 on conflict), without resorting to "you always" statements or blaming each other. Try his way, and then her way, if you can't agree on a plan. See which one works better and under which circumstances. If you can agree, make sure what each of you will do and when is spelled out clearly, and then stick to it. Many times when a couple agrees to a certain sleep routine, mom then changes it unilaterally because something didn't work and she was the first one awake when the child began to cry. This change often leads to mom feeling resentment ("Why am I always the one who gets out of bed?") and to dad feeling shut out ("Why should I bother? She undoes our joint decisions and changes things to her way anyway."). Make sure you both have had a chance to act on the plan, and then you can make changes more flexibly once the feelings about how it is going are mutual. This is also a time for mom to be careful not to be a gatekeeper—that is, to think her way is best. And dad needs to make an effort to stay involved and be a partner in whatever plan the couple agrees on.

Toddler Sleep

Because so much more of life is within the reach of a toddler—now that he is walking and talking—there is more world to leave when he beds down. Consequently, most self-respecting toddlers put up some kind of struggle. This is often dispiriting because parents may have enjoyed months of a "normal" sleep routine, only to see their hard-won peace disappear again in toddlerhood. To complicate matters, many pediatricians are concerned about what they feel is a growing population of sleep-deprived toddlers. This change in sleep behavior and the crankiness that accompanies it tend to show up as "oppositional" behavior, not the exhaustion that it's more likely to be. Sending a toddler off to bed by himself after a long day of saying "No!" (you and him) may be your dream, but it's more likely his nightmare. So is "falling asleep in his tracks"—a technique employed by more than one worn-out parent who is so spent from fighting with her toddler about sleep and the endless routine that precedes it that she lets her child "go and go" until he literally drops from exhaustion. The problem comes when the child awakens; he can be almost "psychotic" as he's being transported from wherever he dropped to his own bed. Either way, it's just too scary or depleting for kids this age to make the transition from awake to asleep on their own.

Doing a half-hour of something special together usually works best to get them decelerating at a rate sufficient to avoid the unwelcome, but common train wreck before bed. Stories, simple games, quiet play, with a little educational content on the side—these are mothers' typical favorites. Fathers tend to be more physical and interactive—often establishing the day's first real one-to-one, emotionally available contact with the child. Both of these types of interactions can work, depending on the child and how affirming the parents are of each other's different approaches, as long as dad doesn't let the play become so exciting that soporific turns to hypomanic. Watching TV or, for that matter, any screen media at this juncture, will simply set you up for a fall. Toddlers need the people they love to help them get to sleep, not advertisers, 'toons, or puppets. They turn your toddler *on*, not down. Giving your child a warm bath, singing to her, or looking together through family photo albums work far better and are more benign.

Toddler sleep can also slip off the rails when routines are interrupted by illness, summer vacations, cutting teeth, holidays, losing the favorite stuffed animal, parental absences, or dreams (which occur at around fourteen to sixteen months for most children). Parents often have widely varying tolerances for these perturbations, quibbling about how much trouble the kids really should have getting to sleep. Common complaints range from, "He's not trying hard enough to get himself to sleep" and "He's playing us again" to "He used to be such a good sleeper—he can do it again himself." But helping your toddler get back on track will be good for everyone, so don't worry if you find yourself relying on some of the rituals he preferred when he was younger. Reassure him that monsters are not real, preferably with words and hugs, not "monster spray" (which only delays the sad truth that there is no magic). The toddlers' fears can also be alleviated by sweeping out the closet or under the bed to show there is nothing there, using a night light, and playing soft music.

Preschooler Sleep
Reading your child a bedtime story can be one of life's sweeter moments. Thanks to the growing language skills of the preschooler, the ritual can help ease him into sleep. The child can understand and anticipate the predictable rhythms of the beginning, middle, and end of a story; recognize if it's new or familiar, render editorial comments; and tell when you digress from the text and are improvising (a desecration of the natural order for many preschoolers).

However, because more mothers than fathers tend to be recreational readers, nighttime story reading can, by default, become a gendered activity (mothers read, fathers play) without anyone noticing. You can tell this has happened when it begins to feel "weird" for Dad to read the story. Or your child only wants mom or dad to read, preferring one style to the other. That's OK for a few nights. But getting into that rut is a bad idea; kids should feel that dad is every bit the wordsmith mom is, or vice versa. This may be especially true for boys.

The other new aspect of sleep during this time is the strong response many preschoolers have to their dreams. Most will sleep through the night regardless, but for many children, there is a sharp increase in the number of scary dreams. Then everybody's up. Such dreams typically occur in the second half of the night, and the child will be scared and crying and need the following reassurances from a parent:

▼ what awakened her was the dream,
▼ it's over now,
▼ it's not real,
▼ it won't come back,
▼ and can't hurt her. Period.

Fear may make it hard for her to resume sleeping, so just accept that it will take however long it takes to settle her back down. And don't get too preoccupied with conversation or dream interpretation; it's your close presence that works the magic, not your ability to help her understand the mysteries of her experience. The other thing that helps is just growing up. Most children only have occasional nightmares after they are age six.

A child's nightmares occur in the darkest hour of the night, without warning, shattering the parents' rest. Our defenses are down, our heart is palpitating from the sudden interruption of our own sleep and dreams, and we are hardly at our best emotionally. So it's pretty common to be both scared and frustrated, even angry, when you finally get into the child's room and bark, "You're too old for this; you'll wake up your brother; get yourself back to sleep; it's just a dream." These responses don't help the situation because they're not particularly rational, coming from him or you. The child will need all his wits to get himself calmed down and back to sleep without being upset by your anger. Fathers are more prone to this hard-liner approach, but in our experience, personality trumps gender, so it usually depends more on which parent is the heavier sleeper or who needs more rest.

Other Things That Go Bump in the Night

Dreams aren't the only thing to go bump in the night for preschoolers. Periodically, a preschooler will *seem* to awaken suddenly, usually within a few hours of going to sleep, be very distressed, open-eyed, and thrashing about when one of you gets to her, yet she doesn't appear to notice that you are even there! She doesn't seem to be dreaming or even awake. This is not a nightmare; she's in the grip of a "night terror." Whatever you do to try to settle her, it fails. She's sweating, seems terrified, pushes you away when you try to comfort her. And then, as suddenly as it began, it's over, and back to sleep she goes, peaceful and calm, having never really awakened. Unlike a nightmare, she will remember none of this the next day, though you will.

You are the one left bewildered, heart racing, and wondering what happened. Night terrors are scary to witness, and the impulse is often to interrupt or interfere with the physical thrashing about and forcibly awaken the child to "snap her out of it" and stop this distressing behavior. It's better to wait. Don't try to communicate with the child since she usually won't remember any of this anyway. Just keep her safe until it passes, which it always does. Don't ask her about it in the morning, because it will only confuse her and make her wonder if something is wrong or if she's normal. Eventually, your child will outgrow night terrors. This one really is just a stage.

Are there co-parenting implications? There isn't a way to handle this differently. It is best to leave gender and parenting style out of it, and just follow the prescription.

Other sleep disruptions in young children can stress the family at night. Sleepwalking can make its debut, though more typically it appears around age five or six; about 15 percent of children will sleepwalk at least once a year during this phase of development.[4] It is not a disorder but a variation on the theme of "my bladder is full, I don't want to wet my bed, and I can't get sufficiently awake to find the bathroom, but I'm trying." Children are not bent on ruining your sleep, so forget about disciplining them for these nocturnal excursions. Just lead them to the toilet and then guide them back to bed without discussion or insisting they awaken; that only increases the stimulation or creates confusion, when neither is helpful. You need to keep them safe, so check the sturdiness of the gate at the top of the stairs, clear the staircase of clutter, and add some extra nightlights in the hallway if necessary. One creative father added some sleigh bells to his sleepwalking daughter's door so he knew when she was on the move. He found it a rather pleasing sound.

Older Children's Sleep Disruptions

The kind of shift in sleep habits we have been describing often manifests in the preschool years, but not always. Sometimes it occurs later, when a child is ready to start school. It may take the shape of a nightmare or the child just feeling less safe in his own room and bed.

Sam and Alexi had enjoyed a "charmed life" as parents, given that both of their sons had been good eaters, sleepers, and talkers, until their older one, Darius, just five, began to come into the parental bed about an hour after his mom and dad went to sleep. He crawled in from the foot of the bed, inserting himself "like a hotdog in a roll" between his sleeping parents. Calm at first, he slowly increased his activity—throwing an arm around his mom while pushing his dad's legs away with his feet. Sam would eventually sigh, get out of bed, mutter something, go into his son's vacant bed, and sleep out the rest of the night. In Sam's view, he "didn't really mind much and got more sleep that way. There is no fighting—just sleep."

But over time, Darius was sleeping less, thrashing about while in bed with Alexi, and having frequent nightmares "full of monster dinosaurs chasing him." Kicking his father out of his parents' bed turned out not as easy as it first seemed. His conquest of the parental bed had left him feeling confused and anxious, and taking his father's place next to his mother had left him feeling more frightened than relaxed and reassured. His parents jointly concluded that what they had considered as the "easy way out" was "anything but" and that they needed to reclaim their bed from the "little intruder." Darius put up stiff resistance. He would stand in the doorway and make sounds until someone awakened or let on that they were listening. He would bring in pillows and blankets and make himself a bed on the floor by his mom's feet and then make noise so everyone knew he was there. He would ask for a hug and kiss and to be tucked in, and then creatively drag it out for fifteen to thirty minutes, until one or both parents were annoyed at him.

His parents started his "sleep retraining" by taking turns moving him to a cot on their floor when he came in. Next, they'd move him back to his bed, again alternating the job of walking him back when he tried to gain access to the parental bed. Incentives that he helped choose during the day (cooking with dad, bowling with mom) helped strengthen his resolve, as did a big fancy sticker chart—just fancy enough to evoke envy in his little brother. Darius wanted to solve this problem, too, and had asked for help (during the day; at night he had less resolve). In the end, it worked because his parents were the bosses; they made it clear they were acting on what they knew he needed, and whether he liked it or not wasn't relevant.

Over time, and after his parents spent a "pretty sleepless two months retraining him to sleep on his own again," Darius came to feel safer in his room and slept deeper and better in his own bed.

Here again, we see the importance of helping children sleep best by relearning how to go to sleep, stay asleep, and go back to sleep on their own. We know that most children sleep deeper and better alone. In addition, sleeping with mom and dad mathematically compounds the frequent awakenings and sleep-state changes caused by group sleeping and is almost always an avoidance of something: the child learning how to be alone, or how to master a fear of the things that go bump in the night, or perhaps mom and dad welcome a visitor because they've turned away from intimacy themselves. In the end, the co-parenting co-sleeping dilemma is solved by determining—after joint consideration—what works best for you as a couple with your particular child to ensure that *everyone* in the family gets sufficient sleep.

Bed-wetting

Bed-wetting (enuresis)—a common medical problem that has nothing to do with willpower—can be a prickly problem, given that it tends to arouse strong feelings in parents about their children's self-control, development, and mastery over bodily functions. The parents' response frequently settles into a good-cop/bad-cop routine, with one parent taking the child's side, saying, "He's just not ready to control this impulse at night yet"; and the other saying, "We've got to get him to take more responsibility for himself." For starters, know that your child is not wetting the bed on purpose and that this is a common medical problem for children under the age of eight.

Pediatricians and nurse practitioners use many approaches that can be helpful—limiting liquids after dinner, encouraging your child during the day to "try to wait a little longer before peeing" to increase bladder capacity, and having him pee just before he goes to sleep. If this gets you nowhere, ask your health care provider about conditioning techniques that can help, such as wetting alarms. In the end, this is just one more skill to master. Both parents need to take care not to make it a point of shame.

Mothers and fathers can avoid that problem by doing *their* homework; be comfortable enough with the topic by discussing it together first, then as a medical issue second, and only finally as a family inconvenience. Often a family history of enuresis in one or both parents' families necessitates some airing, given whose family might be to "blame" and whether it was all handled well (or not) by the previous generation. The previous generation was more likely to take the position that this was a problem that required tough love or just "growing out of it," and the less said about it, the better. The current generation might react against such treatment with more patience—even indulgence, but also with some guilt and shame. That just makes it harder for you to deal with your child, as the whole topic seems so guilt-laden and taboo. Resenting and criticizing your child's bed-wetting lower the chances for the child's successful management of the problem. If your instinct has been to discipline or punish, you're not alone, but this is simply the wrong approach. You'll need to start over with your child, this time at her side, not in her face. She needs to hear you say you want to work with her to help her manage her nighttime wetting (*without* the rolled eyes, long sighs, and dramatic changing of sheets), and get to work on the plan you all have devised with the pediatrician or nurse. She'll be less embarrassed when you are more comfortable and matter of fact, treating this as just another one of those things to outgrow.

Adult Sleep Deprivation

Like fevers and burping cloths, sleep deprivation seems to be an inescapable part of parenting in the early years. One of the problems with sleep deprivation is that it renders parents marginally—and one hopes tempo-rarily—less competent. The eighty-hour-a-week work rule for hospital in-terns and residents was nixed because of concern over documented errors in judgment that sleep-deprived house officers were making in caring for their patients, including slower response times, errors in memory, attention lapses, poor problem solving, EKG reading errors, irritability, and loss of patience. Sound familiar? The same holds true for sleep-deprived parents operating with what our family calls "baby brain." Your child and your mar-riage regularly deserve a good rest, and the peace that comes with it.

We conclude with a simple list of the ten most common co-parenting problems in getting your child to sleep, and what to do about them:

Common Sleep Problems and Co-parenting Solutions

1. **You disagree about what to do once you've entered the baby's room when he's crying.**

   Discuss in advance how you will decide if he's hungry and if he should be picked up, then both stick to the plan.

2. **You disagree about how long to wait when the toddler or preschooler is crying before going in to his room, so he keeps playing the odds, like a slot machine, hoping to get lucky.**

   First try the plan of the parent who takes the harder line to see if it works or makes things worse (but do not keep score; it adds a competitive edge where none is needed).

3. **One parent uses the time at night to compensate for time spent away from the child during the day.**

   The other parent should go in to handle the majority of nocturnal awakenings.

4. **Your spouse leaves the bedroom and sleeps with your toddler after she awakens; you think that's the wrong approach.**

   Ask your spouse to explain why she is doing this. Who is it really for? How does she know? See if you can agree on another way to make up that time or find that closeness. Chart how your child is responding—is she crying more frequently or waking up less often?—so you both have an accurate picture of what is happening and whether it is helping or not.

5. **One of you admits you cannot say no to your child about being alone at night because you know just how it feels from your childhood; the other doesn't see it as an issue.**

   This is one of those "it's your problem, not the child's" that you can gently help your partner recognize. Hold your mate tight when she wants to jump out of bed and be the person she turns to for comfort instead of the child.

6. **You have just moved to a new home, and your child has returned to more regressive behaviors, including not sleeping in her own bed and saying she's scared.**

Talk to your child together and find out what's scaring her. Is it the change? Is the room darker, bigger, further from yours? Then you and your spouse tell her you will figure out together how to make it feel safer. Both of you have the next conversation together with her and outline the plan—including her input if she's old enough (age three or older)—that you've come up with together. Think of others ways she can cope, besides coming into your room, such as putting a flashlight beside the bed, buying a simple music player that can be turned on with one button, installing day-glo stars on the ceiling, and so on.

7. **You disagree about how much time it should take to get your child to sleep at night.**

Agree on a set of sleep rituals and a maximum time that you should spend on them. Have it be an amount both of you can live with, then stick to the plan until it becomes routine.

8. **Mom wants to regularly put the infant to sleep, but dad wants mom to pump more so he can give a bottle more often.**

Have dad give a bottle at least once per night if he is to feel as close to his child as he would like. Make sure mom pumps or dad uses formula for the feeding to allow that. Agree ahead of time which feeding he will do, preferably one in the night and another one in the day, which is often easier on mom.

9. **Your child wants only one of you to put him to sleep; he has chosen one parent over the other.**

From toddlerhood through preschooler, let your child take the lead as much as possible. Talk to him about it, and encourage him to allow the other parent to perform the ritual. Both of you tell him how much mommy or daddy misses putting him to bed. Try doing it together for awhile. Take turns reading a passage or being different characters. If none of that works, you'll need to wait it out while being supportive of the other parent, who probably feels rejected.

10. **You disagree about whether the bottle needs to be warm at night. Dad gives it cold, mom gives it warm. The child has begun to reject the cold milk, and dad is unhappy about it.**

Is this the baby's concern or yours? Some babies really reject cold milk, and warming it makes a big difference in how willing they are to feed. Others do what has been taught them, and they are fine taking it cold, unless given a choice. If your baby wants it warm, you both have to get with the program. You can make it easier by putting the milk in a cooler in your room, with a mini-heater next to it so you don't have to go to the kitchen. If the baby will drink it either way, leave it cold. If you have already given her a choice, and now she wants it warm, you can try for a short while to retrain her, but you may be stuck with warming up the milk until she gets older. Don't sweat it. You did offer her a choice, and she presumed you meant it. How was she to know she fell smack into the middle of a co-parenting issue? She shouldn't have to pay for that.

As we've emphasized throughout, it's much easier to work out the everyday parenting challenges when you and your spouse are operating as a team. In explaining how they manage their household with three young children, one mother said:

> "We are a really good balance for each other. Things that make me anxious don't bother him, and vice versa. Believe me, our kids are lucky they have both of us. Like last night when Cal [their three-and-a-half-year-old] wouldn't go to bed—it went on and on—I turned to my husband and said, 'I just can't take this anymore. He can stay in his room and just scream it out as far as I'm concerned.' [My husband] went in and began the bed-time routines from the top—read to him, rocked him, and they both were calm in just a few minutes. It's like we complement each other really well, so we never both lose it at precisely the same time."

Now, get some rest . . . .

Safety
From Within and Without

Won't you pick me up, please?
I could use a hug and a squeeze . . . from you

Little Bitty Baby

David Alpert

Won't you pick me up please   I could use a hug and a squeeze   from __   you

SO GOES THE CHORUS of our family's favorite comfort song, written
by David Alpert for his Toddler Music collection. Even our sophisticated
ten-year-old will hum a few bars softly when she is feeling needy and
within earshot of the parent who can—for the time being—still pick her
up, fold her "in two," and deliver on the "hug and a squeeze from you"
promise. The song reminds us every time of how small children can feel
in the grown-up world, and how the longing to be safe and protected just
never goes away.

Mothers and fathers agree completely that delivering on this promise
"to keep you safe, no matter what" is at the core of their job as parents.
But who delivers the protection and how and when is open to lively interpretation in many families. The widely accepted stereotype casts fathers

as taking the more casual, even cavalier approach to parental vigilance, with mothers being more eagle-eyed. As previously discussed, fathers defend this approach, explaining that kids need to learn how to handle novel situations on their own so that they can better manage the surprises the world will eventually hurl at them. Researcher Eleanor Maccoby has documented fathers' tendency to want to "harden" their kids to circumstances where there may be some physical or social challenge that they eventually have to master.[1]

> In Frank's view, "When Ben eats lunch at school, no one's going to cut the crust off his sandwich for him, or call 911 if someone snatches the baseball cap off his head. It's better to teach him how to handle this stuff on his own. Nobody wants to buddy-up with a baby."
>
> Jennifer plays out the contrasting stereotype—that of the more vigilant "crossing-guard" parent, as Frank calls her. In her view, "Frank is a bit too tough. Sure, Ben needs to defend himself, but our job is to make sure he feels safe until he is ready to do that. The world will toughen him up. His parents don't need to." She feels strongly that kids "should not have to feel any more scared than is absolutely necessary for them to stay safe." She adds that she would rather "comfort or soothe sooner than later, because letting him figure it out by himself when he's scared will backfire and turn him off to the challenge rather than help him cope with it."

Research supports these contrasting viewpoints, depicting mothers as constructing more restrictive safety zones for their children than fathers do. That is, mothers offer a smaller space (and opportunity) for risk taking.

In our experience, this applies not only to the child's physical safety but to his emotional well-being too. For the sake of clarity, we will consider the child's physical safety and emotional safety separately, knowing full well that these two categories are distinct in name only. In the real lives of young children, separating mind from body is completely unrealistic. That's what makes them so different from us grown-ups and so infinitely interesting.

Standard Safety

When it comes to babies, there is little disagreement between mothers and fathers on what's essential for baby's safety. Once there are toddlers in the house, however, there is more room for interpretation—given that the kids are now on the move and intervention is more essential. Discuss the following list of safety practices with your spouse to see if either of you thinks any are "over the top" (that is, not really necessary for every kid) or "standard issue" safety practice (it's the least a parent must do).

The car:

▼ The child sits only in the backseat in a properly installed, appropriately sized car seat *versus* an occasional "let them sleep in the back of the wagon or van on long trips."

▼ The child is never left alone in the car, even if it's in your driveway with the doors locked *versus* let them finish their carseat nap in a safe neighborhood.

▼ The child doesn't leave his car seat once the vehicle begins moving *versus* he can get out to pick up the book he dropped.

The home:

▼ Windows that can open have secure barriers or screens that exceed the toddler's physical strength to push or break through them. All stairways have gates on them. (Parents routinely underestimate children's ingenuity and strength, whether a boy or a girl.)

▼ Cabinets containing household toxins (there are twice as many as you think—check labels!) need safety locks that are hard even for you to open.

▼ Ipecac syrup is kept in all bathrooms, and poison control numbers are at each phone (including cell phones). Even if parents agree on this, who is going to actually implement this and make sure babysitters and anyone else in the home understand?

▼ Electrical outlets are capped with safety covers. (Many parents confess they are far more likely to do this for their first child than the second.)

▼ The child is not allowed to go near kitchen appliances, heaters of any kind, and irons.

The bedroom:

▼ The crib is far from any draperies or electrical cords.

▼ Nothing in or near the crib can be stacked up and used by the child to climb out.

▼ The crib mattress is kept at its lowest level. The higher crib sides make it harder to climb out.

▼ If the child is able to climb out of the crib, she is moved to a low bed that is accessible even though her legs are short. (Is one parent stalling because he or she is not quite ready to get rid of the degree of control that the crib offers?)

The playroom:

▼ The child has no toys that need electricity in order to work, including motorized riding toys that require charging (this includes that neat toy that grandpa gave him).

Water:

▼ You never take your eyes or hands off your toddler for a second near large sinks, bathtubs, wading pools, fish ponds, or any other body of water.

Outside:

▼ Anywhere near traffic or water, there are fenced-off areas where the child can safely play on his own—because anything can happen in a split second—*versus* "I'm always watching."

▼ Playground equipment is safe and in good repair, and is mounted securely on impact-absorbent surfaces, such as wood chips, grass, or crushed rubber matting. (This involves work, maintenance, and costs.)

The child-care center:

▼ The center should be at least as safe as your home, if not more so, given the number of accidents-waiting-to-happen in the form of more kids per square foot.

▼ Drop-off and pick-up areas are completely safe *versus* "there's not enough parking so you have to cross a busy street with your child." Or there is no fence around the perimeter so an excited child could run out of the yard.

▼ The space has first-aid kits and fire extinguishers; sandboxes and trash containers are covered (when not in use); staff and parents enforce no-smoking policies; there is no peeling paint; kids are never left alone; and playground equipment is safe and in good condition. In other words, cost-cutting measures are not tolerated. These safe conditions are recognized as being as important as the quality of the relationships within.

Did you both have the same responses? Or did you have some answers that were so far apart you thought the other was kidding? These safety recommendations are within the guidelines set by the American Academy of Pediatrics for toddler homes, and all are safety requirements every family should follow. If there are significant discrepancies between your answers, the two of you should talk about why. If you have different toler-ances for risk, how far are you willing to compromise, where your child's physical safety is concerned? Keeping the peace or not doing more than your share are two common compromises that can have serious consequences in this area—for your child's safety and your co-parenting alliance.

Firearms

Kyle grew up in the Plains and the Midwest of the United States, where his father would hunt during both the bow and gun seasons. Boys were expected to learn how to use these weapons well and safely, which is still standard in many communities. Children can get hurt playing with their parents' guns, and safety locks are not always as secure as parents think. Having a gun in the home places every family member at much greater risk of being killed, more so than from someone invading the home with a gun. Children accidentally shoot themselves; impulsive, despondent teenagers commit homicide or suicide with a too-convenient weapon, and domestic violence turns fatal quickly.

Getting rid of the gun at home is best for all concerned. If for some reason you choose not to, for the safety of your family, you should take the following precautions:

▼ Keep *unloaded* guns locked in a cabinet with an obscure combination, known only to you.
▼ Do the same with ammunition, locked up in a separate location.
▼ Install trigger locks on each gun.
▼ Teach your children that guns are not toys; they are to turn and walk away from anyone who offers to show or let them touch a gun. You should role play this periodically; don't assume they already know it or will not forget it.

Men and women frequently disagree on the whole issue of firearms. Men are far more likely to have a gun, feel strongly about owning it, and eventually want to teach their children to love the sport (whether it is target shooting or hunting). Marsha once had a couple come to see her because the mother said she was willing to divorce over this issue. If you can't work out this disagreement, it's unlikely to be the only contentious issue in your partnership. It raises specters of power and control. Why wouldn't you bow to the other's wishes, when safety is so readily implicated?

If the two of you feel so differently that you cannot reach a solution, try these variations: Could your spouse keep his gun at the community gun club, instead of at home? If the gun is in the house—with both parents aware of where and how it is stored and where the ammunition is—could each of you have a key so the more concerned spouse can check periodically?

If these variations don't work, a counselor can help. Get a referral from someone you know, your child's pediatrician, a school guidance counselor, a social worker, or a psychologist.

Fire

Handling firearms is closely related to handling fire. Pediatricians have found that before children—especially boys—reach age ten, the odds are strong that they will play with fire in some form (matches, lighters, and so on). Parents are unlikely to know about it, unless something goes terribly wrong.[2] We are talking about children from across the social spectrum. Remember your child's eyes the first time she understood fire? Whether the fire is birthday candles, the family-room fireplace, a campfire, or July 4th bonfire, it mesmerizes and enchants. The preschooler thinks, 'Why not try to make it on my own sometime? Let's see, where do mom and dad keep the matches?'

What to do? Don't make it just a guy thing. Preschoolers in particular need to hear from both parents on the topic. When you are firing up the grill, tell your children, "Mom and Dad are very careful with fire because it's very hot and it hurts people, even though it looks pretty." By kindergarten, children need to hear again that "fire is for adults. Even though it might seem simple to handle, it gets out of control very fast." When your children are around eight years old, both parents should have a serious conversation with them about playing with fire, followed up by a trip to the fire station. Why age eight? By then, most boys and girls are able to physically manage starting a fire on their own and clever enough to do it without getting caught, especially if it's summer when normally vigilant parents are more relaxed. Keep sulfur matches, lighters, and "instant matches" (propane) locked up and only for adult use until the kids are twelve. After that, they should be used only with adult supervision. Isn't twelve way too old? No. Even though boys and girls have the dexterity to light a match or a fire well before that age, until then they remain largely clueless about how to manage when something *catches* fire, such as their clothes or your house. Boys are more prone to play with fire than girls. For everyone's sake, these guidelines need to be followed by both parents of boys and girls.

Water

For young children, water safety is essential. Here again, there are many generalities about parental attitudes regarding swimming and water play. Many men have said in our presence, "Just throw 'em in—they'll learn or sink. And they won't really sink, they always learn. Of course, you've got to be standing right there, but kids are natural swimmers." Well, not quite. Though she was a good athlete, Kyle's mother, who was "taught" that way, never learned to swim because she was unable to master her panic over being unable to breathe underwater. No one took the trouble to teach her to slowly and calmly hold her breath, duck under the surface, and *not* exhale until she lifted her face out of the water—and to do all this when *she* was ready.

So if your spouse and you feel differently about when your child is ready for swimming, there is a way to deal with this. Talking it out isn't the best way. Instead, the parent who is ready to help the child learn to swim sooner should take the initiative in showing the more conservative or less convinced parent that he is correct about timing. He (assuming it's dad) should give (or take the child to) the swim lessons and take responsibility for getting him taught. This isn't an invitation for gate-keeping, with mom looking over dad's shoulder, waiting to disapprove when he doesn't do it her way, or when the child signals he isn't as ready as dad thinks. Be open to the possibility that the child is more ready than mom thinks. Have this conversation: "OK, if you are so keen on his swimming at this early age, then you teach him safely and in a way that he's not so scared he can't learn. I'm sure we would both want that for him, so I'm leaving it to you to do, since I know I'm not quite ready." Then, mom should back off.

Here's how to encourage your young child's love of swimming.

▼ Get in the water with your kids often. Even if you're just splashing around in the kiddie pool with your ten-month-old, make it a family event.

▼ The warmer the water, the better for little bodies that don't have a lot of fat layers for insulation. The heat relaxes the muscles and eases the mood.

▼ Suits with built-in flotation devices may make you feel more secure, but they don't replace a vigilant adult. Water wings are not a good idea because they alter the child's balance in the water.

▼ Stay wet, calm, and supportive. Kids typically progress after seeming stuck for weeks or months, only to have their fear of the water return the next time they go swimming. Wait out their fear. Eventually their delight in joining the water world will more than repay your patience.

▼ Join a baby swim class so you can see what other kids your child's age are doing. And you'll get a second opinion (the teacher's) about whether your child is really the superstar like you think.

▼ True swim lessons are a good idea after your child begins putting her head in the water of her own accord, kicking, and showing a real desire to move across the pool. Even then, she has to be old enough and coordinated enough to move arms and legs together. Some children are ready by age three, though the majority do best at age four.

Bicycle Riding

Thanks to trail-behind wheeled enclosures for toddlers, tow bars, and tag-a-longs, kids can be part of family biking from early on. Pedal-less training bikes can help them to practice balance and gliding until they are ready for training wheels. Most kids long to get their training wheels with the same passion that they want to ride well without them. It's important to keep up with how proficient they are as riders.

They should all begin this journey from the same spot: the fitting of the *parent's* helmet. (What you *do* as a parent largely eclipses the less potent influences of what you say or buy.) Then it's the child's turn. His helmet should be level when it's on his head—neither a skullcap nor a sunshade, an adult finger-width above the eyebrows. It needs to be snug enough not to dislodge when the child shakes his head side to side. Stop by the local bike shop and have one of the service folks check out the fit.

Teaching kids to ride a bike is as good a metaphor for parenting as you'll ever find. You have to get them up to speed to keep them safe while they don't know what they're doing, and then let go, just at the moment when they are learning that they have to pedal to keep their balance.

We've heard some great fights between parents about whether their child is ready for a two-wheeler. It doesn't matter *who* is right. The question is, is your *child* scared, ready to fly, or not scared enough? Are you holding him back with your own fears, or are you ignoring his tenuousness, his hesitation, his headstrong hubris? He'll eventually be the one who decides what feels safe. For now, you need to hold on a bit longer, even though your arms are killing you, and make the decision about when you should let go based on what you are learning from him moment to moment. There are plenty of other parenting moments when your judgment alone should rule the day, but this is not one of them. You and your child are partners in this decision, not just your spouse. If you and your mate disagree about where the child is on the bike-learning continuum, chances are one of you is not really paying sufficient attention to the young rider. There is no reason to be in a hurry. It will happen when it happens, and the victory is the child's. Remember, there is always next summer.

Sledding

Like biking, sledding can be a favorite family activity, but safety is not guaranteed. There are as many mothers as there are fathers on "Hospital Hill" (the actual name of our favorite sledding spot), but more of the fathers are riding and more of the mothers are shouting instructions and warnings. If you and your spouse disagree about whether your child is ready to fly down the hill, here are some safety pointers that should be a bottom line for both of you, as the ambulance visits the hill far too often:

▼ The course and its run-out must be clear of trees, rocks, and traffic.
▼ No one under five rides alone.
▼ Winter sports helmets are essential for children. It doesn't hurt parents to wear them, too, and you'll be setting a good example to help your child overcome any resistance to wearing such head gear.
▼ The sled should be steerable with good strong handholds, and designed to encourage the child to sit up, face forward. Forget the disc type of sled; they are accidents waiting to happen.
▼ Wait until the run-out is clear of people and pets before launching (screaming works well before and during descent).

If either or both of you follow these precautions, then your differences are probably due to your own comfort zones rather than from true peril on your child's part. If she is smiling and having a good time, lighten up and bite your tongue if you have to. If she is saying she's afraid, then slow your spouse down by helping your child say loud and clear that she is afraid. Suggest a smaller hill and friends in tow who are at the same level. This takes things down a notch.

Exercise and Team Sports

Jennifer and Frank both grew up in families where participation in team sports was valued. But that's where the similarity ended. Jennifer, who played basketball, said, "I was pretty good for my size, and my teams usually had winning seasons. I loved when my parents came to my games, but nobody was sports-crazy. That's just the way I want to set it up for our kids. Good exercise, family focused, and socially meaningful." She didn't expect her son Ben to be playing basketball or any other sport at age five, but she wanted him to be swimming, doing gymnastics, anything that kept him active.

Frank's family was hard core by comparison. He and his brothers played Little League, and his father coached. As Frank remembers it, "Entire summers passed without a family dinner together because of practice, games, and road trips for one, if not all of us—the whole nine yards. I loved it, and so did my dad. My mom . . . not so much. But she was proud of us, and that mattered a lot to me. I'd love for Ben to feel the intense pleasure of giving your team your last drop of blood. It was so great."

Jennifer responded, "That's nuts, honey. Who needs to spill blood to develop a healthy body and a sense of being part of a team? Especially before high school."

Raise-your-pulse exercise is an essential part of your children's physical and mental health. But it needs to be fun and a time for family togetherness. If it's indoors, mats and large balls generally do the trick. Keep them away from your exercise equipment.

Outside is better, weather, season, and safety permitting. If, however, your kindergartener or first-grader is interested in a team sport, she should sample more than one; she's much too young to start focusing on a single sport. It's premature to believe that a child of this age has real talent and should play more frequently and with older kids. Your kid will not get a head start on an athletic scholarship; more likely, he'll wind up with a sprained ankle or other injuries. In addition, the confidence that comes with playing well will be overshadowed by the fact that he's the smallest, youngest, and often least socially desirable child on the team. So lay off the hard-driving T-ball. We helped Frank realize that he was confusing his own childhood dreams with those of his young son. Eventually, Ben might play a team sport when he's older, but for now, as a five-year-old, it's more appropriate for him to play catch in the backyard with mom and dad.

A few years ago, *Sports Illustrated* featured an article on the astounding rise in popularity of lacrosse. The author, a coach himself, explained that the sport was relatively new to most American families, and most parents didn't yet know the rules or the game well enough to ruin it for their kids by overfocusing on its competitive aspects (ouch!).[3] This message—that parents need to keep their competitive juices to themselves—is strongly supported by pediatricians, good coaches, orthopedic surgeons, child psychiatrists, and experts in sports medicine.

Kindergarteners are not ready for competition. What they *are* ready for is that you pay attention to the skills they enjoy mastering. Running around with a bunch of reasonably healthy and happy kids, chasing or hitting a ball, and starting to get the hang of something called "the game" is plenty to have on your plate at this age. Her central nervous system, eye-hand coordination, memory, level of patience, and ability to focus are far from ready to hone her competitive edge. The strength, eye-hand coordination, endurance, and mental toughness of twenty-year-olds are still evolving. Kids are at least age nine before they fully comprehend the concept of winning and losing, and if how they and their team played is even remotely related to the outcome. Furthermore, precious little evidence shows that the early years of anybody's life offer a reliable forecast of future athletic prowess. Frank's son might not even like baseball. If he doesn't, we'd encourage his parents to either back off team sports altogether for the time being or see if there's another sport he'd like to try—lacrosse, perhaps.

What our experience as parents and athletes has taught us is that often the most valuable thing kids learn from team sports is how to manage failure, loss, and erratic rule enforcement in a social context—pretty good preparation for life, eh? Meanwhile, balancing your individual or co-parental support between praise and constructive criticism is the key to helping kids get the most out of this experience. Kyle had a legendary cigar-smoking swim coach named Jim Clark who would bellow after a diver missed a dive or a swimmer missed a turn, "There are no mistakes, only lessons . . . only lessons."

The premier co-parenting lesson we've learned is that when one parent pushes too hard or too fast on this athletic issue, and the other parent disagrees overtly or covertly, the child pays—by quitting the sport just when he or she is old enough to distinguish him- or herself from other kids in a way that might matter to coaches and teammates. Or quitting just when she is ready to handle the competition, solidifying the friendships and skills that can serve as protective factors against risk-taking behaviors in preadolescence and beyond. When your child is young, the question is how to help her enjoy the benefits that accrue in her life *now*: getting good exercise, being part of a team, sticking with something you care about, and learning to follow the rules, without feeling overwhelmed by competition that is too hard to handle. At this age, losing is often accompanied by tears, denial, and heartfelt protest that the other team cheated.

As co-parents, if your child is acting overwhelmed, it's time to work with your spouse to help your child. If she's complaining about the sport itself or her other parent's intensity about it to you, don't conspire or collude. Talk to your child to understand what she's feeling and why. If she feels pushed by the other parent, don't just listen; insist that your child talk to the other parent about how she feels and offer to help her if she's reluctant. Do it together, after giving your spouse a heads-up. (A surprise "ambush" would more likely invoke tension between you and him about being "ganged up on," than cooperation about listening carefully to what your child needs to say.) The confided-in parent should then bow out of the three-way conversation until the two-way is resolved. Encourage an open discussion of whether your child just has to push through her uncertainty or discouragement (you may have the same fight about music lessons) and help your child not to quit. Together with your spouse, come to an understanding about what your child is actually complaining or hurting about and why, as opposed to whether this team thing is just too much, too fast. This will help you decide who wants this anyway—you or your child? After you agree about the parameters for continuing to play full steam, pull back, or quit, and how you will handle meltdowns over disappointments, then it is a time for another three-way discussion with your child.

If you can't get to this point together, it's time to get help from friends, family, or if all else fails, a professional.

Stranger Danger and Other Scary Stuff

It's hard not to be paralyzed by the frightening media stories about missing and abducted children, but you don't want to pass your fears of this statistically rare event directly to your kids, who have no perspective on the likelihood or proximity of danger to them. Of course, we want to be responsible about preparing them for the world we inhabit and to help them make their way safely in it. How to do this thoughtfully involves many illuminating co-parenting conversations, which are heavily influenced by the parent's own experiences and beliefs about personal safety. It takes considered judgment to help kids feel secure, while agreeing on the way to get there.

Most five-year-olds feel anxious when instructed simply "Don't talk to any strangers." They are new social animals at this age, and to have your parents or other trusted adults tell you that most of the human world is off-limits because danger lurks everywhere that's unfamiliar is neither encouraging news nor sensible. Instead, offer positive guidance and a simple, short reason: "Hold Mommy's hand in the store. It's busy and you don't want to get lost." Your kids are smart enough to understand that there is reason for concern, but it is your job to get the scale and magnitude of worry right. Terrorism has its place in the world, but not in this conversation. One of our kid's friends, who lived in Manhattan before and after 9/11, sternly told our children that they "must never go around the corner in any hotel hallway without a grown-up, because terrorists are all around." Our kids, who are no strangers to hotels or the wider world, told us later about all they learned from this family friend, some of which was flat-out misinformation. The amount of worry and anxiety contained in information that children cannot quite digest is palpable.

Jennifer and Frank worked together well on this issue. When asked how they handled security issues, Jennifer responded, " . . . like pros. We taught Ben to stay in the store if he ever got lost, and find the grown-up in a uniform or the one wearing a name tag. We practiced for weeks whenever we went shopping to find the 'name-tag people.' This made it more of a puzzle to solve than a safety drill, but it calmed Frank and me down to see him get it right every time. It mattered only once when we got separated in a busy train station. He found an Amtrak rep with a name tag. He was fine, but it's still in my nightmares."

Parents often give mixed messages about security, including: encouraging your children to hug or kiss someone *they* don't know (how well *you* know the person is basically irrelevant); striking up conversations with children *you* don't know, which contradicts what you tell them about not talking to strangers (you really mean strange adults and much bigger kids); or always locking the car doors, yet telling the kids they live in a really safe neighborhood.

Regarding strangers, tell your kids: "When you want to talk to a grown-up who's not in our family, ask mom/dad/babysitter if it's okay. They'll say yes or no. Wanna practice?" As your children age, they will want, and be able to manage, increasing levels of guidance and *calm* reassurance, according to their growing ability to understand the ways of the world. Limiting TV exposure—especially to the news—helps to contain the issue.

Co-parenting advice on this one? Be calm and consistent. One of you is more likely than the other to be concerned; maybe you are more of a worrier, or maybe you grew up in a big city or had a frightening experience as a child. Don't give wildly differing messages about how worrisome the world really is. Your child will watch and decide, "I don't have to follow the 'no talking to strangers' rule with Daddy because Mommy is the only one who really worries." Being consistent helps your child most so that she doesn't see one adult's worry as valid and the other's as invalid. Agree on the important issues to emphasize, and let the others go until the child is a bit older.

Media

What are some co-parenting approaches to safe exposure to screen and technological media? Ten years ago, this was a far more gendered issue. Even now, more families leave technology purchase, maintenance, and installation issues up to dad. But whoever manages the remotes in your household needs to feel the support of his or her spouse because the issue about screen time (TV and/or computer) can get hot and heavy fast, even with very young children.

First, how much is too much? Have you had your co-parenting discussion about time limits? Have that talk first and then check out this finding: Eminent pediatrician T. Berry Brazelton and child psychiatrist Stanley Greenspan suggest no screen time until *after* family time, playing with friends, and homework—and then no more than thirty minutes per day for children five and under, and no more than two hours per day for six- to nine-year-olds.[4] We recommend far less.

Young children in particular need to be protected from screen time's very powerful sensory magnet. For the three-year-old, the programming—even children's programming—instantly stimulates them; then the nervous system routinely adapts and "habituates" (becomes accustomed to the stimulus) to whatever is on the screen, 'educational' or not. It appears that they are "enjoying watching." But once the set is turned off, there is often an "explosion" as the nervous system tries to download quickly all the accumulated tension from this troubling combination of physical passivity with the visual excitement of watching.[5] It can happen after watching TV, playing on the computer, or seeing a video or DVD.

> When Rose was two and Ben was six, Jennifer and Frank had trouble compromising on screen-time rules. Frank wanted to watch the evening news on the kitchen TV because world events affected many of the companies with whom he consulted, but Jennifer felt the news was just too violent for the kids. Ben was curious about everything on TV, and Rose just repeated what he said and thought about it all. Frank thought Jennifer was being "too protective; besides, they already had their hour of kid's TV. Ben, at least, is old enough to know how the world works." Jennifer replied, "Not yet, he isn't."

Frank wanted Jennifer to concede that the two children should be treated differently because of their ages. His general inclination was to expose Ben to the wider world—the good along with manageable doses of the not-so-good. Jennifer was frustrated that his view wasn't nuanced. He thought she was too rigid across the board, without taking into account the specifics of a particular situation.

On this issue, Jennifer is right. Decades of research show that watching violence on a screen—whether the source is a TV, computer, video game, handheld toy, or a DVD (Disney included)—teaches kids to care progressively less and less about the consequences of interpersonal violence. The victims eventually vanish from their awareness, be they Wile E. Coyote or wartime child refugees. The violence affects kids' attitudes toward victims in the real world, whether it's due to bullying, wars, armed conflict, or street crime. In other words, children need to be protected.[6] But that's just the beginning. The more screen time young children "enjoy," the less interested they are in reading and in creative and imaginary play, the very bedrock of school readiness. Equally worrisome is the undermining effect screen time has on physical activity as a whole and exercise in particular. This is all the more alarming in the face of America's childhood obesity epidemic. Rose is not too young to be affected.

We encouraged Jennifer and Frank to rethink their habits and use a delayed recording device so Frank could watch the news after the little ones were in bed, or just wait for the 10 p.m. news. In addition, there are a growing number of organizations and their websites designed to help parents think about preparing their children to be media literate—an essential skill in this era of endless games, advertising, and social networks. A couple of our favorites are the Media Education Foundation (www.mediaed.org) and the National Association for Media Literacy Education (www.namle.net). This will ensure that kids don't turn into numbed-out, thumb-weary feeders at the vast digital trough that is electronic/digital media.

Bullying

Not all violence is on the screen. Parents must also help their kids manage social and emotional violence too, particularly in its most common form: bullying. Again, mothers' and fathers' separate childhood experiences with bullying play powerful roles in shaping their views about how to deal with the perpetrator and the victim. In our experience working with families, the most common error we see is assuming that you know your partner's views on handling bullies and the rationale. Often you don't, so stop right here and have that conversation, beginning with:

▼ What do you consider bullying among little children?
▼ What should we do if our child is bullying her younger sibling, someone at day care, or the family pet? Be specific about which behaviors fall into the "just siblings working it out" category, and which ones, to a younger child, are experienced as intensely as bullying by a stranger.
▼ At what age should we begin to talk to our child about this subject? (By the way, by the time your child is three, you should explain how his behavior hurts other children's feelings.)

Odds are you may have both bullied and been bullied yourselves, in and outside your families, and that you have strong feelings about these experiences. Chances are that you both feel as if your past experiences are at least in part gender-related, so the gender of your child is likely to play a role in what you want to eventually impart to him about managing this piece of social behavior.

Jessie and Sal were talking about their daughter Sara, who is just shy of her sixth birthday, and one particularly aggressive playmate whose parents live in the neighborhood and share a common social circle with them.

Jessie commented, "When I see Sara playing with Phoebe—and working so hard to comply with her demands and insolence—I want to fold Sara in my arms, tell her that she's fabulous, it's Phoebe that's being the jerk, not to take her crap, and to go play with the other nicer kids. Then, I want to take out my cell phone, call her parents and ask, 'What the hell!?' Sara is just too sweet to protect herself from that kind of meanness at this age."

Sal said, "I know what you mean, sweetie, but rescuing her is not going to help her learn how to handle bullies, even though it might make you feel better. We need to teach her what to say and do to not get hurt and upset by the Phoebes of the world—and there are a lot of them out there."

Here, Sal is right. Are there "bully-proofing" programs for schools and preschools? They do exist, but they have not enjoyed the tide-turning success for which parents and teachers may have hoped. Some researchers[7] have concluded that their greatest value is in reassuring parents that something is actually being done. Ultimately, kids have to discourage bullying at the source—their *reaction* to the jerk.

Bullying is the purposeful repetitive taunting or intimidation of one child by another. Of course, when it's physical, adults need to intervene. But most bullying is verbal and social and happens away from the grown-ups. It often takes a subtle but just as intimidating turn when kids (girls especially) use social situations to reward or punish other children through inclusion or exclusion. Sometimes it's just part of learning about how the social world works. But when your child is the only one not invited to a particular party or is ignored in front of other kids by the child who spent six hours at your home playing happily last weekend, the behavior has crossed a line.

If we're honest (and able to remember young life with siblings), we'll also admit there's a certain perverse pleasure in pushing another person's buttons. Getting that "rise" out of a brother or a classmate can be surprisingly powerful and gratifying experience in a "dark side" kind of way. It also helps to compensate for one's own insecurities. That's why it's so common and so effective.

But what if it doesn't work? What if a bully can't find the buttons to push, or if when he or she does push the buttons, nothing happens? Then it's no fun, game over, on to the next kid.

What the bully wants is to witness his victim's obvious distress; without it, he's lost the game. New York school psychologist Izzy Kalman[8] outlines an approach to deflecting bullying that involves the use of laughter, indifference, and agreement—all to take the wind out of the bully's sails, leaving him adrift, right where you want him. Sal had similar ideas for how Sara might react to Phoebe when she sneers, "*You* don't play with dolls right," Sara could respond:

"I do, too. And I don't care if you like it or not."

"OK, you teach me your way and I'll teach you mine!"

"Chloe likes my way; I'll go play with her. Bye!"

"That's funny, Phoebe; dolls don't *care* how you play with them!"

"I'm done playing with you for now, Phoebe. Bye."

Sal needs to enlist Jessie in this approach, and then together they can start role playing these conversations with Sara.

Sal [in Phoebe's role]: "I am not going to play with you, Sara, if you don't let me go first."

Sara: "Then don't play with me."

Sal: "Good, honey. Now what if she says, 'Then nobody else will be your friend either.'"

Sara tears up. "She *does* do that, Daddy. And then the other kids don't play with me."

Sal: "OK. So now you say . . . what?"

Sara: "I don't know."

Sal: "Here are some of my favorites . . . 'Oh, that won't last. They'll see you for the bossy little girl you're being right now,' or 'My real friends won't listen to you,' or how about 'Are you afraid to just be mad at me yourself, so you have to go tell other people to be on your side?'"

When we tried a similar approach a few years back, our second-grade daughter told us that she "knew what to do with bullies because Kowndry told her." Kowndry, her imaginary friend, was a gifted and timely ally in these and other emotionally laden matters. Nearly two-thirds of kids three to seven years old report having an imaginary pal, maybe for just such moments. We encouraged her to keep Kowndry close to shore herself up until she found a sympathetic ear in her parents or friends of flesh and blood. It's excellent practice in thinking for one's self, not depending on grown-ups for everything, and—as the PBS character D.W., Arthur's little sister, would tell you perfectly normal and great fun.

There is no topic more important for you and your spouse to discuss than your child's internal (emotional) and external safety. Rely together on the known expertise that's around for some of the these safety decisions. The rest you get to cobble together from your own and you kids' delights and worries as life goes on.

11

▼

Education
The Co-parenting Foundation to Lifelong Learning

THERE ARE NO MISTAKES—only lessons." This aphorism from Kyle's swim coach, whom we met in the previous chapter, has stuck with us long after other aphorisms have faded because of this truth: a child's education begins with lessons learned from everyday life with his mother and father as his first teachers. Those lessons span from learning how to get your needs met and what tastes, feels, or sounds good—not from what you did 'wrong'—to whom you can trust and why it's not a good idea to go down the stairs headfirst. Getting burned teaches you to stay away from hot burners because they hurt, not because mom or dad disapproves. And there's great delight inherent in mastering a lesson. Praise from a happy, relevant adult can punctuate an experience, but doesn't add a dram of learning. So why are parents such important teachers?

Mothers and fathers are wise to ponder this question separately and together, well before they place their children in the hands of the next teacher, at school or day care. How do you know if your child is ready for:

▼ Her first bed?
▼ Play dates?
▼ Training wheels?
▼ Attending a birthday party without you?
▼ A sleepover?
▼ Trying to read?
▼ Summer camp?

Chances are, your answers to the first three are based on a guess combined with your own readiness for your child's next developmental stage, while the last four are more informed by something rooted in your understanding of your child at this time in his life. Of course, the closer you and your spouse are to your child, the better you'll both be at reading the signs that he *is* ready to take on something new and harder to master. This mutual support for your child's inner readiness to take on a new challenge makes parents such important teachers. You, after all, know so well what he loves and hates to do, what makes him happy or frustrated, how much he wants to do on his own, and when he needs you very close. That hard-won knowledge makes you the perfect explainer of what is confusing and the perfect challenger and supporter when he is ready to expand a skill or try something different. Development itself ensures that a child will be ready for novelty; the tricky question is *when*. The signs are clear to one or both of you—something you read in his mood, voice, or body when he watches another child doing it, or it emerges as the child's idea or yours. Where it will *not* originate is in some parenting textbook of guidelines. You'll also be the first to know when you've misread intrigue for readiness: The training wheels sit idle for another season, or the musical instrument gathers dust.

In your heart, you probably know that this movement to a new stage of development cannot be accelerated or pushed along, any more than you can yell at a tomato to 'hurry up and ripen.' There's a multibillion dollar industry on the other side of this truth, waiting for you to try to speed up your child's brain development by buying a certain gizmo or DVD. You have better ways to spend your money. Children's basic developmental needs remain the same: That they be treasured and loved, capable of treasuring and loving back, and that they be protected, taught, and enriched according to who they—as unique individuals—simply *are*.

Opportunities for Learning

Stop fretting about accelerating your child's readiness for school. Speeding up this process to ensure that your child is one of the smartest in the class is not a co-parenting argument worth having, even if your spouse sees it differently. Your child started developing competence before she ever saw the light of day. Brain growth is fueled by nutrition, genes, and experience—all of which are readily available in the womb. Maybe that explains those fleeting "knowing glances" you see in your baby's eyes after she learns to focus beyond fourteen inches. In this chapter, we discuss the various opportunities for learning, from your home to formal school settings to after-school programs.

Music to My Ears . . .

For more obvious proof of an infant's readiness to learn, look at her appetite for music, something many babies seem to carry over from their predelivery life. This may be especially true if the pregnant mother frequently exposed her unborn child to music (no research yet on maternal iPod usage) and/or if the father made an effort to sing to the baby *in utero.*

There is an educational opportunity to be enjoyed in music—any music—though few mothers or fathers recognize its value beyond entertainment. If you feel that the joy of music should have something more to show for itself (in addition to the joy), know that children who enjoy daily music also develop stronger memory and language and problem-solving skills. (This is not to be confused with the oft-touted but ill-supported "Mozart effect," the theory that listening to Mozart strengthens memory and abstract reasoning. Evidence for this does exist, but the effect lasts for only two weeks in college students and has nothing to do with young children.) Music is so durable a form of communication it can outlast the intellect in old age. Sometimes following a speech-ending stroke in old age or the onset of Alzheimer's, sung communication is still possible, while spoken is not.

One of you is probably more musical than the other, though ethnomusicologists contend that there is no such thing as a nonmusical human being. Our son wryly commented that "Mommy has a song for everything, even though she can't sing." Although carrying a tune is not her strength, Marsha's love of lyrics teaches the kids about music, and their father's keen musicality adds another dimension. So they get something from each of us. Songs—the ones you know and love—should be a part of everyday routines, like bathing, eating, and playing. They are as good for you as they are for your kids, and, while you're at it, emphasize the beat physically (by tapping or bouncing). It helps children learn to concentrate while listening.

If you use recorded music, mix yours in with theirs. A significant amount of so-called kids' music is saccharine swill or poorly played or sung, so they often prefer songs with texture, character, beat, and surprises—Rossini, the Beatles, Scott Joplin, Gershwin, Beach Boys, Prokofiev, Flat & Scruggs, Orff, Saint-Saens, Frankie Valli and the Four Seasons, Bach, John Williams, and Coltrane, to name a few of our favorites. Keep a basket of the following music makers (or at least ones you can best tolerate) handy: bells, tambourines, triangles, harmonicas, xylophones, drums, shakers, slide whistles, and kazoos are irresistible and effective diversions. Kids can benefit from your involvement, so get in the conga line and move; it'll feel like a homemade musical.

If you prefer a more formal setting, check out some music classes. Ask around about which classes have the best teachers; a good teacher trumps the curriculum ten to one. For the toddler family, this can help engage the less musical parent who is having a harder time getting into the rhythm. For the child, the musical goal is learning to sing in tune (eventually) and keep a beat while still having fun. If your child shows interest and wants more, consider a trip to a local music school fair where he can try out a bunch of instruments. As with reading, a passion for music must be his, not yours, in order for it to endure.

A Picture Says a Thousand Words

Another pillar of the home academy with tangible educational benefits is the world of art. Picasso's aphorism that it took him merely a few decades to draw like Raphael but a lifetime to draw like a child is amusing but, even more to the point, underscores what makes drawn or painted art so important. The child's inherent, natural artistic instincts, not her potential for greatness, are to be encouraged and celebrated now, when they matter to *her*. But do mothers and fathers need to be their kids' patrons, even if they themselves are not particularly artistic?

Although many parents believe their kids harbor some artistic genius—and that's a loving way to look at your own child—most young kids simply enjoy the process of making art. Pushing a marker across a sheet of paper and creating something that wasn't there before is a pleasurable experience. It's also important brainwork in encouraging the eye and hand to cooperate. Drawing takes concentration, awakens a certain wonder, and evokes a drive to repeat a task until it's done. All these skills help the child to become ready for the kind of group learning that takes place in school. Here are some ways to encourage that process:

▼ Have a space dedicated to making art. Whether newsprint or a white board affixed to the staircase or bedroom wall, or a folding card table in a small apartment, devote its main use to making art. An author of children's books we know installed a blackboard wall in his dining room. Both his ideas and his children's art find an outlet there.

▼ Children seem encouraged to create by using good materials, introduced a few at a time. Fat, easy-to-grip, water-based markers, crayons, bright tempera paints, and some oil pastels are plenty. Make sure you have an oilcloth (available in fabric shops) to protect the floors and a smock or 'big old daddy shirt' to protect your child's clothes.

▼ Help children get their ideas off the ground by suggesting things you know *they* already love (fish, planes, dogs, ice cream), or prime the pump with a few interesting objects from their world—key chain, small stuffed animal, toy car, or toothbrush. Mirrors are especially cool ways to get kids looking at things a different way. Then back off. Random scribbles start off late in the first year and early in the second, proceeding to more controlled drawings by age three. Identified or labeled scribbles follow in the fourth year. Somewhere between ages five and seven, they become representational—the tadpole stays a tadpole once it's drawn. But whatever the child's age, the ordered progression from random and plain to schematic and detailed stays the same.

▼ If you feel you must say *something* about what they are doing (and most of us do), keep it descriptive only, along the lines of, "I see lots of dots" and "I notice you like boxes." This is not instruction, it is adventure, and there is no wrong way to do it. But more important than what you say is your appreciation and attention that silently conveys the message, "I just love it, and I love being with you. You are a wonder, no matter what this creation turns out to be."

▼ If your child tells you what she is "doing," don't get too invested in it. Odds are the meaning and design will change within minutes anyway.

A computer-savvy relative complicated (enriched?) this approach by putting our four-year-old on his lap and teaching him to make "art" on his laptop. This presented a dilemma—and introduced some unanticipated co-parenting struggles of our own. Is the computer a boon or bane for the young child's creativity and education? Will or should its seductive programming replace paper and crayon and human assistant as tools of the young artist's trade? Arguments abound more in the scientific literature than they do around the kitchen table. As we know from recent surveys,[1] most parents of young children hold computers in high regard as educational technology and feel that they have a responsibility to introduce their children to them early on. Most level-headed experts will tell you that a balanced media diet is best—including paper and crayons/markers—given that the amount of useful and interesting interactive programming now available makes computers more educationally creative than TV, at least for now.[2]

The First Formal Educational Experience

As you watch your children delight in learning to use their eyes, ears, hands, bodies, voices, and feelings, it's natural to leap ahead to the next phase and consider more formal educational settings for them outside the home. The alternatives are seemingly limitless: family or nonfamily day care, preschool, co-op nursery school, "educare" (the flashy new name for child care plus learning environments). What's right for your family and your particular child, and how will you and your spouse decide together?

Whether you think your child is ready to be away from you for a few hours a day in the care of another adult and in the presence of other children is more critical than whether you think he or she is smart enough or even eager enough to start learning in groups of kids to whom she is not related. Couples rarely reach the identical conclusion at exactly the same moment for exactly the same reasons. Statistically, the separation from home care to some form of group care tends to happen most often in toddlerhood. As previously discussed, this developmental phase can be an especially trying time for the co-parenting alliance because of the couple's differing views on autonomy and dependency, so it's important to look at this event from the male versus female perspectives. Here's a typical example:

> A group of smart, well-educated mothers sits around a table in a coffee shop. Millie is telling her friends that she wants Jacob, her three-year-old, to start preschool. Though she had decided to work part-time to be with him, she thinks he is bored just being with her, despite her attempts to keep him engaged. But Kenny, her husband, feels she should keep him home longer and that it is too soon for Jacob to go into a group setting. In Kenny's view, "He has his whole life to be away from his parents and home. We agreed to give him a good foundation—us."
>
> Millie is upset that Kenny is pressuring her, insinuating that she is making this decision because she wants more freedom. "He isn't the one with him all day," she tells her sympathetic friends. "He doesn't see, as I do, that he is ready for more. It's one thing to have a certain value about what is good for your child, but

when you see who he actually is, it isn't always the way you expected or even dreamed it would be."

The problem isn't whether he goes to group care or not; odds are that he'd adapt either way. His parents' different perceptions and desires, not to mention Millie's—and most mothers'—own ambivalence make this one of the more agonizing decisions parents face.

How do you know your child is ready for her "second school"? (You were her first, remember?) One of you is likely more enthusiastic about this move than the other. Sometimes the question of being ready is spurious, because the grown-ups have pressing career and/or job concerns and short- and long-range logistics that simply call the question. But if you are able to also factor in the child's readiness, look for some of these signs:

▼ He's curious about the kids he sees playing in groups outside of child-care settings and asks what they are doing, who they are, or "can he play, too?"
▼ His play skills and appetites seem to be outgrowing his toys and your playroom.
▼ She is very attentive to peers she encounters in her daily rounds, and can't get enough of her regular neighborhood chums.
▼ Her interest in books, art, and music is accelerating, as is her demand for more.
▼ "Big boy" or "big girl" talk is increasing, as is the richness of her imaginary play.

Not all of these behaviors have to occur at once for you to consider school, but in various combinations, they suggest he is ready to widen his world, with your help and permission.

Choosing a Program

What should you look for when considering a program? The good ones are focused on helping families introduce their children to the adventure of peer learning in small groups, for a limited time, in a safe, stimulating, and loving environment. A program that scrimps on any of these qualities is not worth its salt, no matter who else sends their children there.

Quality programs aim to broaden the child's social circle outside the family under the watchful eye of caring and competent adults, which involves much more than simply being kind. The *quality* of those adults' understanding of children makes a huge difference in the richness of your child's experience. Most children enjoy being around other kids, so your child's enjoyment alone should not be the main factor in deciding where to send her.

Learning should build on the power of your child's natural curiosity (that's why water tables are so popular) and should heavily emphasize play. Here are some additional pointers:

▼ For two- and three-year-olds, small classes are best because they need close adult supervision. State licensing regulations vary, but there should be no more than eight to ten children under the care of two skilled adults.

▼ It's acceptable for four-year-olds to be in slightly larger groups because they require a little less direct supervision.

▼ Teachers and their aides should have training in early child development and/or education. This does not mean a few continuing education weekend workshops, but well-supervised training lasting over a year, preferably longer. Continuing opportunities for teacher education should be built into the program and expected.

▼ Staff turnover rates should be low; if there is rapid turnover, move on and don't look back.

▼ Though both parents should be welcome any time, the school (and parents) should avoid disruptive visits. Nap or quiet time is never a good moment to show up; lunch is better. You can learn a lot while listening to the kids talk around the table.

▼ Disciplinary methods should fit with your beliefs and be clear, consistent, and readily explained.

▼ Sick-child policies should be clear and adhered to.

▼ The physical plant should be safe and hygienic; the teachers should be trained in basic first-aid, CPR, and choking management.

One of the best ways to tell if a program is of high quality is to see how it handles separations. That's the most vulnerable moment for you and your child, so the staff's ability to help both of you reveals the strength of the connection between their hearts and minds in tending to your child. Mothers find this especially important, because children generally separate from fathers more easily. But fathers should be just as vigilant about the school's policies, because those policies indicate much about its values and philosophy. Your spouse's comfort with the policies and how they are handled will strengthen the co-parenting alliance. Look for a clear policy about drop-offs, good-byes, and pick-ups.

When your child begins a new program, you should be welcome to stay for portions of the first few days or week, diminishing your presence gradually. When it's time to go, don't linger. Help your child cope by leaving when he is ready for you to go. Is there a "good-bye window" from which kids can watch you wave and then *leave you* as they turn back to their morning activities? Are teachers tuned in to handling your clinging child *and* you as you writhe in guilt and ambivalence about leaving her there? Do they emphasize punctual pick-ups for your child's well-being or the staff's convenience?

Even when you and your spouse basically agree on the kind. of atmosphere you want for your child, choosing such a place can be confusing and stressful. Classroom visits are subjective experiences, so it's nearly impossible to compare differences in approaches and philosophies. Don't they all say they are "child-centered" and "developmentally driven" with "individualized approaches to the needs of each child?" The kind of setting you each want for your child will be based on your childhood memories of what worked for you when you were little; your beliefs about what education is (and is not); whether delight or accomplishment is more important; and what you can afford—financially, logistically, and maritally.

A typical parental exchange goes something like this: Mom says, "I just want Sam to be able to play. Childhood is so short; it should be sweet." And dad responds, "I just want Sam to love learning; it's so important to lay that foundation in early childhood." And of course they are both right.

In our combined four decades of preschool and school consultation experience, we have routinely heard the following mantra from the best directors we've known: *Most children will thrive in preschool—regardless of its philosophy—if the staff is experienced, loving, creative, and flexible.* In other words, if the relationships between teachers, between teachers and parents, and most importantly, between teachers and kids are great, then so is the preschool. Is it irrelevant which philosophy is being followed? To mom and/or dad . . . unlikely.

There are five basic if somewhat overlapping approaches rooted in slightly different philosophical ideas about how children learn in groups. We describe them here—not for endorsements or marketing—to stimulate a discussion between you and your spouse about what you each believe is best for your child and family. Then you can go out and get it, or reevaluate your child's current situation, because as your child develops you may need to consider Plan B. Here are the five approaches:

Co-op. In cooperative centers, teams of parents and teachers offer toddlers and preschoolers a robust educational experience. They tend to be less expensive, with modest facilities. The richness of the experience comes from having periodic access to one's own mother or father, as well as exposure to a developing community of teachers and other kids' parents who help keep the co-op going. A co-op requires a major time commitment from parents, and the relationships can be intense and demanding, depending on the number (and group dynamics) of families cycling through the schedule.

Play-based. The most commonly used philosophy in American preschools, its premise is simple: Playful, partially supervised learning encourages social and problem-solving development as kids of (roughly) the same age experiment in small groups to practice preliteracy language, social, emotional, and motor development. The building is usually more elaborate and furnished with unbranded (non-PBS, non-Nickelodeon, non-Disney) toys and games that are rotated often. Teachers support and facilitate play when it gets stuck, but play is mostly driven by the children's ideas.

Montessori. The ideologue Maria Montessori believed that children learn to think for themselves when the value of toys is minimized and children instead work independently in calm, uncluttered places with formally introduced "manipulatives" in the presence of other kids of different ages. (Manipulatives are the carefully designed array of specific puzzles, block collections, musical bells and gongs, and so on that Montessori schools are required to use to encourage creative play in children; they are never referred to as "toys.") Teacher-child ratios are larger, given the emphasis on autonomy, and the rules—often prized by the kids themselves—can be a tad off-putting to the democratically inclined parent. In America, "Montessori" often can mean "Montessori-influenced" because the classic Montessori classroom requires extensive supervision that some American schools don't offer. For the kids who love this approach, and there are many, most parents feel the need to supplement their experience with additional social play opportunities outside school.

Reggio Emilia. An idealistic Italian import named for the small city where, in the 1960s, families, teachers, and town officials reinvented schooling for the young. Working in teams, teachers structure and "curricularize" play-based experience with a primary emphasis on "intentionality." After extensive (videotaped) observations of your child's natural play, the school develops week- to month-long lesson plans to capitalize on and extend the ideas and interests already on your child's mind. There is a strong emphasis on community, and art projects are incredibly expansive. To date, the few such preschools that exist across the United States are confined to major cultural centers, but their influence is growing significantly.

Waldorf. Devoid of competition and pressure to perform, young children will naturally learn from imaginative, peaceful, low-tech surroundings, according to the Austrian philosopher, Rudolf Steiner. Daily storytelling rooted in fairy tales, fables, and myths (yes, there's often a spiritual tone) often leads to exploring the cycles and rhythms of nature and music. Toys are wooden, cloth, and straw (no plastic or rubber) and deliberately anticommercial. The approach discourages media exposure (in and out of preschool), because physical and imaginative growth is what really matters in the first five to six years. Though the teachers often read aloud, they do not encourage preliteracy skills until age five, and don't support reading and writing until kids are six or seven years old.

ULTIMATELY, THE CHOICE of approach is best made based on who you and your spouse agree your child is *now*, and which setting you feel would help him *thrive*, not just grow. He'll do that anyway. We underscore though that all children grow up, and most kids who come from families interested in education generally do well in school. When young children thrive, their brain growth, imaginations, and abilities to cope all get an extra boost. So settling for an OK experience for your child because it is convenient and/or you are not sure what else to do should be carefully considered. Why not make every effort to offer him an enriching experience while you have the chance? You'll have a lot less say in his later school experiences as he ages and attends progressively larger educational facilities. If any of the program descriptions sound right for the son or daughter *you* know, and if you are lucky enough to have some choices, visit the schools together.

Kids and Chores

Before your child begins the next phase of his education (kindergarten), chances are a classic co-parenting dilemma/opportunity will arise: kids' chores.

Around the age of three, children start to ask if they can "help." Of course, if you are in an exhausted multitasking frenzy, the answer is no, even if your lips say yes. It can seem very inefficient to find a way for a child to be meaningfully involved. However, if you are thinking about self-esteem, autonomy, and independence, the answer is, "Of course! I'd love your help." To a child, being useful to the ones you love is the path to positive self-regard, though it is rarely neat, straight, or efficient. Nevertheless, letting kids help leads them to feel good about themselves. Most young kids see helping out with family as a chance to join the family community not as a consumer or a "baby," but as a "big kid" helper. At this age, to them it is an opportunity, a job, maybe a potential profession. Even if it taxes your patience, try to remember that chores can be an important part of your child's wider education. Invite your child into this side-by-side world of esteemed family accomplishment, be it weeding, folding laundry or drying lettuce.

The rub in co-parenting comes not so much from whether you think your child should be allowed to help, but when, how, and for what in return. Parents often have very different ideas about what to expect of their kids or what is acceptable behavior. You and your spouse should discuss and resolve some of these issues before you assign chores so you can support each other when things don't go as planned. Consider:

▼ Should chores be mandated, encouraged, or subsidized?
▼ Should they be rewarded, or is belonging to the community of family its own reward?
▼ Should children be allowed to help with certain tasks even if they are likely to spill, break, or make a mess as much as help?
▼ What do you each think of jobs for kids of a certain age?

Here are some ways to incorporate your child's enthusiasm to help out at home. (Take it while the getting is good; it often disappears just when you are ready to declare your child chore-ready and could use her help.) The jobs should be within the child's physical abilities, just slightly challenging, have a real outcome he can see, and have some real value to you, the child, and the family.

Under twos can pay enough attention to, and largely complete, simple tasks such as:

▼ Wash produce at the sink.
▼ Use a small watering can or hose to water the garden.
▼ Help to brush a (sufficiently patient) dog and fill its food dish.
▼ Push the carpet sweeper (just the mechanical type; they aren't ready to use a vacuum cleaner yet).

Under threes, whose skills are expanding daily, can:

▼ Sort some laundry and silverware (no sharp knives).
▼ Put the toys away in their baskets.
▼ Dust and sweep with a child-sized pan and broom.
▼ Wipe down a counter.
▼ Mash and/or stir food.
▼ Spread jelly or peanut butter.

Under fours are now aware that helping is valued by others. They like to:

▼ Pour water for the table from a small pitcher.
▼ Set the family table.
▼ Use a rolling pin or sifter.
▼ Dig, weed, plant, and water in the garden.

Under fives take great pride in a job done responsibly. They can be relied on to:

▼ Fold laundry.
▼ Hang washed clothes on a clothesline.
▼ Handle a whisk, potato masher, and manual juicer in the kitchen.
▼ Use a sanding block and small hammer at the tool bench (under supervision, of course).

Under sixes are searching for a sense of confidence and are aware of cause and effect in connection with the workings of household tools and tasks. They can ably:

▼ Take out trash from smaller cans.
▼ Ride along for dump or recycling errands.
▼ Run the vacuum with help getting started.
▼ Use the DustBuster (and a real favorite: remove the bag and watch the dust fly!).

Under sevens like to be seen as self-sufficient, and they are beginning to develop early reading and math skills. They can:

▼ Notice for themselves what needs to be done (such as setting the table) and actually do it.
▼ Help younger siblings with chores and read them a story to keep them occupied.
▼ Use measuring cups in cooking and caps for laundry soap or the dispensing of pet food (basically, any measuring task is an adventure).

At these ages, helping out does not need to be mandated, given that it usually comes naturally from the child's passion to master things that matter in daily family life. Also, these jobs do not necessarily need to be compensated. In fact, some developmental economists say that rewarding kids monetarily is counterproductive, because community-building tasks are their own reward. But it's important for you and your spouse to figure out what's right for your family.

> Frank's working-class family taught him at a young age that hard work is important and that kids should be paid for doing chores so that they will want to work all their lives. Jennifer's family took the stance that chores begin at age ten and should be separate from allowance. The two didn't realize they were playing out these experiences, until one day six-year-old Ben told Jennifer he wasn't going to work for her anymore, just for his daddy.
> "Why is that?" she asked him.
> "Because Daddy pays me and you don't."
> It was the first time they realized they each had been operating under different assumptions without checking with the other.

Maybe you found yourself thinking that these decisions play out differently for sons and daughters, just as they do for mothers and fathers. And you would be right. Here's what research has shown[3]:

▼ Boys' brains generally differ from girls' brains in that boys grow more neuronal connections between the areas of the brain that control large muscle movements. The areas of the brain devoted to making spatial and mechanical connections are larger and more fully developed. They develop the ability to write and read about eighteen months later, on average, than do girls. Emotions are processed more slowly through words.

▼ Girls' brains generally differ from boys' brains in that the regions of the brain responsible for verbal fluency (and eventually writing fluency) and for recognizing emotion mature sooner and grow larger. Fine motor skills develop earlier and more extensively. The emotional integration region of the brain is connected earlier and more extensively with word-processing and word-handling skills.

With these differences, it stands to reason that you will involve daughters in some tasks and sons in others. If you have one or more children of each gender, be careful not to let these trends slip into routinely reinforced stereotypes. These early developmental differences tend to even out as children start school.

Don't forget that personality and temperament are as influential as gender—if not more so—in shaping who a child is and what might interest him, in or out of school. So as you deliberate together about where to send your child to kindergarten, remember to place his unique needs and abilities at the top of his list of attributes—not his gender.

The Big K: Kindergarten

How important is kindergarten? "Big school," as it's known in our family, refers to the experience of being one of the "little kids" in a big place where learning and achieving are very big deals indeed. Even though your child may have had years of pre-K or other group learning experience under her belt, now she is expected to be more grown up *and* responsible. As thrilled as she may be to finally be in real school with her new backpack and sneakers, she'll be reminded that she's just starting a race that the big kids have been in for years, and there's just no escaping that occasional feeling that the harder you try, the behinder you get.

After her second week of kindergarten, our youngest daughter sighed that it made her "really tired to be a big little kid." All the readiness talk is tested in a place where the teacher seems more remote and unavailable than she ever did in pre-K. Most early childhood experts agree that probably the hardest adjustments kids have to make (before the preteen hurdle) are to kindergarten and first grade. This surprises many parents who are so proud and relieved that their kid is finally going to regular school—life is good, right? The children aren't going to be quite so needy now that they've reached this threshold. Wrong! If you sense another very important, transitional, co-parenting moment, you're right.

Mothers and fathers are often taken aback by the return of neediness and fearfulness when kindergarten gets underway, but they are often surprised to differing degrees.

> A couple with a new kindergartener was explaining their worry that their son was in the wrong school for him.
>
> Mom: "Ian used to bounce out of bed in the morning and get himself dressed for pre-K. Now we both spend an hour getting his PJ's off and his underwear on. He says he doesn't like school, has no one to eat snack or lunch with, and no one plays with him at recess. On the other hand, he comes home with great artwork, and his teacher says he's a bright spot in her day—talkative, helpful, and eager to learn. I'm worried the fit is wrong for him."
>
> Dad: "I think he's jerking our chain. When I pick him up, I can hardly get him in the car he's so social. Then he asks if we can drive by his old school and gets all whiny when he sees other kids playing on what he calls "my old" jungle gym. At pick-up I try to keep my eye out for potential buddies for him, but he nixes

the idea of a play date and says he doesn't like anyone in his class. I think he's missing the old days and isn't quite ready to move on. He'll eventually get it together no matter where he is."

Ian is anxious about whether he'll be able to make it in the big school while he's still part little kid. Regression alternates with progression as he does his best for his teacher, then brings home all the old "baby" worries to his parents: "Will you still cuddle me and baby me when I need it?" alternates with "I can do it—don't treat me like a baby!" Bed-wetting, tummy aches, and intensified sibling aggression may all recur temporarily. This dilemma was summed up by our nephew, who came home from his first day of kindergarten, kicked off his shoes, flopped down on the couch, and said disappointedly, "I didn't learn to read today."

Although mothers and fathers may feel they want to handle this regression differently, they should understand the significance of this adjustment period for their kids. You need to notice first that most kids whine more with one parent than with the other. They prefer to be babied (usually by mom) only sometimes, making parents' views quite different. Either or both parents can do the following:

▼ Start early (a few weeks or so) to talk with him about kindergarten as the next place to go to learn. Let him know that the routines and the daily schedule will change, but that he'll probably have some of his friends and/or neighbors in his class.

▼ A day or two ahead of opening day, take him to the school and preferably inside to see his classroom. It helps most kids to meet the new teacher and see his classroom during the few open-school days that typically precede the official start. This dry run helps reduce the worry about not knowing where to go, getting lost, "no one knows me," finding the bathroom, etc.

▼ A thorough physical examination by your pediatrician is required in most states. It's also important and symbolic to your child too, that she is growing up, and her vision, hearing, overall physical development, and immunizations are under the watchful eye of caring health professionals. These are milestones you can point to as indicators of her readiness for big school.

▼ Before school starts, reintroduce pencils and paper by asking for help with shopping lists, decorating name cards for dinner, checking off errands on your to-do lists, etc. This is not strictly academic work in nature, but so much of kindergarten table or desk work assumes that this pencil-handling motor skill—with its necessary eye-hand coordination—is in place, so it's a good idea to refresh it for your kids. Besides, it's a good antidote to the "pencil anxiety" so many kindergarten teachers see in the first months of school (forming the letters sufficiently so that they can be recognized as actual letters or numbers by the child and others).

Once school finally starts, your child's needs change. She'll require even more of your attention, not less, and that means spending time alone with each parent doing an activity of her choice, no cell phones or multitasking allowed. It helps your child over the insecurity hump that comes from making this developmental leap and helps her to know that you are involved in her first real school. Volunteer to read to the class, go along on field trips, and let her know you will help her to belong. Finally, let her show off her competencies, old and new. It's a good time to pull out the scrapbooks and old videos of her growing up and celebrate her remarkable progress to date as a marvelous human being. Her creative and imaginative powers are surging ahead, neck and neck with her rigid, concrete stubbornness. She needs to know that you both understand how scary and exciting it is to have these parts of herself harnessed together, and that you are right *there* with her—dependable and loving as ever— even for the new "big little kid."

We haven't focused on discrepancies or gaps between mothers and fathers in their approaches to their children's early schooling because the data show that moms and dads typically both put energy into the teaching, role modeling, and moral training of their kids of both genders at this age. Schools today generally incorporate fathers more than they did a generation ago, offering alternative parent-teacher conference schedules for working parents and inviting fathers for show-and-tell, story reading and telling, welcoming involvement in PTA/PTOs, and so on. If yours does not, figure out why and change it, starting with the principal; your kids need both of you there and engaged. One minor mother/father variation regarding schooling is that a father may place a slightly heavier emphasis on his kid's intellectual achievement.[4] This may simply reflect an attitude difference, not a behavioral one, because there is little observable difference between the ways mothers and fathers support their children's school achievement per se.[5]

Fathers can be effective family representatives if a problem crops up between teacher and child. One of the common indicators of trouble is when your child complains that his teacher "doesn't like me," "doesn't call on me," "doesn't help me with my lunch," or "won't let me go to the bathroom when I really have to go." Typically, these comments mean that he's having some trouble adjusting to the less nurturing, hands-on style of kindergarten versus pre-K teaching and classroom life. You can gently explore the facts with him and with the teacher, separately first and then together. When fathers support finding a solution, it usually happens, given the educational setting's typical receptivity to paternal involvement. When they don't, it puts a lot of pressure on the co-parental alliance.

This is an area where a worried mom may want to leap to action, but sometimes with less success than when dad joins her in the problem solving.

Wendy had met with Evan's teacher several times to figure out why the first-grader felt his teacher didn't like him. Although there seemed no basis for his feelings, Evan continued to complain at home and be unhappy at school. Finally Wendy's husband John got sick of hearing about it, so he went to school with Wendy. Somehow the teacher talked differently to them this time. Having both of them present added some weight (whether it should is another matter), and John moved to solve the problem more directly.

He suggested that he bring Evan into class early the next day to meet with Evan's teacher. Instead of just talking together about the problem, he started the meeting saying, "I just want to say that Evan is thrilled you're his teacher, but sometimes he needs to know more about how you feel about him." The teacher said a few things that she loved about having Evan in class, and then John pulled out his camera and asked to take a picture of them together. The teacher put her arm around Evan, and John took a few pictures of them hugging each other. Wendy couldn't believe that would be sufficient to solve the problem. But Evan began to seem more relaxed and happy. It may have been because of John's intervention, or just that Evan knew all the adults were in his corner together and that his happiness in school must really be important.

If your child is having a problem, it's best to begin by asking for a teacher conference. Go in with an open mind, not a list of accusations. There are at least two sides to every story (assuming mom and dad can agree on theirs). Listen carefully first, and then share your concerns, sticking to the facts. Your child's charms, strengths, and weaknesses as you see them should be part of the conversation with the teacher, who is—until proven otherwise—your child's ally. Usually this tactic is sufficient to open a constructive dialogue, and soon your child will feel more comfortable, knowing his team is right there for him. If not, approach the principal or school guidance counselor.

It's Not Whether You Win or Lose . . .

In co-parenting, we've noticed that fathers feel that children should be able to handle losing at anything, whether it's a game, not being invited to a party, or not being called on in class. Mothers seem more invested in helping the kid not lose more than is absolutely necessary (preserving self-esteem by avoiding disappointment), but fathers often feel it is their duty to instruct their kids in the art of *handling* losing (learning to manage expectations by suffering the occasional disappointment). Why? Fathers often say it's because most kids will do a lot more losing in their lives than winning. The start of school seems to be when fathers take on this lesson in earnest, given the negative social implications for a kid who is not handling losing well. When you can't, you get labeled, well, a loser. After both of you have discussed this topic, consider the following suggestions together:

▼ Play games with your child that require more cooperation than one winner/one loser outcomes, such as Red Rover, Freeze tag, and Simon Says.

▼ Play card games that rely on luck—not skill—such as War. These are instructive as long as you make it clear that winning requires luck, not cheating.

▼ Games such as Life or Monopoly that are purposefully interminable teach kids that it's OK to throw in the towel without feeling like a loser because it's gotten *so boring*.

▼ Opt to sometimes choose a reward for losing (decided at the outset of play) just to keep the game from getting too competitive and to teach and enjoy irony. This shows that it can be fun to upend convention.

▼ Tic-tac-toe is a game to grow with because it uses many developing skills, is simple, requires no batteries, and can be ended and started over quickly. Most adults can control enough of the moves to encourage winning or at least avoid perpetual losing. The same holds true for Connect-the-Dots and checkers (but not chess).

More important than any of these techniques for winning at losing are your attitude and behavior when *you* lose. Throughout this book. we have emphasized that parental power to positively or negatively influence our children is greatest through what we *do*, not what we *say*—no matter how timely or cleverly it may be uttered. Graceful, honest losers know and teach that there are no mistakes—only lessons.

Add-ons After School

Once school is up and running your family's life, we come face to face with the *after* school beast and must either grab it by the horns or risk being gored. The American debate about overscheduled children is no longer news and will not be settled in our lifetimes. Why? Because there is no "right" answer that will fit all families and all their children. Mothers and fathers are often lost from the beginning of this debate because many are hopelessly embroiled in multitasking lives themselves, rendering a level of personal activity and productivity unimagined by their parents and grandparents. To help mothers and fathers think rationally about this issue—given the chorus of (largely uninvited and ill-informed) advisers screaming "the earlier you get started at ___ the better"—we offer the following observations:

▼ The capacity to be alone and comfortable in one's skin is learned from within and takes practice, time, and solitude. It is also a pillar of mental health.

▼ Starting organized activities (physical or artistic) too early, no matter how stridently requested, is a setup for physical and mental burnout.

▼ Kids' appetites for new and old activities vary widely and often.

▼ Third grade is generally the most promising portal to the busy life, given the emotional and physical maturity third-graders can then bring to the field or the studio. At this point, they (usually) understand that practice is for their skills and competence, not your happiness.

▼ Varied diets of activity are healthier and more fun. One physical (soccer), one artistic (art, band), one social (scouts), and one moral (religious or spiritual education) are a good mix and something the family and child can generally handle logistically. The child has equally demanding needs (including homework and the need for some down or alone time—see first point).

▼ Multitasking for kids is acceptable only until it starts creating even slightly *un*manageable levels of stress. Then it quickly becomes overwhelming and counterproductive, instead of useful training for a rich and complex life.

The range of development that is the focus of this book obviously figures largely into the equation of how much and how soon. But because many parents feel so hectored by this issue, you should think about this together to get the balance right for your child. Know that you may make some mistakes—and learn some lessons—along the way. Some other variables that influence what should eventually make it onto the family calendar include:

▼ Your child's energy and passion level (weekly activities can be seasonal, offering a welcome break during other times of the year, or year-round, depending on the child).
▼ *Your* inherent activity or energy level.
▼ Your values as an individual and a couple regarding "finishing what you start" versus "experimenting while the child is young."
▼ Your own tolerance for multitasking as a way of being productive.
▼ Important activities shared with your child (making music together, sharing a sport) aren't included in the weekly tally because they count as family time, not extracurricular activity.

Top Ten Education-related Mistakes (...er, Lessons) Parents Make
▼

1. Emphasizing achievement at the expense of wonder and delight in learning.
2. Choosing educational experiences based on what your social circle is doing.
3. Selecting options for early-learning possibilities without doing your due diligence. (Your education in this regard is as important at every step as your child's.)
4. Settling for a mediocre preschool experience for your child because it's convenient, "pretty good," or only viewed as "group babysitting."
5. Not exposing your child early enough to daily doses of art, music, and time alone.
6. Letting your worries about the future (e.g., college) dictate your decisions about what your child needs now to stay in love with learning.
7. Ignoring your young child's drive to be a helping, competent member of the family because it slows everything down.
8. Sticking too closely to what worked for you as a child. (He is not you, and you have worked hard to protect him since birth from your less favorable experiences and attributes.)
9. Failing to talk through your differing desires and perceptions as parents about schools; waiting instead until there is a problem. (Don't leave the decision to only one of you, and don't accept the responsibility for being the "decider" at the expense of involving both of you.)
10. Rushing your child into too much, too fast and too soon.

If you are guilty of some of the mistakes listed in the box, don't worry too much—you are hardly alone. There are no mistakes, only lessons. Two heads and hearts are better than one, so work together on adjusting your course of action next time. Meanwhile, the point of a lesson is to learn. Talk with your spouse about what you have learned together, what you will do differently from now on and next time, and how wonderful it is to know you have lots more chances.

12

▼

Epilogue: For Divorce Prevention
Keeping the Parenting Partnership First So It Lasts

We BEGAN THIS BOOK on the premise that co-parenting is good for children *and* their parents, while noting likewise that marital satisfaction drops—often sharply—after couples make the transition to parenthood. But that's hardly end of story; there are many chapters in between, and much can be done to beat the sober statistics of marital brevity.

Wait to Have Another Baby Until You Are Both Ready

If you are reading this book, you probably already have, or are thinking seriously about having, a child. Or another one or two may yet be in the works. For these subsequent children, as well as for all the parenting that lies ahead for the child or children you have, you both should feel ready, as opposed to helplessly bowing to the intimidating pressure of the biological clock. Second and third children can increase family joy (if planned), stress, and complexity beyond most parents' imaginations. One reason marital happiness declines is that both partners don't feel the same about having their lives turned inside out. If parents haven't talked about what they really want in this next phase of their lives, if you disagree about whether to have a child at this particular time, or if one or both of you are ambivalent about even starting or expanding your family, odds are that the marital satisfaction will dip further, if not nose-dive.

A key lesson from James McHale's "Families Through Time" study was the reliable prediction of successful co-parenting that could be made by how and whether the couple had discussions *before* the baby was born. When couples' prebaby notions were disparate, and they didn't agree on how they would handle sticky parenting issues, the study could predict with confidence that the coalition would be shaky by the time the child was two-and-a-half years old The study could also predict the state of the co-parenting alliance when the child was a toddler by looking at whether the parents—especially the mother—referred to their unborn child as "my" baby versus "our" baby. Did mom say to the kicking fetus, "Oh, you are Mama's super-strong girl?" Did dad put his head on her abdomen and talk to "his" son about the Cubs?

Perhaps you and your spouse started off in different places but have since found your footing on a path of your choosing that is taking you in good directions for your family; despite some tensions, you genuinely enjoy family time together and believe it outweighs what you gave up for it. Or maybe one or both of you aren't quite sure yet that this life is making you as happy as you'd hoped. If this is a concern, you may want to review together the advice we've offered throughout this book on ways to nurture your parenting partnership.

Find Lasting Strength in the Co-parenting Alliance

Myriad families who have attended counseling sessions for and about their children have experienced temporary improvement in their kids' behavior and emotions, only to watch them erode weeks or months later after the counseling stops (usually because the insurance runs out or someone decides the crisis is over). There are various reasons for this slippage. One is that you haven't yet reached the root of the problem, and you need more or a different kind of counseling. While treating a child's symptoms can be therapeutic and highly valuable, we maintain that family systems issues are often missed when attention is focused predominantly on the child, excluding of the rest of the family.

Many mental health professionals currently licensed to work with families of young children are heavily preoccupied with "attachment theory." Even those progressive enough to include fathers in parental meetings tend to emphasize repair of "attachment disorders" without sufficient attention given to strengthening the critical infrastructure of the co-parenting alliance. Addressing the needs of the co-parenting alliance and mobilizing and applying its incredible resources on behalf of a vulnerable child can be highly effective. Clearly one piece of advice we are giving is that if you are going to enter counseling, make sure your therapist is knowledgeable and respectful of co-parenting couple relationships. This can be done by working primarily with your child, the two parents as a couple, or your family. It is the therapist's attitude and awareness of the salience of co-parenting issues, not merely his or her theoretical bent, that counts.

For those of you who don't intend to enter into professional counseling, there are things you can do at home to form a closer, healthier partnership. As we discussed in previous chapters, men often have to take responsibility for changing direction and responding to their wives' needs, because of the way gender roles are enacted. When a man can change in a way that his spouse esteems, the benefits are great for both partners and, ultimately, their child. The family gains the benefit of the parenting alliance; the couple gains the benefits of a happier relationship. When the parents stay together not only to "do their time" until their child is older, but with increased appreciation for their partner and marriage, the benefits to the child grow like compound interest. When a relationship is unhappy, everyone loses; women may lose more than men. Women seek to leave relationships more often than do men. A bad marriage is particularly toxic for women. Compared to men, women in bad marriages are more depressed, drink more, have higher cholesterol levels, lower immune functions, and are more likely to have heart attacks and strokes.[1]

Why did we begin with what *fathers* need to do to change? Recall in chapter 1, we learned that in McHale's research into the first few months of a baby's and his family's life, fathers' emotional resources appeared to be particularly important assets for developing a parenting partnership. When fathers were strong in the face of adversity, the family was strong. Now we've discussed that when marriages are unhappy, the mother is likely to bail out first, especially among educated and middle- to high-income parents.

Clearly, both partners should aim to improve their spouse's emotional resilience during tougher times. You can begin by offering your unconditional support when your partner is facing difficulties. Go the extra mile: Put away his laundry even though it irks you. Take out the trash even though it is "his" job. Dads can do the same: Bring her popcorn and a cup of tea while she is doing the bills. Pick up the kids from school and tell her to go to the gym or take a walk alone or with a friend—among many mothers' favorite decompression strategies. Other favorites are: Encourage your spouse to get away for a night or a day with or without you. Get a massage, go out with friends, and spend money on something frivolous, though not out of economic reach. Make sure he has an ice-fishing weekend with his buddies and that she has a hiking weekend in the mountains with just the girls.

Both of you are probably busy all the time, but it may *feel* uneven. Both of you are often starving for time in these early years to focus on yourselves or one another. In his book, *Stumbling on Happiness*, Daniel Gilbert reported that parents rated sleep, eating, shopping, and exercise as more pleasurable than taking care of their children.[2] At first blush you might say to yourself, "That's horrible. Even exercise?" But when you stop and think about it, it isn't always *fun* to take care of toddlers and preschoolers all day long. Even when it is fun, it is also demanding and depleting. Having a few moments to yourself, to do just about anything else, is a highly regarded respite.

It isn't about *not* loving to be with children. Most of us would say that parenting is the most important, most cherished aspect of our lives. But there is a foreground and a background to every piece of art. In early family life, the big picture is quite lovely. But when you look too closely, it can appear like a patch of a pointillism painting: Up close, the dots are but spongy, sloppy little blotches of color. You have to step back to appreciate the whole image. Some tips:

▼ Do the small things that help your spouse stay organized: charge her cell phone when you find it lying around, put his flash drive back in his briefcase where he usually looks for it. These small gestures come back to you both in large rewards.

▼ Agree on some nonverbal signal that indicates to your spouse that you have reached your limit with the kids and need help ASAP. Marsha or Kyle will flash a stupid smile at the other person, who will then pick up the pieces without undermining or making light of the issue, whatever it may be. Marsha has been known to put her head down on the kitchen table and say, "I'm not getting up until you carry me." She doesn't mean it literally, of course, but she does mean she needs help to move on. Getting support in the form of assistance or "a break" quickly and without having to verbalize the specific need can be reassuring and very loving.

▼ When a conflict is brewing, be the parent who chooses to listen first to the other and forgo saying your piece until you've heard and digested your spouse's complaint. This is extremely hard to do, but a good way to avoid "piling on" the grievances ("And another thing . . ."). After you've addressed your spouse's issue, find time in the near future to bring up *your* beef, which is equally valid. Sometimes you can take both issues on at the same time; other days it is just too much to deal with in tandem.

▼ List positive outcomes from some of the most annoying things your partner does and how those annoyances are linked to his or her most endearing traits (for example, by not cleaning up the kitchen when he said he would, he had ten extra minutes that he spent reading to your child).

The Upside of Your Mate's Downfalls
▼

▼ He often runs out of gas in the car, but he does it trying to fit in one more errand for the kids or her. He's always thinking of them.

▼ She loses the most expensive pieces of jewelry he gives her, but she never loses sight of the things that need to be done for his extended family as well as hers.

▼ She doesn't cook very well, but she has taught their children to love trying new foods at home and in restaurants (when her creations really don't work out). They never know what she'll come up with next.

▼ He leaves piles all over the house, but somehow he can always find just what they're looking for.

▼ He never finishes things around the house when he says he will, but one thing that slows him down is the way he involves the kids in every aspect of the task. They have learned so much from him.

▼ She talks too much to the kids, instead of just disciplining them. She drives them a bit crazy, but because of her they understand their feelings and are able to hold their own in an argument with anybody.

Learning from Divorce

Ironically, as we mentioned earlier, co-parenting between couples has mostly been emphasized only after the marriage ends. It is one of the primary concerns of the divorce industry: how to get parents to accept the important status of both parents in the child's life, regard each other more favorably, work together for the benefit of the child, and reduce conflict—especially conflict *regarding* the child. Marsha developed a co-parenting education course for separating or divorcing couples for the Collaborative Divorce Project in Connecticut, which included male and female support groups. The men who participated talked about how compelling it was to be able to share their experiences with other men who were in similar situations. The women commented that hearing about other couples made them see that their ex-spouses were not any better or worse than a lot of other ex-spouses. They realized that many of their co-parenting problems were not attributable to a spouse's lackluster insensitivity but, instead, were a function of how the pace and needs of early family life contributed to a loss of shared views and dreams, leading to a sense of isolation. There is affirming power inherent in seeing that you are not alone, that others experience similar issues, and that there are multiple ways of handling these issues so that they work for both partners.

But creating positive co-parenting can happen just as effectively, and preventively, by couples who are still together. Reinforcing the influential research by McHale and the Gottmans discussed in chapter 1, Penn State University's Mark Feinberg and Marni Kan have shown that couples who support each other's parenting and don't deviate from the agreed-on plan for how to raise their kids make the most successful co-parents.[3] They also report less distress in the parent-child relationship. Both partners, but mothers in particular, report greater personal well-being. The power of groups of the kind Marsha used in her intervention research can stimulate positive communication between couples and positive attitudes in married couples as well, with long-lasting positive impact on the family. Phil and Carolyn Cowan's seminal intervention study *Becoming a Family* followed couples from the initial transition to parenthood through their children's transition to school. It showed how couples' support groups can be used to reinforce the couple's primacy as an influence on positive parenting attitudes and behaviors. The study's support group had beneficial effects on the couples—including on the longevity of their marriage—for many years after.[4] While not all parents are going to find a group they wish to participate in, all parents can learn from the key message that cuts across marriage and divorce research: Namely, paying attention to the co-parenting alliance early in a family's life is important, and talking, listening, and solving problems together inoculate parents from some of the stresses this period of life inevitably provides.

Here are some parenting lessons that can help you avoid letting things get to the point of "no return," while strengthening your children's well-being through a healthy parenting partnership.

Lesson 1: Don't Get Caught in the Fifty-Fifty Trap. Don't let your belief that it is the other parent's turn to do something with or for your child get in the way of doing it yourself. Your child usually does not take an inventory of which parent played with him last or picked him up at school. If one of you is there and can explain why the other one isn't, your child will not feel slighted, as long as this doesn't happen all the time. For example, you could tell your daughter, "Kim, I'm sorry Daddy can't be at your game, but he is excited to hear all about it. We'll tell him everything when we get home."

Lesson 2: Pick Up the Slack. It's the job of each parent to help the other be the best parent he or she can be. This means filling in the gaps. Dad says, "Oops. Mommy meant to make your sandwich, but she got hung up doing something that couldn't wait. Here, I'll make it for you."

Lesson 3: Back Each Other Up. Your child's self-esteem and respect for you are the first and second casualties when you put her in the middle of a spousal disagreement or belittle your spouse in front of her. Leave your anger at the door when you enter your home. One of the great and necessary conditions to sustain among families in Jewish tradition is *Shalom bayit*—peace in the home. Some Talmudic scholars feel it is primarily the father's responsibility.

The wrong way to express your smoldering anger is to say: "Did Daddy pack that bathing suit you don't like anymore? He usually forgets little details like that. He doesn't mean to; he's just always thinking about work. I'll remind him again which one you like." The result: Your child feels as if his father doesn't care enough about him to get the details right, which makes him feel bad about himself for not being worth the trouble to get it right, and angry at his father. Moreover, when he's old enough to realize it, he'll also be mad at mom for reminding him that he wasn't blessed with a dad who puts his child first.

It would be better to say: "Oh, you were embarrassed about that bathing suit Daddy packed. He must have forgotten, but you know he'd never embarrass you on purpose. He'll feel really bad when you tell him." This doesn't let dad off the hook, nor does it seem as if mom is pretending it didn't happen. Instead, mom is leaving it up to the child to take it up with dad (whom she trusts will respond appropriately). This message will be easier for dad to hear because it's coming from his child. This approach also gives father and child a chance to talk about a reminder for next time, which just might improve their communication, help dad remember the details he seems to forget, and keep the conflict out of the parents' relationship. If you married someone who is often insensitive, your child may have a lifetime of living with that, just as you do. So he may as well start dealing with it.

Lesson 4: Listen to Your Child. No one wants you to co-parent effectively as much as your child does. Given half a chance, she will tell you what she thinks you each do best, what the other parent does better, and why she prefers one or the other of you for a particular activity, moment, or reason. She'll have lots of examples that to her are just part of the package and the fun of being lucky enough to have two parents who are raising her. You'll also realize that for every time you feel self-righteous about what your spouse "doesn't do enough of," your child will let you know how you let her down too. More times than not, neither of you let her down hard. You are tougher critics than she'll ever be. So lighten up. It makes parenting more fun.

WE HOPE THAT YOU have come to see that the differences between men and women are, paradoxically, universal. They help make the world go round. You should now have a better understanding of and appreciation for those differences and their great value to your children and your family. We trust that you have developed a better sense of which fights are worth having and which are not, especially over the long haul, and that you have some fresh ideas about how to make sure your child is getting the best of both you and your spouse. Most important, we hope that you are strengthened in the conviction that the family you have created is precious beyond measure and that your parenting partnership will not only endure, but be the source of real satisfaction and happiness.

Appendix A
Ideas About Parenting*

Gertrude Heming, Philip A. Cowan, and Carolyn Pape Cowan

These items describe a number of different ideas about raising children. Please indicate your opinion and what you think is your partner's opinion by using the following scale:

Very much agree		Moderately agree		Neither agree nor disagree		Moderately disagree		Very much disagree
1	2	3	4	5	6	7	8	9

My Opinion   Partner's Opinion

1. _____ _____ I have a definite clear position on how to raise children.
2. _____ _____ If parents are ready to go out for the evening, even if the child reacts by crying and screaming, it is best for them to continue with their plans.
3. _____ _____ I try to stop my child from playing rough games or doing things where he or she may get hurt.
4. _____ _____ The idea that a child should show "respect for authority" is as valid today as it was yesterday.
5. _____ _____ Children should be encouraged to express their anger as well as their more pleasant feelings.
6. _____ _____ I like to see my child dressed so that he or she fits in and looks like other children.
7. _____ _____ In general, parents today reason too much with their children.
8. _____ _____ I think it is best if the father rather than the mother does the serious disciplining of the child.

My Opinion	Partner's Opinion	

9. _____ _____ I feel confident that I know the right way to bring up my children.

10. _____ _____ Too much cuddling spoils a child.

11. _____ _____ With regard to my child(ren), I would characterize my discipline as fairly permissive.

12. _____ _____ I try to anticipate situations that can cause my child pain or discomfort and help my child to avoid them if at all possible.

13. _____ _____ When my child puts off going to bed, I try to be patient even when I am tired.

14. _____ _____ A child should be able to question the authority of his or her parents.

15. _____ _____ I let my child know how ashamed and disappointed I am when he or she misbehaves.

16. _____ _____ I am more concerned about my child being happy than about what he or she accomplishes.

17. _____ _____ It is best for a preschool child to be cared for almost entirely by his or her own parents.

18. _____ _____ I worry about my child a lot when I am not with him/her.

19. _____ _____ I sometimes feel that I am too involved with my child.

20. _____ _____ I would feel quite comfortable buying a doll for my son and a truck for my daughter.

21. _____ _____ I want my child to be different from the crowd.

22. _____ _____ I prefer to avoid fights with my child.

23. _____ _____ Bottle-feeding is more satisfying to a child than breast-feeding.

24. _____ _____ Parents should keep a firm hold on their child's expression of angry feelings.

25. _____ _____ I select certain television programs for my child to watch and do not permit the watching of others.

26. _____ _____ In a preschool, day-care center, or elementary school, a child must learn to conform to the rules and regulations.

27. _____ _____ When I am very angry with my child, I let him/her know it quite clearly.

	My Opinion	Partner's Opinion	
28.	_____	_____	I believe in giving my child considerable choice in selecting clothes to wear for the day.
29.	_____	_____	I express affection by hugging, kissing, and holding my child.
30.	_____	_____	I want to try to tell my child what to do as little as possible.
31.	_____	_____	I talk it over and reason with my child when he/she misbehaves.
32.	_____	_____	When I yell at my child, I often feel bad because I lost my temper.
33.	_____	_____	A child should respect parents because they are parents.
34.	_____	_____	A parent should not allow his or her mind to be changed by a child.
35.	_____	_____	A certain amount of frustration and upset is necessary for a child's emotional growth. Because of this, parents should not be too protective.
36.	_____	_____	Little boys can be expected to cry as often as little girls.
37.	_____	_____	I wish my child did not have to grow up so fast.
38.	_____	_____	Parents can expect to see differences between boy and girl children no matter how much they try to raise them alike.
39.	_____	_____	Children have a right to do what they want with their own toys.
40.	_____	_____	If left frequently with adults other than parents, my child is likely to become insecure.
41.	_____	_____	I react spontaneously to what my child does; I do not try to formulate a general policy beforehand.
42.	_____	_____	I expect a great deal of my child.
43.	_____	_____	It is all right for the mother of a young child to work half-time or more as long as the parents have good child care.
44.	_____	_____	I care less than most parents I know about having my child obey me.
45.	_____	_____	When a child continues to get out of bed after being sent to bed two or three times, he or she should be punished for disobedience.

My   Partner's
Opinion   Opinion

46. _____   _____   Children should be held when they are upset so that they will be secure in their parents' love for them.

47. _____   _____   Taking care of a child is much more work than pleasure.

48. _____   _____   Children are frequently so demanding that their parents have no time for anything else.

49. _____   _____   I encourage my child always to do his or her best.

50. _____   _____   A child should not talk back to a parent.

51. _____   _____   A parent should be direct with a child, even when that leads to open conflict.

52. _____   _____   Mothers have a special knack for raising daughters.

53. _____   _____   A child's needs must come before the parent's needs.

54. _____   _____   I think one has to let a child take many chances as he or she grows up and tries new things.

55. _____   _____   I think it is best if the mother rather than the father is the one with the most authority over the children.

56. _____   _____   If my child has a temper tantrum, I have a great deal of difficulty in quieting him or her down.

57. _____   _____   It is all right for parents to go on a vacation together and leave the child with a good sitter.

58. _____   _____   When a child is called, he/she should come immediately.

59. _____   _____   I encourage my child to be independent of me.

60. _____   _____   Some children can only be made to obey by scolding and punishment.

61. _____   _____   I believe that children should be able to have secrets from their parents.

62. _____   _____   A child should be able to do as he or she likes as much as possible.

63. _____   _____   I control my child by warning about the bad things that can happen to him or her.

64. _____   _____   One of the joys of parenthood is encouraging a child's natural curiosity.

My   Partner's
Opinion   Opinion

65. _____ _____ I like to see a child have opinions and express them, even to adults.

66. _____ _____ I won't insist that my child eat food that he or she really dislikes.

67. _____ _____ I trust my child to behave as he or she should, even when I am not there.

68. _____ _____ An adult cannot expect a child to obey a rule that the child does not understand.

69. _____ _____ Fathers have a special knack for raising sons.

70. _____ _____ I find some of my greatest satisfaction in my child.

71. _____ _____ I expect my child to do well in school academically.

72. _____ _____ I expect my child to get along with his or her school peers.

73. _____ _____ Parents should be directly involved in supervising their children's school work.

The last items describe things that most children do. Using the following code, show the age at which you would expect a child to do them.

A = 3 years old or younger   D = 5 to 6 years old
B = 3 to 4 years old   E = 6 to 7 years old
C = 4 to 5 years old   F = 7 years old or older

My   Partner's
Opinion   Opinion

74. _____ _____ Choose own clothes for school.

75. _____ _____ Resolve a dispute with a friend without help from adults.

76. _____ _____ Go to a neighbor's without supervision.

77. _____ _____ Care for his/her own room.

78. _____ _____ Make his/her own bed.

79. _____ _____ Stop sucking his/her thumb.

	My Opinion	Partner's Opinion	
80.	_____	_____	Help take care of a younger child.
81.	_____	_____	Have a regular role in household duties and responsibilities.
82.	_____	_____	Get ready for bed without help.
83.	_____	_____	Sleep over at another child's house.

*Items adapted from scales by Diana Baumrind, Jeanne Block, and Gertrude Heming

Appendix B
Parental Profile Answers
"What Grown-ups Understand About Child Development"

National Benchmark Survey; "What Grown-ups Understand About Child Development," conducted by DYG, Inc., for Civitas, Brio, and Zero to Three: National Center for Infants, Toddlers and Families, 2000

1. Prenatal age
2. Right from birth
3. First year has major impact
4. One to three months of age
5. a. Definitely false
   b. Definitely false
6. Play is extremely important to ALL ages
7. While science can't give us exact ratings, research tells us that most of these activities are very effective in helping children become good learners. The two exceptions: current computer activities and memory flashcards are the least effective learning prompts
8. A and B are likely; C is not
9. Not misbehaving
10. A and C are likely; B and D are not
11. No, too young
12. Should not be expected
13. Six-year-old not capable
14. Six-month-old too young to spoil
15. B is spoiling
16. Never appropriate
17. Definitely true
18. 18 months or more
19. Definitely false
20. Definitely true
21. Definitely true

Notes

Chapter 1

1. McHale, J.P. (2007). *Charting the Bumpy Road of Coparenthood: Understanding the Challenges of Family Life*. Washington, DC: Zero to Three Press.
2. McHale.
3. Gottman, J., & Gottman, J., (2007). *And Baby Makes Three*. New York: Crown Publishers.
4. McHale.
5. McHale.
6. McHale.
7. McHale.
8. Gottman & Gottman.
9. Levine, J.A. (1998). *Working Fathers: New Strategies for Balancing Work and Family*. New York: Harcourt Brace & Company.

Chapter 2

1. Swain, J., Taskgin, E., Mayes, L., Feldman, R., Constable, R., and Leckman, J. (2008). "Maternal brain response to own baby cry." *Journal of Child Psychology and Psychiatry*, 49, 1042–1052.
2. Yogman, M.W., Kindlon, D. and Earls, F. (1995). "Father involvement and cognitive/behavioral outcomes of preterm infants." *Journal of the American Academy of Child and Adolescent Psychiatry*, 34, 58–66.
3. Cowan, P.A., Cowan, C.P., Ablow, J.C., and Johnson, V.K. (April 2005). *The Family Context of Parenting in Children's Adaptation to Elementary School*. New York: Lawrence Erlbaum.
4. Pruett, K.D. (1987). *The Nurturing Father*. New York: Warner.
5. Pruett, K.D. (2001). *Fatherneed*. New York: Broadway.
6. Farrell, W. (2001). *Father and Child Reunion*. New York: Tarcher/Putnam.
7. Christofferson, M.N. (1995). "Growing Up With Dad: A Comparison of Children 3–5 years old living with their mothers or fathers." *Childhood*, 5, 41–54.
8. Sakardi, A, Kristiansson, R., Oberklaid, F., and Bremberg, S. (2007) "Fathers' involvement and children's developmental outcomes: A systematic review of longitudinal studies." *Acta Paediatrica* 97, no. 2. 153–158. Retrieved online at http://www3.interscience.wiley.com/journal/119405387, April 12, 2009.
9. McHale.

10. Shonkoff, J.P., and Phillips, D.A. (2000). *From Neurons to Neighborhoods; The Science of Early Childhood Development.* Washington, DC: National Academy Press.
11. McHale, 189.
12. Scull, C. and Alongi, D. Bruzgyte, N., and McHale, J. (May 2006). "Infant and family process predictors of ADHD symptoms at 30 months." Paper presented at the meeting of the Association for Psychological Science, New York.
13. Gottman & Gottman.
14. Pruett, *Fatherneed.*
15. Mead, Margaret. (1949, 1967). *Male and Female.* New York: Harper Collins.

Chapter 3

1. McHale, 320.
2. Ball, F.L.J. (1984). "Understanding and satisfaction in marital problem solving: A hermeneutic inquiry." Unpublished doctoral dissertation. University of California, Berkeley.
3. Coontz, S. (2005). *Marriage, A History.* New York: Penguin Books, 282.
4. Levine.

Chapter 4

1. Sand, M., Fisher, W., Rosen, R., Heiman, J., Eardley, I. (2008). "Erectile dysfunction and constructs of masculinity and quality of life in the multinational men's attitudes to life events and sexuality (MALES) study." *Journal of Sexual Medicine,* 5. 583–594.
2. Gottman and Levenson produced a series of articles on this subject from the late 1980s through the mid 1990s. A seminal scholarly paper is Gottman, J.M. and Levinson, R.W. (1992). "Marital processes predictive of later dissolution: Behavior, physiology, and health." *Journal of Personality and Social Psychology,* 63 (2), 221–223.
3. Their work was summarized in a more rudimentary way for the lay audience in Gottman and Gottman's *And Baby Makes Three,* 76–81.
4. Gottman, J.M. (1994). *What Predicts Divorce?* Hillsdale, N.J: Lawrence Erlbaum.
5. Gottman, *Divorce,* 129.

Chapter 5

1. Lamb, M. (1977). "The development of mother-infant attachments in the second year of life." *Developmental Psychology,* 13, 637–648.
2. McHale.
3. See Pruett, M.K., Arthur, L., and Ebling, R. (2007). "The hand that rocks the cradle: Maternal gatekeeping after divorce." *Pace University Law Review,* 27(4), 709–739.
4. Adapted from a gatekeeping questionnaire designed by Kyle and Marsha Pruett for Marsha's The Collaborative Divorce Project.
5. This excerpt was derived from the Mom as Gateway curriculum, developed by Marsha Pruett, Lauren Arthur, and Ryan Barker in conjunction with Chris Brown and Erik Vecere from the National Fatherhood Institute (NFI). Mom as Gateway was developed as a module for the 24/7 Dad™ program of the NFI. It can be obtained from the Internet in its entirety at www.fatherhood.org.

Chapter 6

1. Zero To Three, Civitas, and Brio Corporation. (2000). What Grown-ups Understand About Child Development: A National Benchmark Survey. Washington, DC: Zero to Three Press.
2. Ennemoser, M. and Schneider, W. (2007). "Relations of television viewing and reading: findings from a 4-year longitudinal study." *Journal of Educational Psychology*, 99, 349–368; and Pecora, N., Murray, J., and Wartella, E. (eds.). (2007). *Children and Television: Fifty Years of Research*. New York, Routledge.
3. Zimmerman, F.J. (2007). "Parental influences on youth television viewing." *Journal of Pediatrics*, 151(4), 334–336.
4. Hunziker, U.A. and Barr, R.A. (1986). "Increased carrying reduces infant crying; a randomized controlled trial." *Pediatrics*, 77(5), 641–648.
5. Field, T. (1982). "Social perception and responsivity in early infancy" in Field, T. et al. *Review of Human Development*. New York: Wiley, 20–31.
6. Sroufe, L.A. (1985). "Attachment classification from the perspective of infant/caregiver relationships and infant temperament." *Child Development*, 56, 1–14.
7. McHale, 235.
8. Emde, R.N. and Hewitt, J.K. (eds.). (2001). *Infancy to Early Childhood: Genetic and Environmental Influences on Developmental Change*. New York: Oxford University Press.

Chapter 7

1. Maccoby, E.E. (1999). *The Two Sexes: Growing Up Apart, Coming Together*. Cambridge, MA: Belknap Press of Harvard University Press, 16.
2. Baumrind, D., (1971). "Current patterns of parental authority." *Developmental Psychology*, 4(2), 1–103.
3. Baumrind.
4. Pollack, W. (1999). *Real Boys: Rescuing Our Sons From the Myths of Boyhood*. New York: Owl/Henry Holt.
5. The American Academy of Child and Adolescent Psychiatry. (1998). *Your Child: What Every Parent Needs to Know About Childhood Development from Birth to Preadolescence*. New York: HarperCollins.
6. Lepper M., and Greene, D. (2003). "Undermining children's intrinsic interest with extrinsic reward: A test of the 'overjustification' hypothesis." *Journal of Personality and Social Psychology*, 28(1), 129–137.
7. Coloroso, B. (2002). *Kids Are Worth It*. New York, HarperCollins
8. J. Heinrichs. (2006). "Argue with me!" *Wondertime*, Winter issue.
9. "The U.S. teens market: Understanding the changing lifestyles and trends of 12- to 19-year-olds." (2002). www.packagedfacts.com.

Chapter 8

1. Dorsey, B. "Conscious Fathering." (2000) http://www.parenttrust.org/for-families/education-support/expectant-new-parent-program/concious-fathering. Retrieved March 5, 2009.
2. Field, T.
3. Karp, H., MD (2003). *The Happiest Baby on the Block* DVD, and/or http://www.associatedcontent.com/article/203745/harvey_karp_knows_how.html. Retrieved March 5, 2009.
4. Maccoby, 135.

5. Fivush, R. (1993). "Emotional content of parent-child conversations about the past." in Nelson, C.A. (ed.), *Memory and Effect in Development. Minnesota Symposium on Child Psychology*, 26, 39–78. Minneapolis, University of Minnesota.
6. Dunn, J., Brown, J., and Munn, P. (1987) "Conversations About Feeling States Between Mothers and Their Young Children." *Developmental Psychology*, 23, 132–139.
7. Buck, R. (1975). "Non-verbal communication of affect in children." *Journal of Personality and Social Psychology*, 31, 644–653
8. Pruett, K.D. (1999). *Me, Myself, and I*. New York: Goddard Press.
9. Maccoby.
10. Reese, E. & Fivush, R. (1993). "Parental styles of talking about the past." *Developmental Psychology*, 29, 596–606.
11. Maccoby, 20.

Chapter 9

1. Feldman, R., Swain, J., Mayes, J. (2005). "Interaction Synchrony and Neural Circuits Contribute to Shared Intentionality." *Behavior and Brain Sciences*, 28(5), 697–698.
2. Brazelton, T. Personal communication with Kyle Pruett. See also *Touchpoints: The Essential Reference* (1992). New York: Addison-Wesley, 422–427.
3. American Academy of Pediatrics. (1998). *The Complete Guide to Caring for Your Baby and Young Child*. New York: Bantam.
4. Ferber, R. (1985). *Solve Your Child's Sleep Problems*. New York: Fireside, 160.

Chapter 10

1. Maccoby, 282.
2. Grolnick, W., Cole, R., and Schwartzman,P. (1990). "Playing with Fire: A Developmental Assessment of Children's Fire Understanding and Experience." *Clinical Journal of Child Psychology*, 19(2), 128–135.
3. Wolff, A. (2005). "Get on the Stick." *Sports Illustrated*, April 25, 2005
4. Brazelton, T.B. and Greenspan, S. I. (2000). *The Irreducible Needs of Children: What Every Child Must Have to Grow, Learn, and Flourish*. Cambridge, MA: Perseus, 49.
5. Brazelton and Greenspan,128.
6 Shifrin, D. Three-Year study documents nature of TV violence, *American Academy of Pediatrics News*, August 1998; and July 26, 2000: Joint statement on the Impact of Entertainment Violence on Children, Congressional Public Health Summit.
7. Smith, J and Schneider, B (2004). "The Effectiveness of Whole-School Anti-bullying programs: Synthesis of Evaluation Research." *School Psychology Review*, 33, 548–561.
8. Kalman, I. (2005). *Bullies to Buddies: How to Turn Your Enemies into Friends*. Staten Island, NY: Wisdom Pages Publisher.

Chapter 11

1. PTA/Roper (2007). "Computers/high regard as educational technology". Roper Center Public Opinion Archives, center.uconn.edu/data/access/ipoll/poll.html.
2. Johnson, S. (2005). *Everything Bad is Good for You: How Today's Popular Culture Is Actually Making You Smarter*. New York: Riverhead Books.

3. Tronick, E. (2007). *The Neurobiological and Social-Emotional Development of Infants and Children*. New York: Norton.
4. Gurian, M. and Stevens, K. (2005). *The Mind of Boys: Saving Our Sons From Falling Behind in School and Life*. San Francisco: Jossey-Bass, 146.
5. Coleman, M., Ganong, L., Clark, J.M., and Madsen, R. (1989). "Parenting perceptions in rural and urban families: Is there a difference?" *Journal of Marriage and the Family*, 51, 329–335. Collins and Russell's (1991) summary of studies on the achievement-oriented interactions of mothers and fathers with children did not find a clear difference between the two parents.

Chapter 12

1. Cowan, C.P. and Cowan, P.A. (2000). *When Partners Become Parents*. New York: Lawrence Erlbaum.
2. Gilbert, D. (2005). *Stumbling On Happiness*. New York: Vintage Press.
3. Feinberg, M., and Kan, M. (2008). "Establishing family foundations: Intervention effects on coparenting, parent/infant well-being, and parent-child relations." *Journal of Family Psychology*, 22(2), 253–263.
4. Cowan and Cowan.

Index

Active sleep, 134
Adult sleep deprivation, 146–147
After-baby fights, 52
After-school activities, 188–189
Aggression
    child's, 127
    intensified sibling, 184
Alpert, David, 151
And Baby Makes Three (Gottman and Schwartz), 4
Anger, child's, 127
Arguments
    with child, 109–110
    disciplined, 109–111
    about preschooler's eating habits, 125
    with spouse, 111
    with toddlers, 92–93
Art, learning and, 172–173
Athletics, 159–162
Attachment disorders, 193
Attachment theory, 193
Authoritarian parents, 101–102
Authoritative parents, 102
Authority, discipline and, 99–101
Autonomy, father and children's, 18–21

Babies
    burping, 117
    caring for, 116
    feeding, 117
    handling, 22–23
    joint emotional ownership of, 41
    sleep and, 117
    voice recognition by unborn, 17–18

waking during night, 135–139
    See also Infants
Babyhood, challenges during, 90–91
Back rubs, 114
Ball, Jessica, 41
Baumrind, Diana, 101–102
Becoming a Family study (Cowan), 196
Bedroom safety, 153
Bed-wetting, 146, 184
Before baby fights, 52
Behavior expectations, 85–86
Behavior problems, father involvement and, 28
Bicycle riding, 158–159
Brazelton, T. Berry, x, 138, 164
Breast-feeding, 121–123
    fathers and, 118
    working mothers and, 122–123
Bribery, as discipline method, 107–108
Buck, Robert, 128
Bullying, 165–168
Burping a baby, 117

Calming children, 120–121
Car safety, 153
Child attachment, working parents and, 87
Child care, dividing up, 40–41
Child development
    babies, 90–91
    emotionally engaged father and, xv
    first formal educational experience and, 174
    movement to new stage of, 170

Child development *(continued)*
  preschoolers, 95–96
  toddlers, 92–94
  See also Development
Child-care center safety, 154
Children
  arguments with, 109–110
  of authoritarian parents, 102
  awareness of parents' moods, 83
  behavior expectations, 85–86
  calming and comforting, 120–121
  coping skills and, 18–21
  decision to have, 191–192
  effects of marital dysfunction on, xvi
  effects of parental disagreements on, 84
  effects on marriage, 3–4
  "emotion talk" with, 128
  importance of play for, 84–85
  listening to, 113, 198
  mother's relationship with, 32
  multiple, effect on marriage, 36–37
  overindulged, 112. *See also* Spoiling
  parenting differences as benefit for, 31
  parents and time away from, 9
  physical handling of, 118–120
  routines and, 138
  sleeping. *See* Sleeping children
  styles of interaction with, 24–25
  talking about feelings, 129
Chores, 179–183
Christofferson, Mogens, 28
Clark, Jim, 161
Colic, 4
Collaborative Divorce Project (Kline Pruett), 196
Coloroso, Barbara, 108
Comforting children, 120–121
Commitment, co-parenting. *See* Co-parenting commitment
Communication
  conflict and, 51–52, 53, 62
  gender differences and, 26–27
  nonverbal, with children, 128
  nonverbal signals, 194
Competitive sports, 160–161
Computers, education and, 173
Conflict
  brewing, 195

communication and, 51–52, 62
  contempt and, 54
  criticism and, 54–55
  defensiveness and, 55–56
  emotional flooding and, 60
  gender differences and, 6
  gender wars, 53
  kids' perceptions of parents and, 68–69
  kinds of, 52–53
  managing, 49–63
  negative responses during, 53–54
  overt, 51
  perpetual issues and, 60
  signs of mismanaged, 50–51
  stonewalling and, 57
  value differences and, 58–63, 94
"Conscious Fathering" program (Dorsey), 117
Contempt, conflict and, 54
Coontz, Stephanie, xii
Cooperative preschool centers, 177–178
Co-parenting commitment, strength of, 65–77
Co-parenting Preventive Maintenance Quiz, 44
Co-parenting relationship, 35–47
  balancing work and family, 45–47
  caring together vs. feeling alone, 41–43
  child care and, 40–41
  intimacy and, 43–45
  key components of, 38
  as "kid's team," 38–40
  managing conflict, 47, 49–63
  tips for success, 42–43
Couple
  parents as, 9
  relationship of, father's tie with child and, 29
  two-career, marital stability and, 45–47
Cowan
  Carolyn Pape, xi, 22, 39, 58, 199
  Philip A., xi, 22, 39, 58, 196, 199
Criticism, conflict and, 54–55
Crying
  dealing with baby's, 117
  infant, stress and, xvi
  parents' differing responses to, 138
Cycle of care program, 117

Damon, William, 112
Deep sleep, 134
Defensiveness, conflict and, 55–56
Dessert, 126
Development
  emotional, 127–129
  intellectual, television and,
    86–87
  questions on parenting profile,
    80–81
  See also Child development
Developmental potential, 86–87
Diaper changes, 117
Diet and nutrition, 121–127
  goals for, 126
  for infants, 121–123
  for kindergarteners, 125–126
  for preschooler, 124–125
  for toddlers, 123–124
Discipline
  authority and, 99–101
  gender differences and, 102
  learning and, 106–112
  methods of, 107–112. *See also*
    Discipline methods
  parenting styles and, 101–102
  preventive, 113–114
  questions on parenting profile,
    82
  shame and, 105–106
  steps for co-parenting and,
    112–114
  when kids act up, 103–105
Discipline methods
  arguments with child and,
    109–110
  arguments with spouse and,
    111
  bribery, 107–108
  positive reinforcement, 108
  spanking, 107
  spoiling vs., 111–112
  values, 108–109
Distress, responses to, 23
Divorce
  co-parenting advice and, xiv
  fathers with sole custody and,
    27–28
  gender-based parenting differ-
    ences and, 30
  learning from, 195–196
  See also Divorce prevention
Divorce prevention, 191–198
  lasting strength in co-parenting,
    192–198

  parenting lessons, 196–198
Dorsey, Bernie, 117
Drawing, 172
Dreaming, 134
Dreams, 143
Dunn, Judith, 128

"Educare," 174
Education, 169–190
  after-school activities, 188–189
  art and, 171
  involved dads and, 32–33
  kids and chores, 179–183
  kindergarten, 183–187
  music and, 171
  opportunities for learning,
    171–174
  parental mistakes, 189–190
  preschool, 174–179. *See also*
    Preschool
  winning vs. losing, 187
Emilia, Reggio, 178
Emotion talk, 128
Emotional development, 127–129
Emotional flooding, 53, 60, 128
Emotional issues, fathers and, 128
Emotional maturity, of
  dad-involved children, 33
Employment, effects of, 87–88
Enuresis, 146
Estrogen, 17
Exercise, 159–162
Expectations
  behavior, 85–86
  questions on parenting profile,
    82
Exploration, gender differences
  and, 23–26

Fair fight, rules for, 56
"Families Through Time" study
  (McHale), 4, 39, 192
Farrell, Warren, 27
Fathers
  are not substitute mothers,
    28–30
  as authoritative, 100
  breast-feeding and, 122
  co-parenting and, 11
  emotional availability of, 119
  emotional closeness and, 22
  emotional issues and, 128
  gatekeeping, 70
  hormonal changes in expectant,
    17

Fathers *(continued)*
  "imperative–move on" discipline
    style, 102
  involved, 32, 75–76, 185–186
  as jungle gym, 26
  mother's feelings about compe-
    tence of, 71
  preparation for new, 116–117
  self-credit for family duties, 7
  stay-at-home, 28
  in workforce, 11
Fats, 126
Feeding babies, 117
Feelings, children talking about,
  129
Feinberg, Mark, 196
Field, Tiffany, 87, 118
Fifty-fifty trap, 197
Fights
  before baby vs. after baby, 52
  fair fights, 56
Fire safety, 156
Firearms, 155–156
Fivush, Robyn, 127
Fleck, Stephen, 42
Frustration, child's handling of,
  18–21

Gardening with kids, 126–127
Gatekeeping, 69–75. *See also*
  Maternal gatekeeping
Gender differences
  children's coping skills and,
    18–21
  communication and, 26–27
  conflict and, 6
  discipline and, 102
  in handling baby, 22–23
  hormonal differences, 16–17
  identifying, 5–7
  play, playfulness, and explo-
    ration, 23–26
  pre-baby attitudes and, 21–22
  responses to distress, 23
Gender stereotypes, 130
Gilbert, Daniel, 194
Golden co-parenting rule, 53
Gottman, John, xi, 4, 53, 128, 196
Gottman, Julie, xi, 196
Greene, David, 108
Greenspan, Stanley, 164
Guns, 155–156

Happiest Baby on the Block, The
  (Karp), 120

Heinrichs, Jay, 110
Heming, Gertrude, 199
Home safety, 153
Hormonal changes during preg-
  nancy
  in men, 16–17
  in women, 16
Humor, 114

"I" statements, conflict and, 55, 94
"Ideas About Parenting" questionnaire (Cowan), 39, 58, 199–
  204
"Imperative–move on" discipline
  style, 102
Infant-care skills, 117
Infants
  crying, stress and, xvi
  feeding, 121–123
  parents' nighttime schedule for,
    122
  physical care of, 40, 117
  readiness to learn, 171
  working mothers and, 122–123
  See also Babies
Intensified parenting, 33
Intentionality, 178
Intimacy, co-parenting relationship
  and, 43–45
Intimacy gap, 5

Kalman, Izzy, 167
Kan, Marni, 196
Karp, Harvey, 120
Kids Are Worth It (Coloroso), 108
Kindergarten, 183–187
  child neediness and fearfulness
    and, 183–184
  child with problem in, 185–186
  child's anxiety and, 183–184
  diet and nutrition for children
    in, 125–126
  parental involvement and, 185

Lamb, Michael, 69
Learning
  discipline and, 106–112
  opportunities for, 171–174
  preschool and, 176
  See also Education
LeMasters, E.E., xv
Lepper, Mark, 108
Levenson, Bob, 53
Lincoln, Abraham, 113
Listening to child, 113, 198

Maccoby, Eleanor, 100, 127, 129, 152
"Madonna position," 22
Magic trio, 114
Manipulatives, 178
Marital dysfunction, effects on children of, xvi
Marriage, effects of children on, 3–4
Materialism, disregard for, 113
Maternal gatekeeping
  defined, 69
  motivations for, 70
  quiz for moms, 72–73
  rigid, 71
  unconscious, 74
Mate's downfalls, upside of, 195
Math skills, involved dads and, 33
McHale, James, xi, 4, 10, 39, 90, 192–193, 196
Mead, Margaret, 33
Media Education Foundation, 165
Media exposure, 163–165
Montessori preschool, 178
Moral behavior, expectations of child's, 85–86
Mothers
  are not substitute fathers, 28–30
  as gatekeeper, 69
  man's relationship with, 31
  "negotiable-sociable" discipline style, 102
  relationship with children, 32
  safety zones and, 152
"Mother tongue," power of, 128
"Mozart effect," 171
Music, 114
  educational opportunity in, 171–172
  infant's appetite for, 171
Mutual caring, 41–43

National Association for Media Literacy Education, 165
National Institute of Child Health and Human Development, 87
"Negotiable-sociable" discipline style, 102
"Neurons to Neighborhoods" report (Shonkoff), 121
Night terrors, 143
Nightmares, child's, 143
Nonverbal signals, 194
Nurturing, as human instinct, 30

Oppositional behavior, sleep and toddlers', 141–142
Outside safety, 154
Overindulged children, 112. See also Spoiling
Oxytocin, 16

Parallel play, 129
Parental differences
  responses to infant cries, 138
  tolerance for privacy, 140
Parental tone, 118–119
Parenthood
  general preparation for, 88
  transition from partnership to, xv
Parenting
  intensified, 33
  as relationship, 33
Parenting differences
  as benefit for children, 31–34
  fathers not substitute mothers, 28–30
  gender differences, 16–27
  mothers not substitute fathers, 28–30
  not deficiencies, 27–28
  personality differences, 30–31, 66–69
  personality styles, 57–58
  See also Gender differences
Parenting partnership
  children's understanding of, 31–32
  determine strength of your, 12–13
  good fathering and, 11
  resilience and, 10
  sharing and, 11
  strong family and, 10
  what is?, xviii
  See also Partnership parenting
Parenting profile, 80–83
Partnership, transition to parenthood from, xv
Partnership parenting
  building the partnership, 9–12
  elements of, 8–9
  See also Parenting partnership
Passive parents, 102
Perpetual issues, 60
Personality differences, 57–58
  child's preferences and, 67–68
  personality attributes, 66–69

Philadelphia Child Guidance
    Clinic, xvii
Plato, 28
Play
    gender differences and, 23–26
    importance of, for children,
        84–85
    parallel, 129
    rough-and-tumble, 26
    winning vs. losing and, 187
Play-based preschool, 178
Playfulness, gender differences
    and, 23–26
Playground safety, 154
Playroom safety, 154
Positive reinforcement, 108
Postpartum blues, 4
Pregnancy, hormonal changes
    during, 16–17
Preschool
    approaches to, 177–179
    challenges during, 95–96
    choosing a program, 175–179
    as first formal educational expe-
        rience, 174–179
    staff of, 177
Preschool gourmand, 124
Preschoolers
    diet and nutrition for, 124–125
    sleep and, 142–144
Preventive discipline, 113–114
Progesterone, 16
Prolactin
    expectant fathers and, 17
    pregnant women and, 16

Quiz
    co-parenting preventive mainte-
        nance, 44
    maternal gatekeeping, 72–73

Reinforcers, 109
Relationship
    couples', father's tie with child
        and, 29
    professional help with, 94
    questions on parenting profile,
        83
    See Co-parenting relationship
Relationship hormone, prolactin
    as, 17
Relationship triangle, 37
REM sleep, 134
Resentments, building, 34
Resilience, 10

Routines, children and, 138

Safety issues, 151–168
    basics, 152–155
    bedroom, 153
    bicycle riding, 158–159
    bullying, 165–168
    car, 153
    child-care center, 154
    exercise and team sports,
        159–162
    fire, 156
    firearms, 155–156
    home, 153
    media exposure, 163–165
    outside, 154
    playground, 154
    playroom, 154
    sledding, 159
    strangers, 162–163
    water, 154, 156–158
Schwartz, Julie, 4
Sears, Robert, 33
Separation
    child's mastering of, 18–21
    sleep as, 135
    working parents and, 87
Sexual behavior, new parents
    and, 5
Shalom bayit, 197
Shame, discipline and, 105–106
Sharing, 11
Shonkoff, Jack, 121
Sledding safety, 159
Sleep
    babies and, 117
    baby's troubles with, 4
    problems and solutions,
        147–149
    as separation, 135
    types of, 134
Sleep deprivation
    adult, 146–147
    crying infant and, xvi
Sleep retraining, 145
Sleeping children, 133–149
    adult sleep deprivation and,
        146–147
    babies wake during night,
        135–139
    bed-wetting, 146
    dreams, 143
    night terrors, 143
    older children, 144–147
    preschoolers, 142–144

sleep as transition, 134–139
sleepwalking, 144
toddlers, 141–142
together with parents, 139–140
Sleepwalking, 144
Snacks, 126
Social development, 129–132
parental role models and,
131–132
stereotypes and, 130
Socialization goals, 104
Spanking, 107
Spoiling
discipline vs., 111–112
expectations about, 87
questions on parenting profile,
82
Sports, competitive, 160–161
Spouse, arguments with, 111
Sroufe, Alan, 87
Stay-at-home dads, 28
Steiner, Rudolf, 179
Stereotypes, social development
and parental, 130
Stonewalling, conflict and, 57
Strangers, talking to, 162–163
Stress, crying infant and, xvi
Stumbling on Happiness (Gilbert),
194
"Super marriages," 4
Sweets, 126
Swimming, 156–158

Team sports, 159–162
Television, 86–87, 164–165
Tender touch, 118–120
Testosterone, 17
Toddler Music collection, 151
"Toddler Property Laws," 130
Toddlers
challenges with, 92–94
feeding, 123–124

manners for, 124
oppositional behavior and,
141–142
sleeping, 141–142
strong parenting partnership
and, 31–32
Two-career couples, marital stability and, 45–47

Value differences, 58–63
Values
discipline methods and,
108–109
parents' competing, 93–94
Verbal skills, involved dads and, 32
Violence, watching, 164–165
Voice recognition, by unborn
babies, 17–18

Waldorf preschool, 179
Water safety, 154, 156–158
"What Grown-ups Understand
About Child Development"
survey, 79
answers to, 205
Winning vs. losing, children and,
187
Women
hormonal changes during pregnancy, 16
intimacy and, 43–45
Work, balancing family and, 45–47
Workforce
both parents in, 45–47
fathers in, 11
Working parents
child attachment and, 87
decisions for, 122–123

"Yes, but...," 75
Yogman, Michael, 18

About the Authors

Kyle Pruett, MD, is an eminent child psychiatrist at the Yale Child Study Center and the nation's top expert on fatherhood. An award-winning author, he frequently conducts lectures and appears in the national media. **Marsha Kline Pruett, PhD, MSL**, a Chaired Professor at the Smith College School for Social Work, has conducted landmark research on co-parenting. She lectures and consults on co-parenting issues to mental health and family law professionals. The Pruetts have two young children and four young grandchildren and live in Northampton, Massachusetts.